ABOUT THIS PUBLICATION

FOR SERVICE ASSISTANCE

Customer Service Department
704.898.0770

North Carolina General Statues is published by The Muliti-Media Group of Greater Charlotte in Charlotte, North Carolina. Copyright 2015 by the Multi-Media Group of Greater Charlotte. This book or parts thereof may not be reproduced in any form, stored in a retrieval system, or transmitted in any form by any means—electronic, mechanical, photocopy, recording or otherwise—without prior written permission of the publisher, except as provided by United States of America copyright law.

The records required by U.S. Code 2257(a) through (c) and the pertinent regulations 28 C.F.R. Cli. 1, Part 75 with respect to this publication and all materials associated with such records are maintained by The Multi-Media Group of Greater Charlotte, Publisher and available for review by Attorney General.

www.visionbooks.org

Copyright © 2015 by MMGGC
All rights reserved!

TID: 5015454
ISBN (10) digit: 1502485818
ISBN (13) digit: 978-1502485816

123-4-56789-01234-Paperback
123-4-56789-01234-Hardback

First Edition

090520140547

Printed in the United States of America

2015 EDITION

North Carolina Criminal Law And Procedure-Pamphlet # 18

Printed In conjunction with the Administration of the Courts

North Carolina Criminal Law and Procedure
Pamphlet Reference Guide

Chapters	Pamphlet
Chapter 1 Civil Procedure	1
Chapter 1 Civil Procedure (Continue)	2
Chapter 1A Rules of Civil Procedure	2
Chapter 1B Contribution.	2
Chapter 1C Enforcement of Judgments.	2
Chapter 1D Punitive Damages.	2
Chapter 1E Eastern Band of Cherokee Indians.	2
Chapter 1F North Carolina Uniform Interstate Depositions and Discovery Act.	2
Chapter 2 - Clerk of Superior Court [Repealed and Transferred.]	3
Chapter 3 - Commissioners of Affidavits and Deeds [Repealed.]	3
Chapter 4 - Common Law	3
Chapter 5 - Contempt [Repealed.]	3
Chapter 5A - Contempt	3
Chapter 6 - Liability for Court Costs	3
Chapter 7 - Courts [Repealed and Transferred.]	3
Chapter 7A – Judicial Department	3
Chapter 7A – Continuation (Judicial Department)	4
Chapter 7A – Continuation (Judicial Department)	5
Chapter 7B - Juvenile Code	5
Chapter 8 - Evidence	6
Chapter 8A - Interpreters for Deaf Persons [Recodified.]	6
Chapter 8B - Interpreters for Deaf Persons	6
Chapter 8C - Evidence Code	6
Chapter 9 - Jurors	6
Chapter 10 - Notaries [Repealed.]	6
Chapter 10A - Notaries [Recodified.]	6
Chapter 10B - Notaries	6
Chapter 11 - Oaths	6
Chapter 12 - Statutory Construction	6
Chapter 13 - Citizenship Restored	6
Chapter 14 - Criminal Law	7
Chapter 14 –Criminal Law (Continuation)	8
Chapter 15 - Criminal Procedure	9
Chapter 15A - Criminal Procedure Act (Continuation)	10
Chapter 15A - Criminal Procedure Act (Continuation)	11
Chapter 15B - Victims Compensation	11
Chapter 15C - Address Confidentiality Program	11
Chapter 16 - Gaming Contracts and Futures	11
Chapter 17 - Habeas Corpus	11

Chapter 17A - Law-Enforcement Officers [Recodified.]	11
Chapter 17B - North Carolina Criminal Justice Education and Training System [Recodified.] Chapter 17C - North Carolina Criminal Justice Education and Training Standards Commission	11
	11
Chapter 17D - North Carolina Justice Academy	11
Chapter 17E - North Carolina Sheriffs' Education and Training Standards Commission	11
Chapter 18 - Regulation of Intoxicating Liquors [Repealed.]	12
Chapter 18A - Regulation of Intoxicating Liquors [Repealed.]	12
Chapter 18B - Regulation of Alcoholic Beverages	12
Chapter 18C - North Carolina State Lottery	12
Chapter 19 - Offenses against Public Morals	12
Chapter 19A - Protection of Animals	12
Chapter 20 - Motor Vehicles	13
Chapter 20 - Motor Vehicles (Continuation)	14
Chapter 20 - Motor Vehicles (Continuation)	15
Chapter 20 - Motor Vehicles (Continuation)	16
Chapter 21 - Bills of Lading	17
Chapter 22 - Contracts Requiring Writing	17
Chapter 22A - Signatures	17
Chapter 22B - Contracts Against Public Policy	17
Chapter 22C - Payments to Subcontractors	17
Chapter 23 - Debtor and Creditor	17
Chapter 24 – Interest	17
Chapter 25 – Uniform Commercial Code	18
Chapter 25 – Uniform Commercial Code (Continuation)	19
Chapter 25A – Retail Installment Sales Act	20
Chapter 25B - Credit	20
Chapter 25C - Sales of Artwork	20
Chapter 26 - Suretyship	20
Chapter 27 - Warehouse Receipts [Repealed.]	20
Chapter 28 - Administration [Repealed.]	20
Chapter 28A - Administration of Decedents' Estates	20
Chapter 28B - Estates of Absentees in Military Service	20
Chapter 28C - Estates of Missing Persons	20
Chapter 29 - Intestate Succession	21
Chapter 30 - Surviving Spouses	21
Chapter 31 - Wills	21
Chapter 31A - Acts Barring Property Rights	21
Chapter 31B - Renunciation of Property and Renunciation of Fiduciary Powers Act	21
Chapter 31C - Uniform Disposition of Community Property Rights at Death Act	21
Chapter 32 - Fiduciaries	21
Chapter 32A - Powers of Attorney	21
Chapter 33 - Guardian and Ward [Repealed and Recodified.]	21

Chapter 33A - North Carolina Uniform Transfers to Minors Act	21
Chapter 33B - North Carolina Uniform Custodial Trust Act	21
Chapter 34 - Veterans' Guardianship Act	22
Chapter 35 - Sterilization Procedures	22
Chapter 35A - Incompetency and Guardianship	22
Chapter 36 - Trusts and Trustees [Repealed.]	22
Chapter 36A - Trusts and Trustees	22
Chapter 36B - Uniform Management of Institutional Funds Act [Repealed.]	22
Chapter 36C - North Carolina Uniform Trust Code	22
Chapter 36D - North Carolina Community Third Party Trusts, Pooled Trusts	23
Chapter 36E - Uniform Prudent Management of Institutional Funds Act	23
Chapter 37 - Allocation of Principal and Income [Repealed.]	23
Chapter 37A - Uniform Principal and Income Act	23
Chapter 38 - Boundaries	23
Chapter 38A - Landowner Liability	23
Chapter 39 - Conveyances	23
Chapter 39A - Transfer Fee Covenants Prohibited	23
Chapter 40 - Eminent Domain [Repealed.]	23
Chapter 40A - Eminent Domain	23
Chapter 41 - Estates	23
Chapter 41A - State Fair Housing Act	23
Chapter 42 - Landlord and Tenant	23
Chapter 42A - Vacation Rental Act	23
Chapter 43 - Land Registration	23
Chapter 44 - Liens	24
Chapter 44A - Statutory Liens and Charges	24
Chapter 45 - Mortgages and Deeds of Trust	24
Chapter 45A - Good Funds Settlement Act	24
Chapter 46 - Partition	24
Chapter 47 - Probate and Registration	25
Chapter 47A - Unit Ownership	25
Chapter 47B - Real Property Marketable Title Act	25
Chapter 47C - North Carolina Condominium Act	25
Chapter 47D - Notice of Settlement Act [Expired.]	25
Chapter 47E - Residential Property Disclosure Act	25
Chapter 47F - North Carolina Planned Community Act	25
Chapter 47G - Option to Purchase Contracts	25
Chapter 47H - Contracts for Deed	25
Chapter 48 - Adoptions +	26
Chapter 48A - Minors	26
Chapter 49 - Bastardy	26
Chapter 49A - Rights of Children	26
Chapter 50 - Divorce and Alimony	26
Chapter 50A - Uniform Child-Custody Jurisdiction and	

Enforcement Act	26
Chapter 50B - Domestic Violence	26
Chapter 50C - Civil No-Contact Orders	26
Chapter 51 - Marriage	26
Chapter 52 - Powers and Liabilities of Married Persons	27
Chapter 52A - Uniform Reciprocal Enforcement of Support Act [Repealed.]	27
Chapter 52B - Uniform Premarital Agreement Act	27
Chapter 52C - Uniform Interstate Family Support Act	27
Chapter 53 - Banks	27
Chapter 53A - Business Development Corporations and North Carolina Capital Resource Corporations	28
Chapter 53B - Financial Privacy Act	28
Chapter 54 - Cooperative Organizations	28
Chapter 54A - Capital Stock Savings and Loan Associations [Repealed.]	28
Chapter 54B - Savings and Loan Associations	29
Chapter 54C - Savings Banks	29
Chapter 55 - North Carolina Business Corporation Act	30
Chapter 55A - North Carolina Nonprofit Corporation Act	31
Chapter 55B - Professional Corporation Act	31
Chapter 55C - Foreign Trade Zones	31
Chapter 55D - Filings, Names, and Registered Agents for Corporations, Nonprofit Corporations, and Partnerships	31
Chapter 56 - Electric, Telegraph and Power Companies [Repealed.]	31
Chapter 57 - Hospital, Medical and Dental Service Corporations [Recodified.]	31
Chapter 57A - Health Maintenance Organization Act [Recodified.]	31
Chapter 57B - Health Maintenance Organization Act [Recodified.]	31
Chapter 57C - North Carolina Limited Liability Company Act.	31
Chapter 58 - Insurance.	32
Chapter 58 - Insurance (Continuation)	33
Chapter 58 - Insurance (Continuation)	34
Chapter 58 - Insurance (Continuation)	35
Chapter 58 - Insurance (Continuation)	36
Chapter 58 - Insurance (Continuation)	37
Chapter 58 - Insurance (Continuation)	38
Chapter 58A - North Carolina Health Insurance Trust Commission [Recodified.]	38
Chapter 59 - Partnership.	39
Chapter 59B - Uniform Unincorporated Nonprofit Association Act.	39
Chapter 60 - Railroads and Other Carriers [Repealed and Transferred.]	39
Chapter 61 - Religious Societies	39
Chapter 62 - Public Utilities	39

Chapter 62 - Public Utilities (Continuation)	40
Chapter 62A - Public Safety Telephone Service And Wireless Telephone Service	40
Chapter 63 - Aeronautics	40
Chapter 63A - North Carolina Global TransPark Authority	40
Chapter 64 - Aliens	40
Chapter 65 – Cemeteries	40
Chapter 66 - Commerce and Business	41
Chapter 67 - Dogs	41
Chapter 68 - Fences and Stock Law	41
Chapter 69 - Fire Protection	41
Chapter 70 - Indian Antiquities, Archaeological Resources and Unmarked Human Skeletal Remains Protection	42
Chapter 71 - Indians [Repealed.]	42
Chapter 71A - Indians	42
Chapter 72 - Inns, Hotels and Restaurants	42
Chapter 73 - Mills	42
Chapter 74 - Mines and Quarries	42
Chapter 74A - Company Police [Repealed.]	42
Chapter 74B - Private Protective Services Act [Repealed.]	42
Chapter 74C - Private Protective Services	42
Chapter 74D - Alarm Systems	42
Chapter 74E - Company Police Act	42
Chapter 74F - Locksmith Licensing Act	42
Chapter 74G - Campus Police Act	42
Chapter 75 - Monopolies, Trusts and Consumer Protection	42
Chapter 75A - Boating and Water Safety	43
Chapter 75B - Discrimination in Business	43
Chapter 75C - Motion Picture Fair Competition Act	43
Chapter 75D - Racketeer Influenced and Corrupt Organizations	43
Chapter 75E - Unlawful Activities in Connection With Certain Corporate Transactions	43
Chapter 76 - Navigation	43
Chapter 76A - Navigation and Pilotage Commissions	43
Chapter 77 - Rivers, Creeks, and Coastal Waters	43
Chapter 78 - Securities Law [Repealed.]	43
Chapter 78A - North Carolina Securities Act	43
Chapter 78B - Tender Offer Disclosure Act [Repealed.]	43
Chapter 78C - Investment Advisers	43
Chapter 78D - Commodities Act	43
Chapter 79 - Strays [Repealed.]	43
Chapter 80 - Trademarks, Brands, etc.	44
Chapter 81 - Weights and Measures [Recodified.]	44
Chapter 81A - Weights and Measures Act of 1975.	44
Chapter 82 - Wrecks [Repealed.]	44
Chapter 83 - Architects [Recodified.]	44

Chapter 83A - Architects	44
Chapter 84 - Attorneys-at-Law	44
Chapter 84A - Foreign Legal Consultants	44
Chapter 85 - Auctions and Auctioneers [Repealed.]	44
Chapter 85A - Bail Bondsmen and Runners [Recodified.]	44
Chapter 85B - Auctions and Auctioneers	44
Chapter 85C - Bail Bondsmen and Runners [Recodified.]	44
Chapter 86 - Barbers [Recodified.]	44
Chapter 86A - Barbers	44
Chapter 87 - Contractors	44
Chapter 88 - Cosmetic Art [Repealed.]	44
Chapter 88A - Electrolysis Practice Act	44
Chapter 88B - Cosmetic Art	45
Chapter 89 - Engineering and Land Surveying [Recodified.]	45
Chapter 89A - Landscape Architects	45
Chapter 89B - Foresters	45
Chapter 89C - Engineering and Land Surveying	45
Chapter 89D - Landscape Contractors	45
Chapter 89E - Geologists Licensing Act	45
Chapter 89F - North Carolina Soil Scientist Licensing Act	45
Chapter 89G - Irrigation Contractors	45
Chapter 90 - Medicine and Allied Occupations	45
Chapter 90 - Medicine and Allied Occupations (Continuation)	46
Chapter 90 - Medicine and Allied Occupations (Continuation)	47
Chapter 90 - Medicine and Allied Occupations (Continuation)	48
Chapter 90A - Sanitarians and Water and Wastewater Treatment Facility Operators	48
Chapter 90B - Social Worker Certification and Licensure Act	48
Chapter 90C - North Carolina Recreational Therapy Licensure Act	48
Chapter 90D - Interpreters and Transliterators	48
Chapter 91 - Pawnbrokers [Repealed.]	48
Chapter 91A - Pawnbrokers Modernization Act of 1989	48
Chapter 92 - Photographers [Deleted.]	48
Chapter 93 - Certified Public Accountants	48
Chapter 93A - Real Estate License Law	49
Chapter 93B - Occupational Licensing Boards	49
Chapter 93C - Watchmakers [Repealed.]	49
Chapter 93D - North Carolina State Hearing Aid Dealers and Fitters Board.	49
Chapter 93E - North Carolina Appraisers Act	49
Chapter 94 - Apprenticeship	49
Chapter 95 - Department of Labor and Labor Regulations	49
Chapter 95 - Department of Labor and Labor Regulations (Continuation)	50
Chapter 96 - Employment Security	50
Chapter 97 - Workers' Compensation Act	50
Chapter 97 - Workers' Compensation Act (Continuation)	51

Chapter 98 - Burnt and Lost Records	51
Chapter 99 - Libel and Slander	51
Chapter 99A - Civil Remedies for Criminal Actions	51
Chapter 99B - Products Liability	51
Chapter 99C - Actions Relating to Winter Sports Safety and Accidents	51
Chapter 99D - Civil Rights	51
Chapter 99E - Special Liability Provisions	51
Chapter 100 - Monuments, Memorials and Parks	51
Chapter 101 - Names of Persons	51
Chapter 102 - Official Survey Base	51
Chapter 103 - Sundays, Holidays and Special Days	51
Chapter 104 - United States Lands	51
Chapter 104A - Degrees of Kinship	51
Chapter 104B - Hurricanes or Other Acts of Nature	51
Chapter 104C - Atomic Energy, Radioactivity and Ionizing Radiation [Repealed and Recodified.]	51
Chapter 104D - Southern States Energy Compact	51
Chapter 104E - North Carolina Radiation Protection Act	51
Chapter 104F - Southeast Interstate Low-Level Radioactive Waste Management Compact [Repealed]	51
Chapter 104G - North Carolina Low-Level Radioactive Waste Management Authority Act of 1987 [Repealed]	51
Chapter 105 - Taxation	51
Chapter 105 - Taxation (Continuation)	52
Chapter 105 - Taxation (Continuation)	53
Chapter 105 - Taxation (Continuation)	54
Chapter 105A - Setoff Debt Collection Act	55
Chapter 105B - Defaulted Student Loan Recovery Act	55
Chapter 106 - Agriculture	55
Chapter 106 - Agriculture (Continue)	56
Chapter 106 - Agriculture (Continue)	57
Chapter 107 - Agricultural Development Districts [Repealed.]	57
Chapter 108 - Social Services [Repealed and Recodified.]	57
Chapter 108A - Social Services	57
Chapter 108B - Community Action Programs	58
Chapter 108C Medicaid and Health Choice Provider Requirements.	58
Chapter 108D Medicaid Managed Care for Behavioral Health Services.	58
Chapter 109 - Bonds [Recodified.]	58
Chapter 110 - Child Welfare	58
Chapter 111 - Aid to the Blind	58
Chapter 112 - Confederate Homes and Pensions [Repealed.]	58
Chapter 113 - Conservation and Development	58
Chapter 113 - Conservation and Development (Continuation)	59

Chapter 113A - Pollution Control and Environment	59
Chapter 113A - Pollution Control and Environment (Continuation)	60
Chapter 113B - North Carolina Energy Policy Act of 1975	60
Chapter 114 - Department of Justice	60
Chapter 115 - Elementary and Secondary Education [Repealed.]	60
Chapter 115A - Community Colleges, Technical Institutes, and Industrial Education Centers [Repealed.]	60
Chapter 115B - Tuition and Fee Waivers	60
Chapter 115C - Elementary and Secondary Education	60
Chapter 115C - Elementary and Secondary Education (Continuation)	61
Chapter 115C - Elementary and Secondary Education (Continuation)	62
Chapter 115C - Elementary and Secondary Education (Continuation)	63
Chapter 115D - Community Colleges	63
Chapter 115E - Private Educational Facilities Finance Act [Recodified]	63
Chapter 116 - Higher Education	63
Chapter 116 - Higher Education (Continuation)	63
Chapter 116A - Escheats and Abandoned Property [Repealed.]	64
Chapter 116B - Escheats and Abandoned Property	64
Chapter 116C - Continuum of Education Programs	64
Chapter 116D - Higher Education Bonds	64
Chapter 117 - Electrification	64
Chapter 118 - Firemen's and Rescue Squad Workers' Relief and Pension Funds [Recodified.]	64
Chapter 118A - Firemen's Death Benefit Act [Repealed.]	64
Chapter 118B - Members of a Rescue Squad Death Benefit Act [Repealed.]	64
Chapter 119 - Gasoline and Oil Inspection and Regulation	64
Chapter 120 - General Assembly	65
Chapter 120 - General Assembly (Continuation)	66
Chapter 120 - General Assembly (Continuation)	67
Chapter 120C - Lobbying	67
Chapter 121 - Archives and History	67
Chapter 122 - Hospitals for the Mentally Disordered [Repealed.]	67
Chapter 122A - North Carolina Housing Finance Agency	67
Chapter 122B - North Carolina Agricultural Facilities Finance Act [Repealed.]	67
Chapter 122C - Mental Health, Developmental Disabilities, and Substance Abuse Act of 1985	67
Chapter 122C - Mental Health, Developmental Disabilities, and Substance Abuse Act of 1985 (Continuation)	68
Chapter 122D - North Carolina Agricultural Finance Act	68

Chapter 122E - North Carolina Housing Trust and Oil Overcharge Act	68
Chapter 123 - Impeachment	69
Chapter 123A - Industrial Development [Repealed.]	69
Chapter 124 - Internal Improvements	69
Chapter 125 - Libraries	69
Chapter 126 - State Personnel System	69
Chapter 127 - Militia [Repealed.]	69
Chapter 127A - Militia	69
Chapter 127B - Military Affairs	69
Chapter 127C - Advisory Commission on Military Affairs	69
Chapter 128 - Offices and Public Officers	69
Chapter 128 - Offices and Public Officers (Continuation)	70
Chapter 129 - Public Buildings and Grounds	70
Chapter 130 - Public Health [Repealed.]	70
Chapter 130A - Public Health	70
Chapter 130A - Public Health (Continuation)	71
Chapter 130A - Public Health (Continuation)	72
Chapter 130B - Hazardous Waste Management Commission [Repealed.]	72
Chapter 131 - Public Hospitals [Repealed.]	72
Chapter 131A - Health Care Facilities Finance Act	72
Chapter 131B - Licensing of Ambulatory Surgical Facilities [Repealed.]	72
Chapter 131C - Charitable Solicitation Licensure Act [Repealed.]	72
Chapter 131D - Inspection and Licensing of Facilities	72
Chapter 131E - Health Care Facilities and Services	72
Chapter 131E - Health Care Facilities and Services (Continuation)	73
Chapter 131F - Solicitation of Contributions	73
Chapter 132 - Public Records	73
Chapter 133 - Public Works	74
Chapter 134 - Youth Development [Recodified.]	74
Chapter 134A - Youth Services [Repealed.]	74
Chapter 135 - Retirement System for Teachers and State Employees; Social Security; Health Insurance Program for Children	74
Chapter 135 - Retirement System for Teachers and State Employees; Social Security; Health Insurance Program for Children	75
Chapter 136 - Transportation	75
Chapter 136 - Transportation (Continuation)	76
Chapter 137 - Rural Rehabilitation [Repealed.]	76
Chapter 138 - Salaries, Fees and Allowances	76
Chapter 138A - State Government Ethics Act	76
Chapter 139 - Soil and Water Conservation Districts	76

Chapter 140 - State Art Museum; Symphony and Art Societies	76
Chapter 140A - State Awards System	76
Chapter 141 - State Boundaries	76
Chapter 142 - State Debt	76
Chapter 143 - State Departments, Institutions, and Commissions	77
Chapter 143 - State Departments, Institutions, and Commissions (Continuation)	78
Chapter 143 - State Departments, Institutions, and Commissions (Continuation)	79
Chapter 143 - State Departments, Institutions, and Commissions (Continuation)	80
Chapter 143A - State Government Reorganization	80
Chapter 143B - Executive Organization Act of 1973	80
Chapter 143B - Executive Organization Act of 1973 (Continuation)	81
Chapter 143B - Executive Organization Act of 1973 (Continuation)	82
Chapter 143C - State Budget Act	83
Chapter 143D - The State Governmental Accountability and Internal Control Act	83
Chapter 144 - State Flag, Official Governmental Flags, Motto, and Colors	83
Chapter 145 - State Symbols and Other Official Adoptions.	83
Chapter 146 - State Lands	83
Chapter 147 - State Officers	83
Chapter 148 - State Prison System	84
Chapter 149 - State Song and Toast	84
Chapter 150 - Uniform Revocation of Licenses [Repealed.]	84
Chapter 150A - Administrative Procedure Act [Recodified.]	84
Chapter 150B - Administrative Procedure Act	84
Chapter 151 - Constables [Repealed.]	84
Chapter 152 - Coroners	84
Chapter 152A - County Medical Examiner [Repealed.]	84
Chapter 152A - County Medical Examiner [Repealed.] (Continuation)	85
Chapter 153 - Counties and County Commissioners [Repealed.]	85
Chapter 153A - Counties	85
Chapter 153B - Mountain Resources Planning Act	85
Chapter 153C - Uwharrie Regional Resources Act	85
Chapter 154 - County Surveyor [Repealed.]	85
Chapter 155 - County Treasurer [Repealed.]	85
Chapter 156 - Drainage	85
Chapter 156 – Drainage (Continuation)	86

Chapter 157 - Housing Authorities and Projects	86
Chapter 157A - Historic Properties Commissions [Transferred.]	86
Chapter 158 - Local Development	86
Chapter 159 - Local Government Finance	86
Chapter 159 - Local Government Finance (Continuation)	87
Chapter 159A - Pollution Abatement and Industrial Facilities Financing Act [Unconstitutional.]	87
Chapter 159B - Joint Municipal Electric Power and Energy Act	87
Chapter 159C - Industrial and Pollution Control Facilities Financing Act	87
Chapter 159D - The North Carolina Capital Facilities Financing Act	87
Chapter 159E - Registered Public Obligations Act	87
Chapter 159F - North Carolina Energy Development Authority [Repealed.]	87
Chapter 159G - Water Infrastructure	87
Chapter 159H - [Reserved.]	87
Chapter 159I - Solid Waste Management Loan Program and Local Government Special Obligation Bonds	87
Chapter 160 - Municipal Corporations [Repealed And Transferred.]	87
Chapter 160A - Cities and Towns	88
Chapter 160A - Cities and Towns (Continuation)	89
Chapter 160B - Consolidated City-County Act	89
Chapter 160C - Baseball Park Districts [Repealed.]	90
Chapter 161 - Register of Deeds	90
Chapter 162 - Sheriff	90
Chapter 162A - Water and Sewer Systems	90
Chapter 162B Continuity of Local Government in Emergency.	90
Chapter 163 Elections and Election Laws.	90
Chapter 163 Elections and Election Laws. (Continuation)	91
Chapter 164 Concerning the General Statutes of North Carolina.	92
Chapter 165 Veterans.	92
Chapter 166 Civil Preparedness Agencies [Repealed.]	92
Chapter 166A North Carolina Emergency Management Act.	92
Chapter 167 State Civil Air Patrol [Repealed.]	92
Chapter 168 Persons with Disabilities.	92
Chapter 168A Persons With Disabilities Protection Act.	92

Chapter 25.

Uniform Commercial Code.

Article 1.

General Provisions.

PART 1.

GENERAL PROVISIONS.

§ 25-1-101. Short titles.

(a)   This Chapter may be cited as the Uniform Commercial Code.

(b)   This Article may be cited as Uniform Commercial Code - General Provisions. (1965, c. 700, s. 1; 2006-112, s. 1.)

§ 25-1-102. Scope of Article.

Except as provided in G.S. 25-1-301, this Article applies to a transaction to the extent that it is governed by another Article of this Chapter. (2006-112, s. 1.)

§ 25-1-103. Construction of this Chapter to promote its purposes and policies; applicability of supplemental principles of law.

(a)   This Chapter shall be liberally construed and applied to promote its underlying purposes and policies, which are:

(1)   To simplify, clarify, and modernize the law governing commercial transactions;

(2)   To permit the continued expansion of commercial practices through custom, usage, and agreement of the parties; and

(3)   To make uniform the law among the various jurisdictions.

(b)   Unless displaced by the particular provisions of this Chapter, the principles of law and equity, including the law merchant and the law relative to capacity to contract, principal and agent, estoppel, fraud, misrepresentation, duress, coercion, mistake, bankruptcy, and other validating or invalidating cause supplement its provisions. (1917, c. 37, s. 56; C.S., s. 4039; 1941, c. 353, s. 18; G.S., s. 55-98; 1955, c. 1371, s. 2; 1965, c. 700, s. 1; 2006-112, s. 1.)

§ 25-1-104. Construction against implied repeal.

This Chapter being a general act intended as a unified coverage of its subject matter, no part of it shall be deemed to be impliedly repealed by subsequent legislation if such construction can reasonably be avoided. (1965, c. 700, s. 1; 2006-112, s. 1.)

§ 25-1-105. Severability.

If any provision or clause of this Chapter or its application to any person or circumstance is held invalid, the invalidity does not affect other provisions or applications of this Chapter that can be given effect without the invalid provision or application, and to this end the provisions of this Chapter are severable. (1965, c. 700, s. 1; 2006-112, s. 1.)

§ 25-1-106. Use of singular and plural; gender.

In this Chapter, unless the statutory context otherwise requires:

(1)   Words in the singular number include the plural, and those in the plural include the singular; and

(2)   Words of any gender also refer to any other gender. (1965, c. 700, s. 1; 2006-112, s. 1.)

§ 25-1-107. Section captions.

Section captions are part of this Chapter. The subsection headings in Article 9 of this Chapter are not parts of this Chapter. (1965, c. 700, s. 1; 2000-169, s. 4; 2006-112, s. 1.)

§ 25-1-108. Relation to Electronic Signatures in Global and National Commerce Act.

This Article modifies, limits, and supersedes the federal Electronic Signatures in Global and National Commerce Act, 15 U.S.C. § 7001, et seq., except that nothing in this Article modifies, limits, or supersedes Section 7001(c) of that Act or authorizes electronic delivery of any of the notices described in Section 7003(b) of that Act. (2006-112, s. 1.)

PART 2.

GENERAL DEFINITIONS AND PRINCIPLES OF INTERPRETATION.

§ 25-1-201. General definitions.

(a)   Unless the context otherwise requires, words or phrases defined in this section, or in the additional definitions contained in other Articles of this Chapter that apply to particular Articles or Parts thereof, have the meanings stated.

(b)   Subject to definitions contained in other articles of this Chapter that apply to particular articles or parts thereof:

(1)   "Action," in the sense of a judicial proceeding, includes recoupment, counterclaim, setoff, suit in equity, and any other proceeding in which rights are determined.

(2)   "Aggrieved party" means a party entitled to pursue a remedy.

(3)   "Agreement," as distinguished from "contract," means the bargain of the parties in fact, as found in their language or inferred from other circumstances, including course of performance, course of dealing, or usage of trade as provided in G.S. 25-1-303.

(4)   "Bank" means a person engaged in the business of banking and includes a savings bank, savings and loan association, credit union, and trust company.

(5)   "Bearer" means a person in control of a negotiable electronic document of title or a person in possession of a negotiable instrument, negotiable tangible

document of title, or certificated security that is payable to bearer or indorsed in blank.

(6) "Bill of lading" means a document of title evidencing the receipt of goods for shipment issued by a person engaged in the business of directly or indirectly transporting or forwarding goods. The term does not include a warehouse receipt.

(7) "Branch" includes a separately incorporated foreign branch of a bank.

(8) "Burden of establishing" a fact means the burden of persuading the trier of fact that the existence of the fact is more probable than its nonexistence.

(9) "Buyer in ordinary course of business" means a person that buys goods in good faith, without knowledge that the sale violates the rights of another person in the goods, and in the ordinary course from a person, other than a pawnbroker, in the business of selling goods of that kind. A person buys goods in the ordinary course if the sale to the person comports with the usual or customary practices in the kind of business in which the seller is engaged or with the seller's own usual or customary practices. A person that sells oil, gas, or other minerals at the wellhead or minehead is a person in the business of selling goods of that kind. A buyer in ordinary course of business may buy for cash, by exchange of other property, or on secured or unsecured credit, and may acquire goods or documents of title under a preexisting contract for sale. Only a buyer that takes possession of the goods or has a right to recover the goods from the seller under Article 2 of this Chapter may be a buyer in ordinary course of business. "Buyer in ordinary course of business" does not include a person that acquires goods in a transfer in bulk or as security for or in total or partial satisfaction of a money debt.

(10) "Conspicuous," with reference to a term, means so written, displayed, or presented that a reasonable person against which it is to operate ought to have noticed it. Whether a term is "conspicuous" or not is a decision for the court. Conspicuous terms include the following:

a. A heading in capitals equal to or greater in size than the surrounding text, or in contrasting type, font, or color to the surrounding text of the same or lesser size; and

b. Language in the body of a record or display in larger type than the surrounding text, or in contrasting type, font, or color to the surrounding text of the same size, or set off from surrounding text of the same size by symbols or other marks that call attention to the language.

(11)   "Consumer" means an individual who enters into a transaction primarily for personal, family, or household purposes.

(12)   "Contract," as distinguished from "agreement," means the total legal obligation that results from the parties' agreement as determined by this Chapter as supplemented by any other applicable laws.

(13)   "Creditor" includes a general creditor, a secured creditor, a lien creditor, and any representative of creditors, including an assignee for the benefit of creditors, a trustee in bankruptcy, a receiver in equity, and an executor or administrator of an insolvent debtor's or assignor's estate.

(14)   "Defendant" includes a person in the position of defendant in a counterclaim, cross-claim, or third-party claim.

(15)   "Delivery", with respect to an electronic document of title means voluntary transfer of control and with respect to an instrument, a tangible document of title, or chattel paper, means voluntary transfer of possession.

(16)   "Document of title" means a record (i) that in the regular course of business or financing is treated as adequately evidencing that the person in possession or control of the record is entitled to receive, control, hold, and dispose of the record and the goods the record covers and (ii) that purports to be issued by or addressed to a bailee and to cover goods in the bailee's possession which are either identified or are fungible portions of an identified mass. The term includes a bill of lading, transport document, dock warrant, dock receipt, warehouse receipt, and order for delivery of goods. An electronic document of title means a document of title evidenced by a record consisting of information stored in an electronic medium. A tangible document of title means a document of title evidenced by a record consisting of information that is inscribed on a tangible medium.

(17)   "Fault" means a default, breach, or wrongful act or omission.

(18)   "Fungible goods" means:

a.   Goods of which any unit, by nature or usage of trade, are the equivalent of any other like unit; or

b.   Goods that by agreement are treated as equivalent.

(19)   "Genuine" means free of forgery or counterfeiting.

(20)   "Good faith," except as otherwise provided in Article 5 of this Chapter, means honesty in fact and the observance of reasonable commercial standards of fair dealing.

(21)   "Holder" means:

a.   The person in possession of a negotiable instrument that is payable either to bearer or to an identified person that is the person in possession;

b.   The person in possession of a negotiable tangible document of title if the goods are deliverable either to bearer or to the order of the person in possession; or

c.   The person in control of a negotiable electronic document of title.

(22)   "Insolvency proceeding" includes an assignment for the benefit of creditors or other proceeding intended to liquidate or rehabilitate the estate of the person involved.

(23)   "Insolvent" means:

a.   Having generally ceased to pay debts in the ordinary course of business other than as a result of bona fide dispute;

b.   Being unable to pay debts as they become due; or

c.   Being insolvent within the meaning of federal bankruptcy law.

(24)   "Money" means a medium of exchange currently authorized or adopted by a domestic or foreign government. The term includes a monetary unit of account established by an intergovernmental organization or by agreement between two or more countries.

(25)   "Organization" means a person other than an individual.

(26) "Party," as distinguished from "third party," means a person that has engaged in a transaction or made an agreement subject to this Chapter.

(27) "Person" means an individual, corporation, business trust, estate, trust, partnership, limited liability company, association, joint venture, government, governmental subdivision, agency, or instrumentality, public corporation, or any other legal or commercial entity.

(28) "Present value" means the amount as of a date certain of one or more sums payable in the future, discounted to the date certain by use of either an interest rate specified by the parties if that rate is not manifestly unreasonable at the time the transaction is entered into or, if an interest rate is not so specified, a commercially reasonable rate that takes into account the facts and circumstances at the time the transaction is entered into.

(29) "Purchase" means taking by sale, lease, discount, negotiation, mortgage, pledge, lien, security interest, issue or reissue, gift, or any other voluntary transaction creating an interest in property.

(30) "Purchaser" means a person that takes by purchase.

(31) "Record" means information that is inscribed on a tangible medium or that is stored in an electronic or other medium and is retrievable in perceivable form.

(32) "Remedy" means any remedial right to which an aggrieved party is entitled with or without resort to a tribunal.

(33) "Representative" means a person empowered to act for another, including an agent, an officer of a corporation or association, and a trustee, executor, or administrator of an estate.

(34) "Right" includes remedy.

(35) "Security interest" means an interest in personal property or fixtures which secures payment or performance of an obligation. "Security interest" includes any interest of a consignor and a buyer of accounts, chattel paper, a payment intangible, or a promissory note in a transaction that is subject to Article 9 of this Chapter. "Security interest" does not include the special property interest of a buyer of goods on identification of those goods to a contract for sale under G.S. 25-2-401, but a buyer may also acquire a "security interest" by

complying with Article 9 of this Chapter. Except as otherwise provided in G.S. 25-2-505, the right of a seller or lessor of goods under Article 2 or 2A of this Chapter to retain or acquire possession of the goods is not a "security interest," but a seller or lessor may also acquire a "security interest" by complying with Article 9 of this Chapter. The retention or reservation of title by a seller of goods notwithstanding shipment or delivery to the buyer under G.S. 25-2-401 is limited in effect to a reservation of a "security interest." Whether a transaction in the form of a lease creates a "security interest" is determined pursuant to G.S. 25-1-203.

(36) "Send" in connection with a writing, record, or notice means:

a. To deposit in the mail or deliver for transmission by any other usual means of communication with postage or cost of transmission provided for and properly addressed and, in the case of an instrument, to an address specified thereon or otherwise agreed, or if there be none to any address reasonable under the circumstances; or

b. In any other way to cause to be received any record or notice within the time it would have arrived if properly sent.

(37) "Signed" includes using any symbol executed or adopted with present intention to adopt or accept a writing.

(38) "State" means a State of the United States, the District of Columbia, Puerto Rico, the United States Virgin Islands, or any territory or insular possession subject to the jurisdiction of the United States.

(39) "Surety" includes a guarantor or other secondary obligor.

(40) "Term" means a portion of an agreement that relates to a particular matter.

(41) "Unauthorized signature" means a signature made without actual, implied, or apparent authority. The term includes a forgery.

(42) "Warehouse receipt" means a document of title issued by a person engaged in the business of storing goods for hire.

(43) "Writing" includes printing, typewriting, or any other intentional reduction to tangible form. "Written" has a corresponding meaning. (1899, c. 733, ss. 25,

56, 191; Rev., ss. 2173, 2205, 2340, 3032; 1917, c. 37, ss. 4, 5, 58; 1919, c. 65, ss. 1, 10, 32, 42; c. 290; C.S., ss. 280, 283, 292, 314, 2976, 3005, 3037, 4037, 4044, 4046; 1941, c. 353, s. 22; G.S., s. 55-102; 1955, c. 1371, s. 2; 1961, c. 574; 1965, c. 700, s. 1; 1967, c. 562, s. 1; 1975, c. 862, ss. 2, 3; 1989 (Reg. Sess., 1990), c. 1024, s. 8(a)-(c); 1993, c. 463, s. 2; 1995, c. 232, s. 3; 2000-169, ss. 5-7; 2006-112, ss. 1, 26.)

§ 25-1-202. Notice; knowledge.

(a)   Subject to subsection (f) of this section, a person has "notice" of a fact if the person:

(1)   Has actual knowledge of it;

(2)   Has received a notice or notification of it; or

(3)   From all the facts and circumstances known to the person at the time in question, has reason to know that it exists.

(b)   "Knowledge" means actual knowledge. "Knows" has a corresponding meaning.

(c)   "Discover," "learn," or words of similar import refer to knowledge rather than to reason to know.

(d)   A person "notifies" or "gives" a notice or notification to another person by taking such steps as may be reasonably required to inform the other person in ordinary course, whether or not the other person actually comes to know of it.

(e)   Subject to subsection (f) of this section, a person "receives" a notice or notification when:

(1)   It comes to that person's attention; or

(2)   It is duly delivered in a form reasonable under the circumstances at the place of business through which the contract was made or at another location held out by that person as the place for receipt of such communications.

(f) Notice, knowledge, or a notice or notification received by an organization is effective for a particular transaction from the time it is brought to the attention of the individual conducting that transaction and, in any event, from the time it would have been brought to the individual's attention if the organization had exercised due diligence. An organization exercises due diligence if it maintains reasonable routines for communicating significant information to the person conducting the transaction and there is reasonable compliance with the routines. Due diligence does not require an individual acting for the organization to communicate information unless the communication is part of the individual's regular duties or the individual has reason to know of the transaction and that the transaction would be materially affected by the information. (1899, c. 733, ss. 25, 56, 191; Rev., ss. 2173, 2205, 2340, 3032; 1917, c. 37, ss. 4, 5, 58; 1919, c. 65, ss. 1, 10, 32, 42; c. 290; C.S., ss. 280, 283, 292, 314, 2976, 3005, 3037, 4037, 4044, 4046; 1941, c. 353, s. 22; G.S., s. 55-102; 1955, c. 1371, s. 2; 1961, c. 574; 1965, c. 700, s. 1; 1967, c. 562, s. 1; 1975, c. 862, ss. 2, 3; 1989 (Reg. Sess., 1990), c. 1024, s. 8(a)-(c); 1993, c. 463, s. 2; 1995, c. 232, s. 3; 2000-169, ss. 5-7; 2006-112, s. 1.)

§ 25-1-203. Lease distinguished from security interest.

(a) Whether a transaction in the form of a lease creates a lease or security interest is determined by the facts of each case.

(b) A transaction in the form of a lease creates a security interest if the consideration that the lessee is to pay the lessor for the right to possession and use of the goods is an obligation for the term of the lease and is not subject to termination by the lessee, and:

(1) The original term of the lease is equal to or greater than the remaining economic life of the goods;

(2) The lessee is bound to renew the lease for the remaining economic life of the goods or is bound to become the owner of the goods;

(3) The lessee has an option to renew the lease for the remaining economic life of the goods for no additional consideration or for nominal additional consideration upon compliance with the lease agreement; or

(4) The lessee has an option to become the owner of the goods for no additional consideration or for nominal additional consideration upon compliance with the lease agreement.

(c) A transaction in the form of a lease does not create a security interest merely because:

(1) The present value of the consideration the lessee is obligated to pay the lessor for the right to possession and use of the goods is substantially equal to or is greater than the fair market value of the goods at the time the lease is entered into;

(2) The lessee assumes risk of loss of the goods;

(3) The lessee agrees to pay, with respect to the goods, taxes, insurance, filing, recording, or registration fees, or service or maintenance costs;

(4) The lessee has an option to renew the lease or to become the owner of the goods;

(5) The lessee has an option to renew the lease for a fixed rent that is equal to or greater than the reasonably predictable fair market rent for the use of the goods for the term of the renewal at the time the option is to be performed; or

(6) The lessee has an option to become the owner of the goods for a fixed price that is equal to or greater than the reasonably predictable fair market value of the goods at the time the option is to be performed.

(d) Additional consideration is nominal if it is less than the lessee's reasonably predictable cost of performing under the lease agreement if the option is not exercised. Additional consideration is not nominal if:

(1) When the option to renew the lease is granted to the lessee, the rent is stated to be the fair market rent for the use of the goods for the term of the renewal determined at the time the option is to be performed; or

(2) When the option to become the owner of the goods is granted to the lessee, the price is stated to be the fair market value of the goods determined at the time the option is to be performed.

(e) The "remaining economic life of the goods" and "reasonably predictable" fair market rent, fair market value, or cost of performing under the lease agreement must be determined with reference to the facts and circumstances at the time the transaction is entered into. (1899, c. 733, ss. 25, 56, 191; Rev., ss. 2173, 2205, 2340, 3032; 1917, c. 37, ss. 4, 5, 58; 1919, c. 65, ss. 1, 10, 32, 42; c. 290; C.S., ss. 280, 283, 292, 314, 2976, 3005, 3037, 4037, 4044, 4046; 1941, c. 353, s. 22; G.S., s. 55-102; 1955, c. 1371, s. 2; 1961, c. 574; 1965, c. 700, s. 1; 1967, c. 562, s. 1; 1975, c. 862, ss. 2, 3; 1989 (Reg. Sess., 1990), c. 1024, s. 8(a)-(c); 1993, c. 463, s. 2; 1995, c. 232, s. 3; 2000-169, ss. 5-7; 2006-112, s. 1.)

§ 25-1-204. Value.

Except as otherwise provided in Articles 3, 4, and 5 of this Chapter, a person gives value for rights if the person acquires them:

(1) In return for a binding commitment to extend credit or for the extension of immediately available credit, whether or not drawn upon and whether or not a charge-back is provided for in the event of difficulties in collection;

(2) As security for, or in total or partial satisfaction of, a preexisting claim;

(3) By accepting delivery under a preexisting contract for purchase; or

(4) In return for any consideration sufficient to support a simple contract. (1899, c. 733, ss. 25, 56, 191; Rev., ss. 2173, 2205, 2340, 3032; 1917, c. 37, ss. 4, 5, 58; 1919, c. 65, ss. 1, 10, 32, 42; c. 290; C.S., ss. 280, 283, 292, 314, 2976, 3005, 3037, 4037, 4044, 4046; 1941, c. 353, s. 22; G.S., s. 55-102; 1955, c. 1371, s. 2; 1961, c. 574; 1965, c. 700, s. 1; 1967, c. 562, s. 1; 1975, c. 862, ss. 2, 3; 1989 (Reg. Sess., 1990), c. 1024, s. 8(a)-(c); 1993, c. 463, s. 2; 1995, c. 232, s. 3; 2000-169, ss. 5-7; 2006-112, s. 1.)

§ 25-1-205. Reasonable time; seasonableness.

(a) Whether a time for taking an action required by this Chapter is reasonable depends on the nature, purpose, and circumstances of the action.

(b) An action is taken seasonably if it is taken at or within the time agreed or, if no time is agreed, at or within a reasonable time. (1899, c. 733, s. 193; Rev., s. 2343; C.S., s. 2978; 1965, c. 700, s. 1; 2006-112, s. 1.)

§ 25-1-206. Presumptions.

Whenever this Chapter creates a "presumption" with respect to a fact, or provides that a fact is "presumed," the trier of fact must find the existence of the fact unless and until evidence is introduced that supports a finding of its nonexistence. (1899, c. 733, ss. 25, 56, 191; Rev., ss. 2173, 2205, 2340, 3032; 1917, c. 37, ss. 4, 5, 58; 1919, c. 65, ss. 1, 10, 32, 42; c. 290; C.S., ss. 280, 283, 292, 314, 2976, 3005, 3037, 4037, 4044, 4046; 1941, c. 353, s. 22; G.S., s. 55-102; 1955, c. 1371, s. 2; 1961, c. 574; 1965, c. 700, s. 1; 1967, c. 562, s. 1; 1975, c. 862, ss. 2, 3; 1989 (Reg. Sess., 1990), c. 1024, s. 8(a)-(c); 1993, c. 463, s. 2; 1995, c. 232, s. 3; 2000-169, ss. 5-7; 2006-112, s. 1.)

PART 3.

TERRITORIAL APPLICABILITY AND GENERAL RULES.

§ 25-1-301. Territorial applicability; parties' power to choose applicable law.

(a) Except as otherwise provided in this section, when a transaction bears a reasonable relation to this State and also to another state or nation the parties may agree that the law either of this State or of such other state or nation shall govern their rights and duties.

(b) In the absence of an agreement effective under subsection (a) of this section, and except as provided in subsection (c) of this section, this Chapter applies to transactions bearing an appropriate relation to this State.

(c) If one of the following provisions of this Chapter specifies the applicable law, that provision governs and a contrary agreement is effective only to the extent permitted by the law so specified:

(c) (1) G.S. 25-2-402;

(2) G.S. 25-2A-105 and G.S. 25-2A-106;

(3) G.S. 25-4-102;

(4) G.S. 25-4A-507;

(5) G.S. 25-5-116;

(6) G.S. 25-8-110;

(7) G.S. 25-9-301 through G.S. 25-9-307. (1965, c. 700, s. 1; 1975, c. 862, s. 1; 1993, c. 157, s. 2; 1997-181, s. 17; 1999-73, s. 2; 2000-169, s. 3; 2004-190, s. 2; 2006-112, s. 1.)

§ 25-1-302. Variation by agreement.

(a) Except as otherwise provided in subsection (b) of this section or elsewhere in this Chapter, the effect of provisions of this Chapter may be varied by agreement.

(b) The obligations of good faith, diligence, reasonableness, and care prescribed by this Chapter may not be disclaimed by agreement. The parties, by agreement, may determine the standards by which the performance of those obligations is to be measured if those standards are not manifestly unreasonable. Whenever this Chapter requires an action to be taken within a reasonable time, a time that is not manifestly unreasonable may be fixed by agreement.

(c) The presence in certain provisions of this Chapter of the phrase "unless otherwise agreed," or words of similar import, does not imply that the effect of other provisions may not be varied by agreement under this section. (1899, c. 733, s. 193; Rev., s. 2343; C.S., s. 2978; 1965, c. 700, s. 1; 2006-112, s. 1.)

§ 25-1-303. Course of performance, course of dealing, and usage of trade.

(a) A "course of performance" is a sequence of conduct between the parties to a particular transaction that exists if:

(1) The agreement of the parties with respect to the transaction involves repeated occasions for performance by a party; and

(2) The other party, with knowledge of the nature of the performance and opportunity for objection to it, accepts the performance or acquiesces in it without objection.

(b) A "course of dealing" is a sequence of conduct concerning previous transactions between the parties to a particular transaction that is fairly to be regarded as establishing a common basis of understanding for interpreting their expressions and other conduct.

(c) A "usage of trade" is any practice or method of dealing having such regularity of observance in a place, vocation, or trade as to justify an expectation that it will be observed with respect to the transaction in question. The existence and scope of such a usage must be proved as facts. If it is established that such a usage is embodied in a trade code or similar record, the interpretation of the record is a question of law.

(d) A course of performance or course of dealing between the parties or usage of trade in the vocation or trade in which they are engaged or of which they are or should be aware is relevant in ascertaining the meaning of the parties' agreement, may give particular meaning to specific terms of the agreement, and may supplement or qualify the terms of the agreement. A usage of trade applicable in the place in which part of the performance under the agreement is to occur may be so utilized as to that part of the performance.

(e) Except as otherwise provided in subsection (f) of this section, the express terms of an agreement and any applicable course of performance, course of dealing, or usage of trade must be construed whenever reasonable as consistent with each other. If such a construction is unreasonable:

(1) Express terms prevail over course of performance, course of dealing, and usage of trade;

(2) Course of performance prevails over course of dealing and usage of trade; and

(3) Course of dealing prevails over usage of trade.

(f) Subject to G.S. 25-2-209, a course of performance is relevant to show a waiver or modification of any term inconsistent with the course of performance.

(g) Evidence of a relevant usage of trade offered by one party is not admissible unless that party has given the other party notice that the court finds sufficient to prevent unfair surprise to the other party. (1965, c. 700, s. 1; 2006-112, s. 1.)

§ 25-1-304. Obligation of good faith.

Every contract or duty within this Chapter imposes an obligation of good faith in its performance and enforcement. (1965, c. 700, s. 1; 2006-112, s. 1.)

§ 25-1-305. Remedies to be liberally administered.

(a) The remedies provided by this Chapter shall be liberally administered to the end that the aggrieved party may be put in as good a position as if the other party had fully performed, but neither consequential or special damages nor penal damages may be had except as specifically provided in this Chapter or by other rule of law.

(b) Any right or obligation declared by this Chapter is enforceable by action unless the provision declaring it specifies a different and limited effect. (1965, c. 700, s. 1; 2006-112, s. 1.)

§ 25-1-306. Waiver or renunciation of claim or right after breach.

A claim or right arising out of an alleged breach may be discharged in whole or in part without consideration by agreement of the aggrieved party in an authenticated record. (1965, c. 700, s. 1; 2006-112, s. 1.)

§ 25-1-307. Prima facie evidence by third-party documents.

A document in due form purporting to be a bill of lading, policy or certificate of insurance, official weigher's or inspector's certificate, consular invoice, or any other document authorized or required by the contract to be issued by a third party is prima facie evidence of its own authenticity and genuineness and of the facts stated in the document by the third party. (1965, c. 700, s. 1; 2006-112, s. 1.)

§ 25-1-308. Performance or acceptance under reservation of rights.

(a) A party that with explicit reservation of rights performs or promises performance or assents to performance in a manner demanded or offered by the other party does not thereby prejudice the rights reserved. Such words as "without prejudice," "under protest," or the like are sufficient.

(b) Subsection (a) of this section does not apply to an accord and satisfaction. (1965, c. 700, s. 1; 1995, c. 232, s. 4; 2006-112, s. 1.)

§ 25-1-309. Option to accelerate at will.

A term providing that one party or that party's successor in interest may accelerate payment or performance or require collateral or additional collateral "at will" or when the party "deems itself insecure," or words of similar import, means that the party has power to do so only if that party in good faith believes that the prospect of payment or performance is impaired. The burden of establishing lack of good faith is on the party against which the power has been exercised. (1965, c. 700, s. 1; 2006-112, s. 1.)

§ 25-1-310. Subordinated obligations.

An obligation may be issued as subordinated to performance of another obligation of the person obligated, or a creditor may subordinate its right to performance of an obligation by agreement with either the person obligated or another creditor of the person obligated. Subordination does not create a security interest as against either the common debtor or a subordinated creditor. (1967, c. 562, s. 1; 2006-112, s. 1.)

Article 2.

Sales.

Part 1.

Short Title, General Construction and Subject Matter.

§ 25-2-101. Short title.

This article shall be known and may be cited as Uniform Commercial Code-Sales. (1965, c. 700, s. 1.)

§ 25-2-102. Scope; certain security and other transactions excluded from this article.

Unless the context otherwise requires, this article applies to transactions in goods; it does not apply to any transaction which although in the form of an unconditional contract to sell or present sale is intended to operate only as a security transaction nor does this article impair or repeal any statute regulating sales to consumers, farmers or other specified classes of buyers. (1965, c. 700, s. 1.)

§ 25-2-103. Definitions and index of definitions.

(1) In this article unless the context otherwise requires

(a) "Buyer" means a person who buys or contracts to buy goods.

(b) Repealed by Session Laws 2006-112, s. 2, effective October 1, 2006.

(c) "Receipt" of goods means taking physical possession of them.

(d) "Seller" means a person who sells or contracts to sell goods. Any manufacturer of self-propelled motor vehicles, as defined in G.S. 20-4.01, is also a "seller" with respect to buyers of its product to whom it makes an express warranty, notwithstanding any lack of privity between them, for purposes of all rights and remedies available to buyers under this Article.

(2) Other definitions applying to this article or to specified parts thereof, and the sections in which they appear are:

"Acceptance."	G.S. 25-2-606.
"Banker's credit."	G.S. 25-2-325.
"Between merchants."	G.S. 25-2-104.
"Cancellation."	G.S. 25-2-106 (4).
"Commercial unit."	G.S. 25-2-105.
"Confirmed credit."	G.S. 25-2-325.
"Conforming to contract."	G.S. 25-2-106.
"Contract for sale."	G.S. 25-2-106.
"Cover."	G.S. 25-2-712.
"Entrusting."	G.S. 25-2-403.
"Financing agency."	G.S. 25-2-104.
"Future goods."	G.S. 25-2-105.
"Goods."	G.S. 25-2-105.
"Identification."	G.S. 25-2-501.
"Installment contract."	G.S. 25-2-612.
"Letter of credit."	G.S. 25-2-325.

"Lot."	G.S. 25-2-105.
"Merchant."	G.S. 25-2-104.
"Overseas."	G.S. 25-2-323.
"Person in position of seller."	G.S. 25-2-707.
"Present sale."	G.S. 25-2-106.
"Sale."	G.S. 25-2-106.
"Sale on approval."	G.S. 25-2-326.
"Sale or return."	G.S. 25-2-326.
"Termination."	G.S. 25-2-106.

(3)   "Control" as provided in G.S. 25-7-106 and the following definitions in other Articles apply to this Article:

"Check"	G.S. 25-3-104.
"Consignee"	G.S. 25-7-102.
"Consignor"	G.S. 25-7-102.
"Consumer Goods"	G.S. 25-9-102.
"Dishonor"	G.S. 25-3-502.
"Draft"	G.S. 25-3-104.

(4)   In addition article 1 contains general definitions and principles of construction and interpretation applicable throughout this article. (1965, c. 700, s. 1; 1983, c. 598; 2000-169, s. 8; 2006-112, ss. 2, 27.)

§ 25-2-104. Definitions: "Merchant"; "between merchants"; "financing agency."

(1) "Merchant" means a person who deals in goods of the kind or otherwise by his occupation holds himself out as having knowledge or skill peculiar to the practices or goods involved in the transaction or to whom such knowledge or skill may be attributed by his employment of an agent or broker or other intermediary who by his occupation holds himself out as having such knowledge or skill.

(2) "Financing agency" means a bank, finance company or other person who in the ordinary course of business makes advances against goods or documents of title or who by arrangement with either the seller or the buyer intervenes in ordinary course to make or collect payment due or claimed under the contract for sale, as by purchasing or paying the seller's draft or making advances against it or by merely taking it for collection whether or not documents of title accompany or are associated with the draft. "Financing agency" includes also a bank or other person who similarly intervenes between persons who are in the position of seller and buyer in respect to the goods (G.S. 25-2-707).

(3) "Between merchants" means in any transaction with respect to which both parties are chargeable with the knowledge or skill of merchants. (1965, c. 700, s. 1; 2006-112, s. 28.)

§ 25-2-105. Definitions: Transferability; "goods"; "future" goods; "lot"; "commercial unit."

(1) "Goods" means all things (including specially manufactured goods) which are movable at the time of identification to the contract for sale other than the money in which the price is to be paid, investment securities (article 8) and things in action. "Goods" also includes the unborn young of animals and growing crops and other identified things attached to realty as described in the section on goods to be severed from realty (G.S. 25-2-107).

(2) Goods must be both existing and identified before any interest in them can pass. Goods which are not both existing and identified are "future" goods. A purported present sale of future goods or of any interest therein operates as a contract to sell.

(3) There may be a sale of a part interest in existing identified goods.

(4) An undivided share in an identified bulk of fungible goods is sufficiently identified to be sold although the quantity of the bulk is not determined. Any agreed proportion of such a bulk or any quantity thereof agreed upon by number, weight or other measure may to the extent of the seller's interest in the bulk be sold to the buyer who then becomes an owner in common.

(5) "Lot" means a parcel or a single article which is the subject matter of a separate sale or delivery, whether or not it is sufficient to perform the contract.

(6) "Commercial unit" means such a unit of goods as by commercial usage is a single whole for purposes of sale and division of which materially impairs its character or value on the market or in use. A commercial unit may be a single article (as a machine) or a set of articles (as a suite of furniture or an assortment of sizes) or a quantity (as a bale, gross, or carload) or any other unit treated in use or in the relevant market as a single whole. (1965, c. 700, s. 1.)

§ 25-2-106. Definitions: "Contract"; "agreement"; "contract for sale"; "sale"; "present sale"; "layaway contract"; "conforming" to contract; "termination"; "cancellation."

(1) In this article unless the context otherwise requires "contract" and "agreement" are limited to those relating to the present or future sale of goods, including layaway contracts. "Contract for sale" includes both a present sale of goods and a contract to sell goods at a future time. A "sale" consists in the passing of title from the seller to the buyer for a price (G.S. 25-2-401). A "present sale" means a sale which is accomplished by the making of the contract. A "layaway contract" means any contract for the sale of goods in which the seller agrees with the purchaser, in consideration for the purchaser's payment of a deposit, down payment, or similar initial payment, to hold identified goods for future delivery upon the purchaser's payment of a specified additional amount, whether in installments or otherwise.

(2) Goods or conduct including any part of a performance are "conforming" or conform to the contract when they are in accordance with the obligations under the contract.

(3) "Termination" occurs when either party pursuant to a power created by agreement or law puts an end to the contract otherwise than for its breach. On

"termination" all obligations which are still executory on both sides are discharged but any right based on prior breach or performance survives.

(4) "Cancellation" occurs when either party puts an end to the contract for breach by the other and its effect is the same as that of "termination" except that the cancelling party also retains any remedy for breach of the whole contract or any unperformed balance. (1965, c. 700, s. 1; 1967, c. 24, s. 6; 1993, c. 340, s. 1.)

§ 25-2-107. Goods to be severed from realty; recording.

(1) A contract for the sale of minerals or the like (including oil and gas) or a structure or its materials to be removed from realty is a contract for the sale of goods within this article if they are to be severed by the seller but until severance a purported present sale thereof which is not effective as a transfer of an interest in land is effective only as a contract to sell.

(2) A contract for the sale apart from the land of growing crops or other things attached to realty and capable of severance without material harm thereto but not described in subsection (1) or of timber to be cut is a contract for the sale of goods within this article whether the subject matter is to be severed by the buyer or by the seller even though it forms part of the realty at the time of contracting, and the parties can by identification effect a present sale before severance.

(3) The provisions of this section are subject to any third-party rights provided by the law relating to realty records, and the contract for sale may be executed and recorded as a document transferring an interest in land and shall then constitute notice to third parties of the buyer's rights under the contract for sale. (1965, c. 700, s. 1; 1975, c. 862, s. 4.)

Part 2.

Form, Formation and Readjustment of Contract.

§ 25-2-201. Formal requirements; statute of frauds.

(1) Except as otherwise provided in this section a contract for the sale of goods for the price of five hundred dollars ($500.00) or more is not enforceable by way of action or defense unless there is some writing sufficient to indicate that a contract for sale has been made between the parties and signed by the party against whom enforcement is sought or by his authorized agent or broker. A writing is not insufficient because it omits or incorrectly states a term agreed upon but the contract is not enforceable under this paragraph beyond the quantity of goods shown in such writing.

(2) Between merchants if within a reasonable time a writing in confirmation of the contract and sufficient against the sender is received and the party receiving it has reason to know its contents, it satisfies the requirements of subsection (1) against such party unless written notice of objection to its contents is given within ten days after it is received.

(3) A contract which does not satisfy the requirements of subsection (1) but which is valid in other respects is enforceable

(a) if the goods are to be specially manufactured for the buyer and are not suitable for sale to others in the ordinary course of the seller's business and the seller, before notice of repudiation is received and under circumstances which reasonably indicate that the goods are for the buyer, has made either a substantial beginning of their manufacture or commitments for their procurement; or

(b) if the party against whom enforcement is sought admits in his pleading, testimony or otherwise in court that a contract for sale was made, but the contract is not enforceable under this provision beyond the quantity of goods admitted; or

(c) with respect to goods for which payment has been made and accepted or which have been received and accepted (G.S. 25-2-606). (1965, c. 700, s. 1.)

PART 2.

FORM, FORMATION AND READJUSTMENT OF CONTRACT.

§ 25-2-202. Final written expression; parol or extrinsic evidence.

Terms with respect to which the confirmatory memoranda of the parties agree or which are otherwise set forth in a writing intended by the parties as a final expression of their agreement with respect to such terms as are included therein may not be contradicted by evidence of any prior agreement or of a contemporaneous oral agreement but may be explained or supplemented

(a)   by course of dealing or usage of trade (G.S. 25-1-205) or by course of performance (G.S. 25-2-208); and

(b)   by evidence of consistent additional terms unless the court finds the writing to have been intended also as a complete and exclusive statement of the terms of the agreement. (1965, c. 700, s. 1.)

§ 25-2-203. Seals inoperative.

The affixing of a seal to a writing evidencing a contract for sale or an offer to buy or sell goods does not constitute the writing a sealed instrument and the law with respect to sealed instruments does not apply to such a contract or offer. (1965, c. 700, s. 1.)

§ 25-2-204. Formation in general.

(1)   A contract for sale of goods may be made in any manner sufficient to show agreement, including conduct by both parties which recognizes the existence of such a contract.

(2)   An agreement sufficient to constitute a contract for sale may be found even though the moment of its making is undetermined.

(3)   Even though one or more terms are left open a contract for sale does not fail for indefiniteness if the parties have intended to make a contract and there is a reasonably certain basis for giving an appropriate remedy. (1965, c. 700, s. 1.)

§ 25-2-205. Firm offers.

An offer by a merchant to buy or sell goods in a signed writing which by its terms gives assurance that it will be held open is not revocable, for lack of consideration, during the time stated or if no time is stated for a reasonable time, but in no event may such period of irrevocability exceed three months; but any such term of assurance on a form supplied by the offeree must be separately signed by the offeror. (1965, c. 700, s. 1.)

§ 25-2-206. Offer and acceptance in formation of contract.

(1)   Unless otherwise unambiguously indicated by the language or circumstances

(a)   an offer to make a contract shall be construed as inviting acceptance in any manner and by any medium reasonable in the circumstances;

(b)   an order or other offer to buy goods for prompt or current shipment shall be construed as inviting acceptance either by a prompt promise to ship or by the prompt or current shipment of conforming or nonconforming goods, but such a shipment of nonconforming goods does not constitute an acceptance if the seller seasonably notifies the buyer that the shipment is offered only as an accommodation to the buyer.

(2)   Where the beginning of a requested performance is a reasonable mode of acceptance an offeror who is not notified of acceptance within a reasonable time may treat the offer as having lapsed before acceptance. (1965, c. 700, s. 1.)

§ 25-2-207. Additional terms in acceptance or confirmation.

(1)   A definite and seasonable expression of acceptance or a written confirmation which is sent within a reasonable time operates as an acceptance even though it states terms additional to or different from those offered or agreed upon, unless acceptance is expressly made conditional on assent to the additional or different terms.

(2) The additional terms are to be construed as proposals for addition to the contract. Between merchants such terms become part of the contract unless:

(a) the offer expressly limits acceptance to the terms of the offer;

(b) they materially alter it; or

(c) notification of objection to them has already been given or is given within a reasonable time after notice of them is received.

(3) Conduct by both parties which recognizes the existence of a contract is sufficient to establish a contract for sale although the writings of the parties do not otherwise establish a contract. In such case the terms of the particular contract consist of those terms on which the writings of the parties agree, together with any supplementary terms incorporated under any other provisions of this chapter. (1965, c. 700, s. 1; 1967, c. 562, s. 1.)

§ 25-2-208: Repealed by Session Laws 2006-112, s. 4, effective October 1, 2006.

§ 25-2-209. Modification, rescission and waiver.

(1) An agreement modifying a contract within this article needs no consideration to be binding.

(2) A signed agreement which excludes modification or rescission except by a signed writing cannot be otherwise modified or rescinded, but except as between merchants such a requirement on a form supplied by the merchant must be separately signed by the other party.

(3) The requirements of the statute of frauds section of this article (G.S. 25-2-201) must be satisfied if the contract as modified is within its provisions.

(4) Although an attempt at modification or rescission does not satisfy the requirements of subsection (2) or (3) it can operate as a waiver.

(5) A party who has made a waiver affecting an executory portion of the contract may retract the waiver by reasonable notification received by the other party that strict performance will be required of any term waived, unless the retraction would be unjust in view of a material change of position in reliance on the waiver. (1965, c. 700, s. 1.)

§ 25-2-210. Delegation of performance; assignment of rights.

(1) A party may perform his duty through a delegate unless otherwise agreed or unless the other party has a substantial interest in having his original promisor perform or control the acts required by the contract. No delegation of performance relieves the party delegating of any duty to perform or any liability for breach.

(2) Except as otherwise provided in G.S. 25-9-406, unless otherwise agreed, all rights of either seller or buyer can be assigned except where the assignment would materially change the duty of the other party, or increase materially the burden or risk imposed on him by his contract, or impair materially his chance of obtaining return performance. A right to damages for breach of the whole contract or a right arising out of the assignor's due performance of his entire obligation can be assigned despite agreement otherwise.

(3) The creation, attachment, perfection, or enforcement of a security interest in the seller's interest under a contract is not a transfer that materially changes the duty of or increases materially the burden or risk imposed on the buyer or impairs materially the buyer's chance of obtaining return performance within the purview of subsection (2) of this section unless, and then only to the extent that, enforcement actually results in a delegation of material performance of the seller. Even in that event, the creation, attachment, perfection, and enforcement of the security interest remain effective, but (i) the seller is liable to the buyer for damages caused by the delegation to the extent that the damages could not reasonably be prevented by the buyer, and (ii) a court having jurisdiction may grant other appropriate relief, including cancellation of the contract for sale or an injunction against enforcement of the security interest or consummation of the enforcement.

(4) Unless the circumstances indicate the contrary, a prohibition of assignment of "the contract" is to be construed as barring only the delegation to the assignee of the assignor's performance.

(5) An assignment of "the contract" or of "all my rights under the contract" or an assignment in similar general terms is an assignment of rights and unless the language or the circumstances (as in an assignment for security) indicate the contrary, it is a delegation of performance of the duties of the assignor and its acceptance by the assignee constitutes a promise by him to perform those duties. This promise is enforceable by either the assignor or the other party to the original contract.

(6) The other party may treat any assignment which delegates performance as creating reasonable grounds for insecurity and may without prejudice to his rights against the assignor demand assurances from the assignee. (1965, c. 700, s. 1; 2000-169, s. 9.)

Part 3.

GENERAL OBLIGATION AND CONSTRUCTION OF CONTRACT.

§ 25-2-301. General obligations of parties.

The obligation of the seller is to transfer and deliver and that of the buyer is to accept and pay in accordance with the contract. (1965, c. 700, s. 1.)

§ 25-2-302. Unconscionable contract or clause.

(1) If the court as a matter of law finds the contract or any clause of the contract to have been unconscionable at the time it was made the court may refuse to enforce the contract, or it may enforce the remainder of the contract without the unconscionable clause, or it may so limit the application of any unconscionable clause as to avoid any unconscionable result.

(2) When it is claimed or appears to the court that the contract or any clause thereof may be unconscionable the parties shall be afforded a reasonable opportunity to present evidence as to its commercial setting,

purpose and effect to aid the court in making the determination. (1971, c. 1055, s. 1.)

§ 25-2-303. Allocation or division of risks.

Where this article allocates a risk or a burden as between the parties "unless otherwise agreed," the agreement may not only shift the allocation but may also divide the risk or burden. (1965, c. 700, s. 1.)

§ 25-2-304. Price payable in money, goods, realty, or otherwise.

(1)   The price can be made payable in money or otherwise. If it is payable in whole or in part in goods each party is a seller of the goods which he is to transfer.

(2)   Even though all or part of the price is payable in an interest in realty the transfer of the goods and the seller's obligations with reference to them are subject to this article, but not the transfer of the interest in realty or the transferor's obligations in connection therewith. (1965, c. 700, s. 1.)

§ 25-2-305. Open price term.

(1)   The parties if they so intend can conclude a contract for sale even though the price is not settled. In such a case the price is a reasonable price at the time for delivery if

(a)   nothing is said as to price; or

(b)   the price is left to be agreed by the parties and they fail to agree; or

(c)   the price is to be fixed in terms of some agreed market or other standard as set or recorded by a third person or agency and it is not so set or recorded.

(2)   A price to be fixed by the seller or by the buyer means a price for him to fix in good faith.

(3) When a price left to be fixed otherwise than by agreement of the parties fails to be fixed through fault of one party the other may at his option treat the contract as cancelled or himself fix a reasonable price.

(4) Where, however, the parties intend not to be bound unless the price be fixed or agreed and it is not fixed or agreed there is no contract. In such a case the buyer must return any goods already received or if unable so to do must pay their reasonable value at the time of delivery and the seller must return any portion of the price paid on account. (1965, c. 700, s. 1.)

§ 25-2-306. Output, requirements and exclusive dealings.

(1) A term which measures the quantity by the output of the seller or the requirements of the buyer means such actual output or requirements as may occur in good faith, except that no quantity unreasonably disproportionate to any stated estimate or in the absence of a stated estimate to any normal or otherwise comparable prior output or requirements may be tendered or demanded.

(2) A lawful agreement by either the seller or the buyer for exclusive dealing in the kind of goods concerned imposes unless otherwise agreed an obligation by the seller to use best efforts to supply the goods and by the buyer to use best efforts to promote their sale. (1965, c. 700, s. 1.)

§ 25-2-307. Delivery in single lot or several lots.

Unless otherwise agreed all goods called for by a contract for sale must be tendered in a single delivery and payment is due only on such tender but where the circumstances give either party the right to make or demand delivery in lots the price if it can be apportioned may be demanded for each lot. (1965, c. 700, s. 1.)

§ 25-2-308. Absence of specified place for delivery.

Unless otherwise agreed

(a)   the place for delivery of goods is the seller's place of business or if he has none, his residence; but

(b)   in a contract for sale of identified goods which to the knowledge of the parties at the time of contracting are in some other place, that place is the place for their delivery; and

(c)   documents of title may be delivered through customary banking channels. (1965, c. 700, s. 1.)

§ 25-2-309. Absence of specific time provisions; notice of termination.

(1)   The time for shipment or delivery or any other action under a contract if not provided in this article or agreed upon shall be a reasonable time.

(2)   Where the contract provides for successive performances but is indefinite in duration it is valid for a reasonable time but unless otherwise agreed may be terminated at any time by either party.

(3)   Termination of a contract by one party except on the happening of an agreed event requires that reasonable notification be received by the other party and an agreement dispensing with notification is invalid if its operation would be unconscionable. (1965, c. 700, s. 1.)

PART 3.

GENERAL OBLIGATION AND CONSTRUCTION OF CONTRACT.

§ 25-2-310. Open time for payment or running of credit; authority to ship under reservation.

Unless otherwise agreed

(a)   payment is due at the time and place at which the buyer is to receive the goods even though the place of shipment is the place of delivery; and

(b) if the seller is authorized to send the goods he may ship them under reservation, and may tender the documents of title, but the buyer may inspect the goods after their arrival before payment is due unless such inspection is inconsistent with the terms of the contract (G.S. 25-2-513); and

(c) if delivery is authorized and made by way of documents of title otherwise than by subsection (b) then payment is due regardless of where the goods are to be received (i) at the time and place at which the buyer is to receive delivery of the tangible documents or (ii) at the time the buyer is to receive delivery of the electronic documents and at the seller's place of business or if none, the seller's residence; and

(d) where the seller is required or authorized to ship the goods on credit the credit period runs from the time of shipment but postdating the invoice or delaying its dispatch will correspondingly delay the starting of the credit period. (1965, c. 700, s. 1; 2006-112, s. 29.)

§ 25-2-311. Options and cooperation respecting performance.

(1) An agreement for sale which is otherwise sufficiently definite (subsection (3) of G.S. 25-2-204) to be a contract is not made invalid by the fact that it leaves particulars of performance to be specified by one of the parties. Any such specification must be made in good faith and within limits set by commercial reasonableness.

(2) Unless otherwise agreed specifications relating to assortment of the goods are at the buyer's option and except as otherwise provided in subsections (1) (c) and (3) of G.S. 25-2-319 specifications or arrangements relating to shipment are at the seller's option.

(3) Where such specification would materially affect the other party's performance but is not seasonably made or where one party's cooperation is necessary to the agreed performance of the other but is not seasonably forthcoming, the other party in addition to all other remedies

(a) is excused for any resulting delay in his own performance; and

(b) may also either proceed to perform in any reasonable manner or after the time for a material part of his own performance treat the failure to specify or to cooperate as a breach by failure to deliver or accept the goods. (1965, c. 700, s. 1.)

§ 25-2-312. Warranty of title and against infringement; buyer's obligation against infringement.

(1) Subject to subsection (2) there is in a contract for sale a warranty by the seller that

(a) the title conveyed shall be good, and its transfer rightful; and

(b) the goods shall be delivered free from any security interest or other lien or encumbrance of which the buyer at the time of contracting has no knowledge.

(2) A warranty under subsection (1) will be excluded or modified only by specific language or by circumstances which give the buyer reason to know that the person selling does not claim title in himself or that he is purporting to sell only such right or title as he or a third person may have.

(3) Unless otherwise agreed a seller who is a merchant regularly dealing in goods of the kind warrants that the goods shall be delivered free of the rightful claim of any third person by way of infringement or the like but a buyer who furnishes specifications to the seller must hold the seller harmless against any such claim which arises out of compliance with the specifications. (1965, c. 700, s. 1.)

§ 25-2-313. Express warranties by affirmation, promise, description, sample.

(1) Express warranties by the seller are created as follows:

(a) Any affirmation of fact or promise made by the seller to the buyer which relates to the goods and becomes part of the basis of the bargain creates an express warranty that the goods shall conform to the affirmation or promise.

(b) Any description of the goods which is made part of the basis of the bargain creates an express warranty that the goods shall conform to the description.

(c) Any sample or model which is made part of the basis of the bargain creates an express warranty that the whole of the goods shall conform to the sample or model.

(2) It is not necessary to the creation of an express warranty that the seller use formal words such as "warrant" or "guarantee" or that he have a specific intention to make a warranty, but an affirmation merely of the value of the goods or a statement purporting to be merely the seller's opinion or commendation of the goods does not create a warranty. (1965, c. 700, s. 1.)

§ 25-2-314. Implied warranty: Merchantability; usage of trade.

(1) Unless excluded or modified (G.S. 25-2-316), a warranty that the goods shall be merchantable is implied in a contract for their sale if the seller is a merchant with respect to goods of that kind. Under this section the serving for value of food or drink to be consumed either on the premises or elsewhere is a sale.

(2) Goods to be merchantable must be at least such as

(a) pass without objection in the trade under the contract description; and

(b) in the case of fungible goods, are of fair average quality within the description; and

(c) are fit for the ordinary purposes for which such goods are used; and

(d) run, within the variations permitted by the agreement, of even kind, quality and quantity within each unit and among all units involved; and

(e) are adequately contained, packaged, and labeled as the agreement may require; and

(f) conform to the promises or affirmations of fact made on the container or label if any.

(3) Unless excluded or modified (G.S. 25-2-316) other implied warranties may arise from course of dealing or usage of trade. (1965, c. 700, s. 1.)

§ 25-2-315. Implied warranty: Fitness for particular purpose.

Where the seller at the time of contracting has reason to know any particular purpose for which the goods are required and that the buyer is relying on the seller's skill or judgment to select or furnish suitable goods, there is unless excluded or modified under the next section [G.S. 25-2-316] an implied warranty that the goods shall be fit for such purpose. (1965, c. 700, s. 1.)

§ 25-2-316. Exclusion or modification of warranties.

(1) Words or conduct relevant to the creation of an express warranty and words or conduct tending to negate or limit warranty shall be construed wherever reasonable as consistent with each other; but subject to the provisions of this article on parol or extrinsic evidence (G.S. 25-2-202) negation or limitation is inoperative to the extent that such construction is unreasonable.

(2) Subject to subsection (3), to exclude or modify the implied warranty of merchantability or any part of it the language must mention merchantability and in case of a writing must be conspicuous, and to exclude or modify any implied warranty of fitness the exclusion must be by a writing and conspicuous. Language to exclude all implied warranties of fitness is sufficient if it states, for example, that "There are no warranties which extend beyond the description on the face hereof."

(3) Notwithstanding subsection (2)

(a) unless the circumstances indicate otherwise, all implied warranties are excluded by expressions like "as is," "with all faults" or other language which in common understanding calls the buyer's attention to the exclusion of warranties and makes plain that there is no implied warranty; and

(b) when the buyer before entering into the contract has examined the goods or the sample or model as fully as he desired or has refused to examine the goods there is no implied warranty with regard to defects which an examination ought in the circumstances to have revealed to him; and

(c) an implied warranty can also be excluded or modified by course of dealing or course of performance or usage of trade.

(4) Remedies for breach of warranty can be limited in accordance with the provisions of this article on liquidation or limitation of damages and on contractual modification of remedy (G.S. 25-2-718 and 25-2-719). (1965, c. 700, s. 1.)

§ 25-2-317. Cumulation and conflict of warranties express or implied.

Warranties whether express or implied shall be construed as consistent with each other and as cumulative, but if such construction is unreasonable the intention of the parties shall determine which warranty is dominant. In ascertaining that intention the following rules apply:

(a) Exact or technical specifications displace an inconsistent sample or model or general langauge of description.

(b) A sample from an existing bulk displaces inconsistent general language of description.

(c) Express warranties displace inconsistent implied warranties other than an implied warranty of fitness for a particular purpose. (1965, c. 700, s. 1.)

§ 25-2-318. Third party beneficiaries of warranties express or implied.

A seller's warranty whether express or implied extends to any natural person who is in the family or household of his buyer or who is a guest in his home if it is reasonable to expect that such person may use, consume or be affected by the goods and who is injured in person by breach of the warranty. A seller may not exclude or limit the operation of this section. (1965, c. 700, s. 1.)

§ 25-2-319. F.O.B. and F.A.S. terms.

(1)   Unless otherwise agreed the term F.O.B. (which means "free on board") at a named place, even though used only in connection with the stated price, is a delivery term under which

(a)   when the term is F.O.B. the place of shipment, the seller must at that place ship the goods in the manner provided in this article (G.S. 25-2-504) and bear the expense and risk of putting them into the possession of the carrier; or

(b)   when the term is F.O.B. the place of destination, the seller must at his own expense and risk transport the goods to that place and there tender delivery of them in the manner provided in this article (G.S. 25-2-503);

(c)   when under either (a) or (b) the term is also F.O.B. vessel, car or other vehicle, the seller must in addition at his own expense and risk load the goods on board. If the term is F.O.B. vessel the buyer must name the vessel and in an appropriate case the seller must comply with the provisions of this article on the form of bill of lading (G.S. 25-2-323).

(2)   Unless otherwise agreed the term F.A.S. vessel (which means "free alongside") at a named port, even though used only in connection with the stated price, is a delivery term under which the seller must

(a)   at his own expense and risk deliver the goods alongside the vessel in the manner usual in that port or on a dock designated and provided by the buyer; and

(b)   obtain and tender a receipt for the goods in exchange for which the carrier is under a duty to issue a bill of lading.

(3)   Unless otherwise agreed in any case falling within subsection (1)(a) or (c) or subsection (2) the buyer must seasonably give any needed instructions for making delivery, including when the term is F.A.S. or F.O.B. the loading berth of the vessel and in an appropriate case its name and sailing date. The seller may treat the failure of needed instructions as a failure of cooperation under this article (G.S. 25-2-311). He may also at his option move the goods in any reasonable manner preparatory to delivery or shipment.

(4)   Under the term F.O.B. vessel or F.A.S. unless otherwise agreed the buyer must make payment against tender of the required documents and the

seller may not tender nor the buyer demand delivery of the goods in substitution for the documents. (1965, c. 700, s. 1.)

§ 25-2-320. C.I.F. and C. & F. terms.

(1)   The term C.I.F. means that the price includes in a lump sum the cost of the goods and the insurance and freight to the named destination. The term C. & F. or C.F. means that the price so includes cost and freight to the named destination.

(2)   Unless otherwise agreed and even though used only in connection with the stated price and destination, the term C.I.F. destination or its equivalent requires the seller at his own expense and risk to

(a)   put the goods into the possession of a carrier at the port for shipment and obtain a negotiable bill or bills of lading covering the entire transportation to the named destination; and

(b)   load the goods and obtain a receipt from the carrier (which may be contained in the bill of lading) showing that the freight has been paid or provided for; and

(c)   obtain a policy or certificate of insurance, including any war risk insurance, of a kind and on terms then current at the port of shipment in the usual amount, in the currency of the contract, shown to cover the same goods covered by the bill of lading and providing for payment of loss to the order of the buyer or for the account of whom it may concern; but the seller may add to the price the amount of the premium for any such war risk insurance; and

(d)   prepare an invoice of the goods and procure any other documents required to effect shipment or to comply with the contract; and

(e)   forward and tender with commercial promptness all the documents in due form and with any indorsement necessary to perfect the buyer's rights.

(3)   Unless otherwise agreed the term C. & F. or its equivalent has the same effect and imposes upon the seller the same obligations and risks as a C.I.F. term except the obligation as to insurance.

(4) Under the term C.I.F. or C. & F. unless otherwise agreed the buyer must make payment against tender of the required documents and the seller may not tender nor the buyer demand delivery of the goods in substitution for the documents. (1965, c. 700, s. 1.)

§ 25-2-321. C.I.F. or C. & F.: "Net landed weights"; "payment on arrival"; warranty of condition on arrival.

Under a contract containing a term C.I.F. or C. & F.

(1) Where the price is based on or is to be adjusted according to "net landed weights," "delivered weights," "out turn" quantity or quality or the like, unless otherwise agreed the seller must reasonably estimate the price. The payment due on tender of the documents called for by the contract is the amount so estimated, but after final adjustment of the price a settlement must be made with commercial promptness.

(2) An agreement described in subsection (1) or any warranty of quality or condition of the goods on arrival places upon the seller the risk of ordinary deterioration, shrinkage and the like in transportation but has no effect on the place or time of identification to the contract for sale or delivery or on the passing of the risk of loss.

(3) Unless otherwise agreed where the contract provides for payment on or after arrival of the goods the seller must before payment allow such preliminary inspection as is feasible; but if the goods are lost delivery of the documents and payment are due when the goods should have arrived. (1965 c. 700, s. 1.)

§ 25-2-322. Delivery "ex-ship."

(1) Unless otherwise agreed a term for delivery of goods "ex-ship" (which means from the carrying vessel) or in equivalent language is not restricted to a particular ship and requires delivery from a ship which has reached a place at the named port of destination where goods of the kind are usually discharged.

(2) Under such a term unless otherwise agreed

(a) the seller must discharge all liens arising out of the carriage and furnish the buyer with a direction which puts the carrier under a duty to deliver the goods; and

(b) the risk of loss does not pass to the buyer until the goods leave the ship's tackle or are otherwise properly unloaded. (1965, c. 700, s. 1.)

§ 25-2-323. Form of bill of lading required in overseas shipment; "overseas."

(1) Where the contract contemplates overseas shipment and contains a term C.I.F. or C. & F. or F.O.B. vessel, the seller unless otherwise agreed must obtain a negotiable bill of lading stating that the goods have been loaded on board or, in the case of a term C.I.F. or C. & F., received for shipment.

(2) Where in a case within subsection (1) of this section a tangible bill of lading has been issued in a set of parts, unless otherwise agreed if the documents are not to be sent from abroad the buyer may demand tender of the full set; otherwise only one part of the bill of lading need be tendered. Even if the agreement expressly requires a full set

(a) due tender of a single part is acceptable within the provisions of this Article on cure of improper delivery (subsection (1) of G.S. 25-2-508); and

(b) even though the full set is demanded, if the documents are sent from abroad the person tendering an incomplete set may nevertheless require payment upon furnishing an indemnity which the buyer in good faith deems adequate.

(3) A shipment by water or by air or a contract contemplating such shipment is "overseas" insofar as by usage of trade or agreement it is subject to the commercial, financing or shipping practices characteristic of international deep water commerce. (1965, c. 700, s. 1; 2006-112, s. 30.)

§ 25-2-324. "No arrival, no sale" term.

Under a term "no arrival, no sale" or terms of like meaning, unless otherwise agreed,

(a) the seller must properly ship conforming goods and if they arrive by any means he must tender them on arrival but he assumes no obligation that the goods will arrive unless he has caused the non-arrival; and

(b) where without fault of the seller the goods are in part lost or have so deteriorated as no longer to conform to the contract or arrive after the contract time, the buyer may proceed as if there had been casualty to identified goods (G.S. 25-2-613). (1965, c. 700, s. 1.)

§ 25-2-325. "Letter of credit" term; "confirmed credit."

(1) Failure of the buyer seasonably to furnish an agreed letter of credit is a breach of the contract for sale.

(2) The delivery to seller of a proper letter of credit suspends the buyer's obligation to pay. If the letter of credit is dishonored, the seller may on seasonable notification to the buyer require payment directly from him.

(3) Unless otherwise agreed the term "letter of credit" or "banker's credit" in a contract for sale means an irrevocable credit issued by a financing agency of good repute and, where the shipment is overseas, of good international repute. The term "confirmed credit" means that the credit must also carry the direct obligation of such an agency which does business in the seller's financial market. (1965, c. 700, s. 1.)

§ 25-2-326. Sale on approval and sale or return; rights of creditors.

(1) Unless otherwise agreed, if delivered goods may be returned by the buyer even though they conform to the contract, the transaction is:

(a) a "sale on approval" if the goods are delivered primarily for use, and

(b) a "sale or return" if the goods are delivered primarily for resale.

(2) Goods held on approval are not subject to the claims of the buyer's creditors until acceptance; goods held on sale or return are subject to such claims while in the buyer's possession.

(3) Any "or return" term of a contract for sale is to be treated as a separate contract for sale within the statute of frauds section of this article (G.S. 25-2-201) and as contradicting the sale aspect of the contract within the provisions of this article on parol or extrinsic evidence (G.S. 25-2-202). (1965, c. 700, s. 1; 2000-169, s. 10.)

§ 25-2-327. Special incidents of sale on approval and sale or return.

(1) Under a sale on approval unless otherwise agreed

(a) although the goods are identified to the contract the risk of loss and the title do not pass to the buyer until acceptance; and

(b) use of the goods consistent with the purpose of trial is not acceptance but failure seasonably to notify the seller of election to return the goods is acceptance, and if the goods conform to the contract acceptance of any part is acceptance of the whole; and

(c) after due notification of election to return, the return is at the seller's risk and expense but a merchant buyer must follow any reasonable instructions.

(2) Under a sale or return unless otherwise agreed

(a) the option to return extends to the whole or any commercial unit of the goods while in substantially their original condition, but must be exercised seasonably; and

(b) the return is at the buyer's risk and expense. (1965, c. 700, s. 1.)

§ 25-2-328. Sale by auction.

(1) In a sale by auction if goods are put up in lots each lot is the subject of a separate sale.

(2) A sale by auction is complete when the auctioneer so announces by the fall of the hammer or in other customary manner. Where a bid is made while the hammer is falling in acceptance of a prior bid the auctioneer may in his discretion reopen the bidding or declare the goods sold under the bid on which the hammer was falling.

(3) Such a sale is with reserve unless the goods are in explicit terms put up without reserve. In an auction with reserve the auctioneer may withdraw the goods at any time until he announces completion of the sale. In an auction without reserve, after the auctioneer calls for bids on an article or lot, that article or lot cannot be withdrawn unless no bid is made within a reasonable time. In either case a bidder may retract his bid until the auctioneer's announcement of completion of the sale, but a bidder's retraction does not revive any previous bid.

(4) If the auctioneer knowingly receives a bid on the seller's behalf or the seller makes or procures such a bid, and notice has not been given that liberty for such bidding is reserved, the buyer may at his option avoid the sale or take the goods at the price of the last good faith bid prior to the completion of the sale. This subsection shall not apply to any bid at a forced sale. (1965, c. 700, s. 1.)

PART 4.

TITLE, CREDITORS AND GOOD FAITH PURCHASERS.

§ 25-2-401. Passing of title; reservation for security; limited application of this section.

Each provision of this article with regard to the rights, obligations and remedies of the seller, the buyer, purchasers or other third parties applies irrespective of title to the goods except where the provision refers to such title. Insofar as situations are not covered by the other provisions of this article and matters concerning title become material the following rules apply:

(1) Title to goods cannot pass under a contract for sale prior to their identification to the contract (G.S. 25-2-501), and unless otherwise explicitly agreed the buyer acquires by their identification a special property as limited by

this chapter. Any retention or reservation by the seller of the title (property) in goods shipped or delivered to the buyer is limited in effect to a reservation of a security interest. Subject to these provisions and to the provisions of the article on secured transactions (article 9), title to goods passes from the seller to the buyer in any manner and on any conditions explicitly agreed on by the parties.

(2)   Unless otherwise explicitly agreed title passes to the buyer at the time and place at which the seller completes his performance with reference to the physical delivery of the goods, despite any reservation of a security interest and even though a document of title is to be delivered at a different time or place; and in particular and despite any reservation of a security interest by the bill of lading

(a)   if the contract requires or authorizes the seller to send the goods to the buyer but does not require him to deliver them at destination, title passes to the buyer at the time and place of shipment; but

(b)   if the contract requires delivery at destination, title passes on tender there.

(3)   Unless otherwise explicitly agreed where delivery is to be made without moving the goods,

(a)   if the seller is to deliver a tangible document of title, title passes at the time when and the place where he delivers such documents and if the seller is to deliver an electronic document of title, title passes when the seller delivers the document; or

(b)   if the goods are at the time of contracting already identified and no documents of title are to be delivered, title passes at the time and place of contracting.

(4)   A rejection or other refusal by the buyer to receive or retain the goods, whether or not justified, or a justified revocation of acceptance revests title to the goods in the seller. Such revesting occurs by operation of law and is not a "sale." (1965, c. 700, s. 1; 2006-112, s. 31.)

§ 25-2-402. Rights of seller's creditors against sold goods.

(1) Except as provided in subsections (2) and (3), rights of unsecured creditors of the seller with respect to goods which have been identified to a contract for sale are subject to the buyer's rights to recover the goods under this article (G.S. 25-2-502 and 25-2-716).

(2) A creditor of the seller may treat a sale or an identification of goods to a contract for sale as void if as against him a retention of possession by the seller is fraudulent under any rule of law of the state where the goods are situated, except that retention of possession in good faith and current course of trade by a merchant-seller for a commercially reasonable time after a sale or identification is not fraudulent.

(3) Nothing in this article shall be deemed to impair the rights of creditors of the seller

(a) under the provisions of the article on secured transactions (article 9); or

(b) where identification to the contract or delivery is made not in current course of trade but in satisfaction of or as security for a pre-existing claim for money, security or the like and is made under circumstances which under any rule of law of the state where the goods are situated would apart from this article constitute the transaction a fraudulent transfer or voidable preference. (1965, c. 700, s. 1.)

§ 25-2-403. Power to transfer; good faith purchase of goods; "entrusting."

(1) A purchaser of goods acquires all title which his transferor had or had power to transfer except that a purchaser of a limited interest acquires rights only to the extent of the interest purchased. A person with voidable title has power to transfer a good title to a good faith purchaser for value. When goods have been delivered under a transaction of purchase the purchaser has such power even though

(a) the transferor was deceived as to the identity of the purchaser, or

(b) the delivery was in exchange for a check which is later dishonored, or

(c) it was agreed that the transaction was to be a "cash sale," or

(d) the delivery was procured through fraud punishable as larcenous under the criminal law.

(2) Any entrusting of possession of goods to a merchant who deals in goods of that kind gives him power to transfer all rights of the entruster to a buyer in ordinary course of business.

(3) "Entrusting" includes any delivery and any acquiescence in retention of possession regardless of any condition expressed between the parties to the delivery or acquiescence and regardless of whether the procurement of the entrusting or the possessor's disposition of the goods have been such as to be larcenous under the criminal law.

(4) The rights of other purchasers of goods and of lien creditors are governed by the articles on secured transactions (article 9) and documents of title (article 7). (1965, c. 700, s. 1; 2004-190, s. 3.)

Part 5.

Performance.

§ 25-2-501. Insurable interest in goods; manner of identification of goods.

(1) The buyer obtains a special property and an insurable interest in goods by identification of existing goods as goods to which the contract refers even though the goods so identified are nonconforming and he has an option to return or reject them. Such identification can be made at any time and in any manner explicitly agreed to by the parties. In the absence of explicit agreement identification occurs

(a) when the contract is made if it is for the sale of goods already existing and identified;

(b) if the contract is for the sale of future goods other than those described in paragraph (c), when goods are shipped, marked or otherwise designated by the seller as goods to which the contract refers;

(c) when the crops are planted or otherwise become growing crops or the young are conceived if the contract is for the sale of unborn young to be born within twelve months after contracting or for the sale of crops to be harvested within twelve months or the next normal harvest season after contracting whichever is longer.

(2) The seller retains an insurable interest in goods so long as title to or any security interest in the goods remains in him and where the identification is by the seller alone he may until default or insolvency or notification to the buyer that the identification is final substitute other goods for those identified.

(3) Nothing in this section impairs any insurable interest recognized under any other statute or rule of law. (1965, c. 700, s. 1; 1967, c. 24, s. 8.)

§ 25-2-502. Buyer's right to goods on seller's repudiation, failure to deliver, or insolvency.

(1) Subject to subsections (2) and (3) of this section and even though the goods have not been shipped, a buyer who has paid a part or all of the price of goods in which he has a special property under G.S. 25-2-501 may, on making and keeping good a tender of any unpaid portion of their price, recover them from the seller if:

a. in the case of goods bought for personal, family, or household purposes, the seller repudiates or fails to deliver as required by the contract; or

b. in all cases, the seller becomes insolvent within 10 days after receipt of the first installment on their price.

(2) The buyer's right to recover the goods under subdivision (1)a. of this section vests upon acquisition of a special property, even if the seller had not then repudiated or failed to deliver.

(3) If the identification creating his special property has been made by the buyer, he acquires the right to recover the goods only if they conform to the contract for sale. (1965, c. 700, s. 1; 2000-169, s. 11.)

PART 5.

PERFORMANCE.

§ 25-2-503. Manner of seller's tender of delivery.

(1)   Tender of delivery requires that the seller put and hold conforming goods at the buyer's disposition and give the buyer any notification reasonably necessary to enable him to take delivery. The manner, time and place for tender are determined by the agreement and this article, and in particular

(a)   tender must be at a reasonable hour, and if it is of goods they must be kept available for the period reasonably necessary to enable the buyer to take possession; but

(b)   unless otherwise agreed the buyer must furnish facilities reasonably suited to the receipt of the goods.

(2)   Where the case is within the next section [G.S. 25-2-504] respecting shipment tender requires that the seller comply with its provisions.

(3)   Where the seller is required to deliver at a particular destination tender requires that he comply with subsection (1) and also in any appropriate case tender documents as described in subsections (4) and (5) of this section.

(4)   Where goods are in the possession of a bailee and are to be delivered without being moved

(a)   tender requires that the seller either tender a negotiable document of title covering such goods or procure acknowledgment by the bailee of the buyer's right to possession of the goods; but

(b)   tender to the buyer of a non-negotiable document of title or of a record directing the bailee to deliver is sufficient tender unless the buyer seasonably objects, and, except as otherwise provided in Article 9 of this Chapter, receipt by the bailee of notification of the buyer's rights fixes those rights as against the bailee and all third persons; but risk of loss of the goods and of any failure by the bailee to honor the nonnegotiable document of title or to obey the direction remains on the seller until the buyer has had a reasonable time to present the document or direction, and a refusal by the bailee to honor the document or to obey the direction defeats the tender.

(5)   Where the contract requires the seller to deliver documents

(a) he must tender all such documents in correct form, except as provided in this article with respect to bills of lading in a set (subsection (2) of G.S. 25-2-323); and

(b) tender through customary banking channels is sufficient and dishonor of a draft accompanying or associated with the documents constitutes non-acceptance or rejection. (1965, c. 700, s. 1; 2006-112, s. 32.)

§ 25-2-504. Shipment by seller.

Where the seller is required or authorized to send the goods to the buyer and the contract does not require him to deliver them at a particular destination, then unless otherwise agreed he must

(a) put the goods in the possession of such a carrier and make such a contract for their transportation as may be reasonable having regard to the nature of the goods and other circumstances of the case; and

(b) obtain and promptly deliver or tender in due form any document necessary to enable the buyer to obtain possession of the goods or otherwise required by the agreement or by usage of trade; and

(c) promptly notify the buyer of the shipment.

Failure to notify the buyer under paragraph (c) or to make a proper contract under paragraph (a) is a ground for rejection only if material delay or loss ensues. (1965, c. 700, s. 1.)

§ 25-2-505. Seller's shipment under reservation.

(1) Where the seller has identified goods to the contract by or before shipment:

(a) his procurement of a negotiable bill of lading to his own order or otherwise reserves in him a security interest in the goods. His procurement of the bill to the order of a financing agency or of the buyer indicates in addition only the seller's expectation of transferring that interest to the person named.

(b)   a nonnegotiable bill of lading to himself or his nominee reserves possession of the goods as security but except in a case of conditional delivery (subsection (2) of G.S. 25-2-507) a nonnegotiable bill of lading naming the buyer as consignee reserves no security interest even though the seller retains possession or control of the bill of lading.

(2)   When shipment by the seller with reservation of a security interest is in violation of the contract for sale it constitutes an improper contract for transportation within G.S. 25-2-504 but impairs neither the rights given to the buyer by shipment and identification of the goods to the contract nor the seller's powers as a holder of a negotiable document of title. (1965, c. 700, s. 1; 2006-112, s. 33.)

§ 25-2-506. Rights of financing agency.

(1)   A financing agency by paying or purchasing for value a draft which relates to a shipment of goods acquires to the extent of the payment or purchase and in addition to its own rights under the draft and any document of title securing it any rights of the shipper in the goods including the right to stop delivery and the shipper's right to have the draft honored by the buyer.

(2)   The right to reimbursement of a financing agency which has in good faith honored or purchased the draft under commitment to or authority from the buyer is not impaired by subsequent discovery of defects with reference to any relevant document which was apparently regular. (1965, c. 700, s. 1; 2006-112, s. 34.)

§ 25-2-507. Effect of seller's tender; delivery on condition.

(1)   Tender of delivery is a condition to the buyer's duty to accept the goods and, unless otherwise agreed, to his duty to pay for them. Tender entitles the seller to acceptance of the goods and to payment according to the contract.

(2) Where payment is due and demanded on the delivery to the buyer of goods or documents of title, his right as against the seller to retain or dispose of them is conditional upon his making the payment due. (1965, c. 700, s. 1.)

§ 25-2-508. Cure by seller of improper tender or delivery; replacement.

(1) Where any tender or delivery by the seller is rejected because nonconforming and the time for performance has not yet expired, the seller may seasonably notify the buyer of his intention to cure and may then within the contract time make a conforming delivery.

(2) Where the buyer rejects a nonconforming tender which the seller had reasonable grounds to believe would be acceptable with or without money allowance the seller may if he seasonably notifies the buyer have a further reasonable time to substitute a conforming tender. (1965, c. 700, s. 1.)

§ 25-2-509. Risk of loss in the absence of breach.

(1) Where the contract requires or authorizes the seller to ship the goods by carrier

(a) if it does not require him to deliver them at a particular destination, the risk of loss passes to the buyer when the goods are duly delivered to the carrier even though the shipment is under reservation (G.S. 25-2-505); but

(b) if it does require him to deliver them at a particular destination and the goods are there duly tendered while in the possession of the carrier, the risk of loss passes to the buyer when the goods are there duly so tendered as to enable the buyer to take delivery.

(2) Where the goods are held by a bailee to be delivered without being moved, the risk of loss passes to the buyer

(a) on his receipt of possession or control of a negotiable document of title covering the goods; or

(b)   on acknowledgment by the bailee of the buyer's right to possession of the goods; or

(c)   after his receipt of possession or control of a nonnegotiable document of title or other direction to deliver in a record, as provided in subsection (4)(b) of G.S. 25-2-503.

(3)   In any case not within subsection (1) or (2), the risk of loss passes to the buyer on his receipt of the goods if the seller is a merchant; otherwise the risk passes to the buyer on tender of delivery.

(4)   The provisions of this section are subject to contrary agreement of the parties and to the provisions of this article on sale on approval (G.S. 25-2-327) and on effect of breach on risk of loss (G.S. 25-2-510). (1965, c. 700, s. 1; 2006-112, s. 35.)

§ 25-2-510. Effect of breach on risk of loss.

(1)   Where a tender or delivery of goods so fails to conform to the contract as to give a right of rejection the risk of their loss remains on the seller until cure or acceptance.

(2)   Where the buyer rightfully revokes acceptance he may to the extent of any deficiency in his effective insurance coverage treat the risk of loss as having rested on the seller from the beginning.

(3)   Where the buyer as to conforming goods already identified to the contract for sale repudiates or is otherwise in breach before risk of their loss has passed to him, the seller may to the extent of any deficiency in his effective insurance coverage treat the risk of loss as resting on the buyer for a commercially reasonable time. (1965, c. 700, s. 1.)

§ 25-2-511. Tender of payment by buyer; payment by check.

(1)   Unless otherwise agreed tender of payment is a condition to the seller's duty to tender and complete any delivery.

(2)   Tender of payment is sufficient when made by any means or in any manner current in the ordinary course of business unless the seller demands

payment in legal tender and gives any extension of time reasonably necessary to procure it.

(3)   Subject to the provisions of this chapter on the effect of an instrument on an obligation (G.S. 25-3-310), payment by check is conditional and is defeated as between the parties by dishonor of the check on due presentment. (1965, c. 700, s. 1; 1995, c. 232, s. 5.)

§ 25-2-512. Payment by buyer before inspection.

(1)   Where the contract requires payment before inspection nonconformity of the goods does not excuse the buyer from so making payment unless

(a)   the nonconformity appears without inspection; or

(b)   despite tender of the required documents the circumstances would justify injunction against honor under this chapter (G.S. 25-5-109(b)).

(2)   Payment pursuant to subsection (1) does not constitute an acceptance of goods or impair the buyer's right to inspect or any of his remedies. (1965, c. 700, s. 1; 1999-73, s. 3.)

§ 25-2-513. Buyer's right to inspection of goods.

(1)   Unless otherwise agreed and subject to subsection (3), where goods are tendered or identified to the contract for sale, the buyer has a right before payment or acceptance to inspect them at any reasonable place and time and in any reasonable manner. When the seller is required or authorized to send the goods to the buyer, the inspection may be after their arrival.

(2)   Expenses of inspection must be borne by the buyer but may be recovered from the seller if the goods do not conform and are rejected.

(3)   Unless otherwise agreed and subject to the provisions of this article on C.I.F. contracts (subsection (3) of G.S. 25-2-321), the buyer is not entitled to inspect the goods before payment of the price when the contract provides

(a)   for delivery "C.O.D." or on other like terms; or

(b)   for payment against documents of title, except where such payment is due only after the goods are to become available for inspection.

(4)   A place or method of inspection fixed by the parties is presumed to be exclusive but unless otherwise expressly agreed it does not postpone identification or shift the place for delivery or for passing the risk of loss. If compliance becomes impossible, inspection shall be as provided in this section unless the place or method fixed was clearly intended as an indispensable condition failure of which avoids the contract. (1965, c. 700, s. 1.)

§ 25-2-514. When documents deliverable on acceptance; when on payment.

Unless otherwise agreed documents against which a draft is drawn are to be delivered to the drawee on acceptance of the draft if it is payable more than three days after presentment; otherwise, only on payment. (1965, c. 700, s. 1.)

§ 25-2-515. Preserving evidence of goods in dispute.

In furtherance of the adjustment of any claim or dispute

(a)   either party on reasonable notification to the other and for the purpose of ascertaining the facts and preserving evidence has the right to inspect, test and sample the goods including such of them as may be in the possession or control of the other; and

(b)   the parties may agree to a third party inspection or survey to determine the conformity or condition of the goods and may agree that the findings shall be binding upon them in any subsequent litigation or adjustment. (1965, c. 700, s. 1.)

Part 6.

Breach, Repudiation and Excuse.

§ 25-2-601. Buyer's rights on improper delivery.

Subject to the provisions of this article on breach in installment contracts (G.S. 25-2-612) and unless otherwise agreed under the sections on contractual limitations of remedy (G.S. 25-2-718 and 25-2-719), if the goods or the tender of delivery fail in any respect to conform to the contract, the buyer may

(a) reject the whole; or

(b) accept the whole; or

(c) accept any commercial unit or units and reject the rest. (1965, c. 700, s. 1.)

§ 25-2-602. Manner and effect of rightful rejection.

(1) Rejection of goods must be within a reasonable time after their delivery or tender. It is ineffective unless the buyer seasonably notifies the seller.

(2) Subject to the provisions of the two following sections on rejected goods (G.S. 25-2-603 and 25-2-604),

(a) after rejection any exercise of ownership by the buyer with respect to any commercial unit is wrongful as against the seller; and

(b) if the buyer has before rejection taken physical possession of goods in which he does not have a security interest under the provisions of this article (subsection (3) of G.S. 25-2-711), he is under a duty after rejection to hold them with reasonable care at the seller's disposition for a time sufficient to permit the seller to remove them; but

(c) the buyer has no further obligations with regard to goods rightfully rejected.

(3) The seller's rights with respect to goods wrongfully rejected are governed by the provisions of this article on seller's remedies in general (G.S. 25-2-703). (1965, c. 700, s. 1.)

§ 25-2-603. Merchant buyer's duties as to rightfully rejected goods.

(1)   Subject to any security interest in the buyer (subsection (3) of G.S. 25-2-711), when the seller has no agent or place of business at the market of rejection a merchant buyer is under a duty after rejection of goods in his possession or control to follow any reasonable instructions received from the seller with respect to the goods and in the absence of such instructions to make reasonable efforts to sell them for the seller's account if they are perishable or threaten to decline in value speedily. Instructions are not reasonable if on demand indemnity for expenses is not forthcoming.

(2)   When the buyer sells goods under subsection (1), he is entitled to reimbursement from the seller or out of the proceeds for reasonable expenses of caring for and selling them, and if the expenses include no selling commission then to such commission as is usual in the trade or if there is none to a reasonable sum not exceeding ten per cent (10%) on the gross proceeds.

(3)   In complying with this section the buyer is held only to good faith and good faith conduct hereunder is neither acceptance nor conversion nor the basis of an action for damages. (1965, c. 700, s. 1.)

§ 25-2-604. Buyer's options as to salvage of rightfully rejected goods.

Subject to the provisions of the immediately preceding section [G.S. 25-2-603] on perishables if the seller gives no instructions within a reasonable time after notification of rejection the buyer may store the rejected goods for the seller's account or reship them to him or resell them for the seller's account with reimbursement as provided in the preceding section. Such action is not acceptance or conversion. (1965, c. 700, s. 1.)

PART 6.

BREACH, REPUDIATION AND EXCUSE.

§ 25-2-605. Waiver of buyer's objections by failure to particularize.

(1) The buyer's failure to state in connection with rejection a particular defect which is ascertainable by reasonable inspection precludes him from relying on the unstated defect to justify rejection or to establish breach

(a) where the seller could have cured it if stated seasonably; or

(b) between merchants when the seller has after rejection made a request in writing for a full and final written statement of all defects on which the buyer proposes to rely.

(2) Payment against documents made without reservation of rights precludes recovery of the payment for defects apparent in the documents. (1965, c. 700, s. 1; 2006-112, s. 36.)

§ 25-2-606. What constitutes acceptance of goods.

(1) Acceptance of goods occurs when the buyer

(a) after a reasonable opportunity to inspect the goods signifies to the seller that the goods are conforming or that he will take or retain them in spite of their non-conformity; or

(b) fails to make an effective rejection (subsection (1) of G.S. 25-2-602), but such acceptance does not occur until the buyer has had a reasonable opportunity to inspect them; or

(c) does any act inconsistent with the seller's ownership; but if such act is wrongful as against the seller it is an acceptance only if ratified by him.

(2) Acceptance of a part of any commercial unit is acceptance of that entire unit. (1965, c. 700, s. 1.)

§ 25-2-607. Effect of acceptance; notice of breach; burden of establishing breach after acceptance; notice of claim or litigation to person answerable over.

(1) The buyer must pay at the contract rate for any goods accepted.

(2) Acceptance of goods by the buyer precludes rejection of the goods accepted and if made with knowledge of a nonconformity cannot be revoked because of it unless the acceptance was on the reasonable assumption that the nonconformity would be seasonably cured but acceptance does not of itself impair any other remedy provided by this article for nonconformity.

(3) Where a tender has been accepted

(a) the buyer must within a reasonable time after he discovers or should have discovered any breach notify the seller of breach or be barred from any remedy; and

(b) if the claim is one for infringement or the like (subsection (3) of G.S. 25-2-312) and the buyer is sued as a result of such a breach he must so notify the seller within a reasonable time after he receives notice of the litigation or be barred from any remedy over for liability established by the litigation.

(4) The burden is on the buyer to establish any breach with respect to the goods accepted.

(5) Where the buyer is sued for breach of a warranty or other obligation for which his seller is answerable over

(a) he may give his seller written notice of the litigation. If the notice states that the seller may come in and defend and that if the seller does not do so he will be bound in any action against him by his buyer by any determination of fact common to the two litigations, then unless the seller after seasonable receipt of the notice does come in and defend he is so bound.

(b) if the claim is one for infringement or the like (subsection (3) of G.S. 25-2-312) the original seller may demand in writing that his buyer turn over to him control of the litigation including settlement or else be barred from any remedy over and if he also agrees to bear all expense and to satisfy any adverse judgment, then unless the buyer after seasonable receipt of the demand does turn over control the buyer is so barred.

(6) The provisions of subsections (3), (4) and (5) apply to any obligation of a buyer to hold the seller harmless against infringement or the like (subsection (3) of G.S. 25-2-312). (1965, c. 700, s. 1.)

§ 25-2-608. Revocation of acceptance in whole or in part.

(1)   The buyer may revoke his acceptance of a lot or commercial unit whose nonconformity substantially impairs its value to him if he has accepted it

(a)   on the reasonable assumption that its nonconformity would be cured and it has not been seasonably cured; or

(b)   without discovery of such nonconformity if his acceptance was reasonably induced either by the difficulty of discovery before acceptance or by the seller's assurances.

(2)   Revocation of acceptance must occur within a reasonable time after the buyer discovers or should have discovered the ground for it and before any substantial change in condition of the goods which is not caused by their own defects. It is not effective until the buyer notifies the seller of it.

(3)   A buyer who so revokes has the same rights and duties with regard to the goods involved as if he had rejected them. (1965, c. 700, s. 1.)

§ 25-2-609. Right to adequate assurance of performance.

(1)   A contract for sale imposes an obligation on each party that the other's expectation of receiving due performance will not be impaired. When reasonable grounds for insecurity arise with respect to the performance of either party the other may in writing demand adequate assurance of due performance and until he receives such assurance may if commercially reasonable suspend any performance for which he has not already received the agreed return.

(2)   Between merchants the reasonableness of grounds for insecurity and the adequacy of any assurance offered shall be determined according to commercial standards.

(3)   Acceptance of any improper delivery or payment does not prejudice the aggrieved party's right to demand adequate assurance of future performance.

(4) After receipt of a justified demand failure to provide within a reasonable time not exceeding thirty days such assurance of due performance as is adequate under the circumstances of the particular case is a repudiation of the contract. (1965, c. 700, s. 1.)

§ 25-2-610. Anticipatory repudiation.

When either party repudiates the contract with respect to a performance not yet due the loss of which will substantially impair the value of the contract to the other, the aggrieved party may

(a) for a commercially reasonable time await performance by the repudiating party; or

(b) resort to any remedy for breach (G.S. 25-2-703 or G.S. 25-2-711), even though he has notified the repudiating party that he would await the latter's performance and has urged retraction; and

(c) in either case suspend his own performance or proceed in accordance with the provisions of this article on the seller's right to identify goods to the contract notwithstanding breach or to salvage unfinished goods (G.S. 25-2-704). (1965, c. 700, s. 1.)

§ 25-2-611. Retraction of anticipatory repudiation.

(1) Until the repudiating party's next performance is due he can retract his repudiation unless the aggrieved party has since the repudiation cancelled or materially changed his position or otherwise indicated that he considers the repudiation final.

(2) Retraction may be by any method which clearly indicates to the aggrieved party that the repudiating party intends to perform, but must include any assurance justifiably demanded under the provisions of this article (G.S. 25-2-609).

(3) Retraction reinstates the repudiating party's rights under the contract with due excuse and allowance to the aggrieved party for any delay occasioned by the repudiation. (1965, c. 700, s. 1.)

§ 25-2-612. "Installment contract"; breach.

(1) An "installment contract" is one which requires or authorizes the delivery of goods in separate lots to be separately accepted, even though the contract contains a clause "each delivery is a separate contract" or its equivalent.

(2) The buyer may reject any installment which is nonconforming if the nonconformity substantially impairs the value of that installment and cannot be cured or if the nonconformity is a defect in the required documents; but if the nonconformity does not fall within subsection (3) and the seller gives adequate assurance of its cure the buyer must accept that installment.

(3) Whenever nonconformity or default with respect to one or more installments substantially impairs the value of the whole contract there is a breach of the whole. But the aggrieved party reinstates the contract if he accepts a nonconforming installment without seasonably notifying of cancellation or if he brings an action with respect only to past installments or demands performance as to future installments. (1965, c. 700, s. 1.)

§ 25-2-613. Casualty to identified goods.

Where the contract requires for its performance goods identified when the contract is made, and the goods suffer casualty without fault of either party before the risk of loss passes to the buyer, or in a proper case under a "no arrival, no sale" term (G.S. 25-2-324) then

(a) if the loss is total the contract is avoided; and

(b) if the loss is partial or the goods have so deteriorated as no longer to conform to the contract the buyer may nevertheless demand inspection and at his option either treat the contract as avoided or accept the goods with due allowance from the contract price for the deterioration or the deficiency in quantity but without further right against the seller. (1965, c. 700, s. 1.)

§ 25-2-614. Substituted performance.

(1)   Where without fault of either party the agreed berthing, loading, or unloading facilities fail or an agreed type of carrier becomes unavailable or the agreed manner of delivery otherwise becomes commercially impracticable but a commercially reasonable substitute is available, such substitute performance must be tendered and accepted.

(2)   If the agreed means or manner of payment fails because of domestic or foreign governmental regulation, the seller may withhold or stop delivery unless the buyer provides a means or manner of payment which is commercially a substantial equivalent. If delivery has already been taken, payment by the means or in the manner provided by the regulation discharges the buyer's obligation unless the regulation is discriminatory, oppressive or predatory. (1965, c. 700, s. 1.)

§ 25-2-615. Excuse by failure of presupposed conditions.

Except so far as a seller may have assumed a greater obligation and subject to the preceding section [G.S. 25-2-614] on substituted performance:

(a)   Delay in delivery or nondelivery in whole or in part by a seller who complies with paragraphs (b) and (c) is not a breach of his duty under a contract for sale if performance as agreed has been made impracticable by the occurrence of a contingency the nonoccurrence of which was a basic assumption on which the contract was made or by compliance in good faith with any applicable foreign or domestic governmental regulation or order whether or not it later proves to be invalid.

(b)   Where the causes mentioned in paragraph (a) affect only a part of the seller's capacity to perform, he must allocate production and deliveries among his customers but may at his option include regular customers not then under contract as well as his own requirements for further manufacture. He may so allocate in any manner which is fair and reasonable.

(c) The seller must notify the buyer seasonably that there will be delay or nondelivery and, when allocation is required under paragraph (b), of the estimated quota thus made available for the buyer. (1965, c. 700, s. 1.)

§ 25-2-616. Procedure on notice claiming excuse.

(1) Where the buyer receives notification of a material or indefinite delay or an allocation justified under the preceding section [G.S. 25-2-615] he may by written notification to the seller as to any delivery concerned, and where the prospective deficiency substantially impairs the value of the whole contract under the provisions of this article relating to breach of installment contracts (G.S. 25-2-612), then also as to the whole,

(a) terminate and thereby discharge any unexecuted portion of the contract; or

(b) modify the contract by agreeing to take his available quota in substitution.

(2) If after receipt of such notification from the seller the buyer fails so to modify the contract within a reasonable time not exceeding thirty days the contract lapses with respect to any deliveries affected.

(3) The provisions of this section may not be negated by agreement except insofar as the seller has assumed a greater obligation under the preceding section [G.S. 25-2-615]. (1965, c. 700, s. 1.)

Part 7.

Remedies.

§ 25-2-701. Remedies for breach of collateral contracts not impaired.

Remedies for breach of any obligation or promise collateral or ancillary to a contract for sale are not impaired by the provisions of this article. (1965, c. 700, s. 1.)

§ 25-2-702. Seller's remedies on discovery of buyer's insolvency.

(1) Where the seller discovers the buyer to be insolvent he may refuse delivery except for cash including payment for all goods theretofore delivered under the contract, and stop delivery under this article (G.S. 25-2-705).

(2) Where the seller discovers that the buyer has received goods on credit while insolvent he may reclaim the goods upon demand made within ten days after the receipt, but if misrepresentation of solvency has been made to the particular seller in writing within three months before delivery the ten-day limitation does not apply. Except as provided in this subsection the seller may not base a right to reclaim goods on the buyer's fraudulent or innocent misrepresentation of solvency or of intent to pay.

(3) The seller's right to reclaim under subsection (2) is subject to the rights of a buyer in ordinary course or other good faith purchaser under this article (G.S. 25-2-403). Successful reclamation of goods excludes all other remedies with respect to them. (1965, c. 700, s. 1; 1967, c. 562, s. 1.)

§ 25-2-703. Seller's remedies in general.

Where the buyer wrongfully rejects or revokes acceptance of goods or fails to make a payment due on or before delivery or repudiates with respect to a part or the whole, then with respect to any goods directly affected and, if the breach is of the whole contract (G.S. 25-2-612), then also with respect to the whole undelivered balance, the aggrieved seller may

(a) withhold delivery of such goods;

(b) stop delivery by any bailee as hereafter provided (G.S. 25-2-705);

(c) proceed under the next section [G.S. 25-2-704] respecting goods still unidentified to the contract;

(d) resell and recover damages as hereafter provided (G.S. 25-2-706);

(e) recover damages for nonacceptance (G.S. 25-2-708) or in a proper case the price (G.S. 25-2-709);

(f) cancel. (1965, c. 700, s. 1.)

§ 25-2-704. Seller's right to identify goods to the contract notwithstanding breach or to salvage unfinished goods.

(1) An aggrieved seller under the preceding section [G.S. 25-2-703] may

(a) identify to the contract conforming goods not already identified if at the time he learned of the breach they are in his possession or control;

(b) treat as the subject of resale goods which have demonstrably been intended for the particular contract even though those goods are unfinished.

(2) Where the goods are unfinished an aggrieved seller may in the exercise of reasonable commercial judgment for the purposes of avoiding loss and of effective realization either complete the manufacture and wholly identify the goods to the contract or cease manufacture and resell for scrap or salvage value or proceed in any other reasonable manner. (1965, c. 700, s. 1; 1967, c. 24, s. 9.)

PART 7.

REMEDIES.

§ 25-2-705. Seller's stoppage of delivery in transit or otherwise.

(1) The seller may stop delivery of goods in the possession of a carrier or other bailee when he discovers the buyer to be insolvent (G.S. 25-2-702) and may stop delivery of carload, truckload, planeload or larger shipments of express or freight when the buyer repudiates or fails to make a payment due before delivery or if for any other reason the seller has a right to withhold or reclaim the goods.

(2) As against such buyer the seller may stop delivery until

(a) receipt of the goods by the buyer; or

(b) acknowledgment to the buyer by any bailee of the goods except a carrier that the bailee holds the goods for the buyer; or

(c) such acknowledgment to the buyer by a carrier by reshipment or as a warehouse; or

(d) negotiation to the buyer of any negotiable document of title covering the goods.

(3) (a) To stop delivery the seller must so notify as to enable the bailee by reasonable diligence to prevent delivery of the goods.

(b) After such notification the bailee must hold and deliver the goods according to the directions of the seller but the seller is liable to the bailee for any ensuing charges or damages.

(c) If a negotiable document of title has been issued for goods the bailee is not obliged to obey a notification to stop until surrender of possession or control of the document.

(d) A carrier who has issued a nonnegotiable bill of lading is not obliged to obey a notification to stop received from a person other than the consignor. (1965, c. 700, s. 1; 2006-112, s. 37.)

§ 25-2-706. Seller's resale including contract for resale.

(1) Under the conditions stated in G.S. 25-2-703 on seller's remedies, the seller may resell the goods concerned or the undelivered balance thereof. Where the resale is made in good faith and in a commercially reasonable manner the seller may recover the difference between the resale price and the contract price together with any incidental damages allowed under the provisions of this article (G.S. 25-2-710), but less expenses saved in consequence of the buyer's breach.

(2) Except as otherwise provided in subsection (3) or unless otherwise agreed resale may be at public or private sale including sale by way of one or

more contracts to sell or of identification to an existing contract of the seller. Sale may be as a unit or in parcels and at any time and place and on any terms but every aspect of the sale including the method, manner, time, place and terms must be commercially reasonable. The resale must be reasonably identified as referring to the broken contract, but it is not necessary that the goods be in existence or that any or all of them have been identified to the contract before the breach.

(3)   Where the resale is at private sale the seller must give the buyer reasonable notification of his intention to resell.

(4)   Where the resale is at public sale

(a)   only identified goods can be sold except where there is a recognized market for a public sale of futures in goods of the kind; and

(b)   it must be made at a usual place or market for public sale if one is reasonably available and except in the case of goods which are perishable or threaten to decline in value speedily the seller must give the buyer reasonable notice of the time and place of the resale; and

(c)   if the goods are not to be within the view of those attending the sale the notification of sale must state the place where the goods are located and provide for their reasonable inspection by prospective bidders; and

(d)   the seller may buy.

(5)   A purchaser who buys in good faith at a resale takes the goods free of any rights of the original buyer even though the seller fails to comply with one or more of the requirements of this section.

(6)   The seller is not accountable to the buyer for any profit made on any resale. A person in the position of a seller (G.S. 25-2-707) or a buyer who has rightfully rejected or justifiably revoked acceptance must account for any excess over the amount of his security interest, as hereinafter defined (subsection (3) of G.S. 25-2-711). (1965, c. 700, s. 1.)

§ 25-2-707. "Person in the position of a seller."

(1) A "person in the position of a seller" includes as against a principal an agent who has paid or become responsible for the price of goods on behalf of his principal or anyone who otherwise holds a security interest or other right in goods similar to that of a seller.

(2) A person in the position of a seller may as provided in this article withhold or stop delivery (G.S. 25-2-705) and resell (G.S. 25-2-706) and recover incidental damages (G.S. 25-2-710). (1965, c. 700, s. 1.)

§ 25-2-708. Seller's damages for nonacceptance or repudiation.

(1) Subject to subsection (2) and to the provisions of this article with respect to proof of market price (G.S. 25-2-723), the measure of damages for nonacceptance or repudiation by the buyer is the difference between the market price at the time and place for tender and the unpaid contract price together with any incidental damages provided in this article (G.S. 25-2-710), but less expenses saved in consequence of the buyer's breach.

(2) If the measure of damages provided in subsection (1) is inadequate to put the seller in as good a position as performance would have done then the measure of damages is the profit (including reasonable overhead) which the seller would have made from full performance by the buyer, together with any incidental damages provided in this article (G.S. 25-2-710), due allowance for costs reasonably incurred and due credit for payments or proceeds of resale. (1965, c. 700, s. 1.)

§ 25-2-709. Action for the price.

(1) When the buyer fails to pay the price as it becomes due the seller may recover, together with any incidental damages under the next section [G.S. 25-2-710], the price

(a) of goods accepted or of conforming goods lost or damaged within a commercially reasonable time after risk of their loss has passed to the buyer; and

(b) of goods identified to the contract if the seller is unable after reasonable effort to resell them at a reasonable price or the circumstances reasonably indicate that such effort will be unavailing.

(2) Where the seller sues for the price he must hold for the buyer any goods which have been identified to the contract and are still in his control except that if resale becomes possible he may resell them at any time prior to the collection of the judgment. The net proceeds of any such resale must be credited to the buyer and payment of the judgment entitles him to any goods not resold.

(3) After the buyer has wrongfully rejected or revoked acceptance of the goods or has failed to make a payment due or has repudiated (G.S. 25-2-610), a seller who is held not entitled to the price under this section shall nevertheless be awarded damages for nonacceptance under the preceding section [G.S. 25-2-708]. (1965, c. 700, s. 1.)

§ 25-2-710. Seller's incidental damages.

Incidental damages to an aggrieved seller include any commercially reasonable charges, expenses or commissions incurred in stopping delivery, in the transportation, care and custody of goods after the buyer's breach, in connection with return or resale of the goods or otherwise resulting from the breach. (1965, c. 700, s. 1.)

§ 25-2-711. Buyer's remedies in general; buyer's security interest in rejected goods.

(1) Where the seller fails to make delivery or repudiates or the buyer rightfully rejects or justifiably revokes acceptance then with respect to any goods involved, and with respect to the whole if the breach goes to the whole contract (G.S. 25-2-612), the buyer may cancel and whether or not he has done so may in addition to recovering so much of the price as has been paid

(a) "cover" and have damages under the next section [G.S. 25-2-712] as to all the goods affected whether or not they have been identified to the contract; or

(b) recover damages for nondelivery as provided in this article (G.S. 25-2-713).

(2) Where the seller fails to deliver or repudiates the buyer may also

(a) if the goods have been identified recover them as provided in this article (G.S. 25-2-502); or

(b) in a proper case obtain specific performance or replevy the goods as provided in this article (G.S. 25-2-716).

(3) On rightful rejection or justifiable revocation of acceptance a buyer has a security interest in goods in his possession or control for any payments made on their price and any expenses reasonably incurred in their inspection, receipt, transportation, care and custody and may hold such goods and resell them in like manner as an aggrieved seller (G.S. 25-2-706). (1965, c. 700, s. 1.)

§ 25-2-712. "Cover"; buyer's procurement of substitute goods.

(1) After a breach within the preceding section [G.S. 25-2-711] the buyer may "cover" by making in good faith and without unreasonable delay any reasonable purchase of or contract to purchase goods in substitution for those due from the seller.

(2) The buyer may recover from the seller as damages the difference between the cost of cover and the contract price together with any incidental or consequential damages as hereinafter defined (G.S. 25-2-715), but less expenses saved in consequence of the seller's breach.

(3) Failure of the buyer to effect cover within this section does not bar him from any other remedy. (1965, c. 700, s. 1.)

§ 25-2-713. Buyer's damages for nondelivery or repudiation.

(1) Subject to the provisions of this article with respect to proof of market price (G.S. 25-2-723), the measure of damages for nondelivery or repudiation by the seller is the difference between the market price at the time when the

buyer learned of the breach and the contract price together with any incidental and consequential damages provided in this article (G.S. 25-2-715), but less expenses saved in consequence of the seller's breach.

(2) Market price is to be determined as of the place for tender or, in cases of rejection after arrival or revocation of acceptance, as of the place of arrival. (1965, c. 700, s. 1.)

§ 25-2-714. Buyer's damages for breach in regard to accepted goods.

(1) Where the buyer has accepted goods and given notification (subsection (3) of G.S. 25-2-607) he may recover as damages for any nonconformity of tender the loss resulting in the ordinary course of events from the seller's breach as determined in any manner which is reasonable.

(2) The measure of damages for breach of warranty is the difference at the time and place of acceptance between the value of the goods accepted and the value they would have had if they had been as warranted, unless special circumstances show proximate damages of a different amount.

(3) In a proper case any incidental and consequential damages under the next section [G.S. 25-2-715] may also be recovered. (1965, c. 700, s. 1.)

§ 25-2-715. Buyer's incidental and consequential damages.

(1) Incidental damages resulting from the seller's breach include expenses reasonably incurred in inspection, receipt, transportation and care and custody of goods rightfully rejected, any commercially reasonable charges, expenses or commissions in connection with effecting cover and any other reasonable expense incident to the delay or other breach.

(2) Consequential damages resulting from the seller's breach include

(a) any loss resulting from general or particular requirements and needs of which the seller at the time of contracting had reason to know and which could not reasonably be prevented by cover or otherwise; and

(b) injury to person or property proximately resulting from any breach of warranty. (1965, c. 700, s. 1.)

§ 25-2-716. Buyer's right to specific performance or replevin.

(1) Specific performance may be decreed where the goods are unique or in other proper circumstances.

(2) The decree for specific performance may include such terms and conditions as to payment of the price, damages, or other relief as the court may deem just.

(3) The buyer has a right of replevin for goods identified to the contract if after reasonable effort he is unable to effect cover for such goods or the circumstances reasonably indicate that such effort will be unavailing or if the goods have been shipped under reservation and satisfaction of the security interest in them has been made or tendered. In the case of goods bought for personal, family, or household purposes, the buyer's right of replevin vests upon acquisition of a special property, even if the seller had not then repudiated or failed to deliver. (1965, c. 700, s. 1; 1967, c. 562, s. 1; 2000-169, s. 12.)

§ 25-2-717. Deduction of damages from the price.

The buyer on notifying the seller of his intention to do so may deduct all or any part of the damages resulting from any breach of the contract from any part of the price still due under the same contract. (1965, c. 700, s. 1.)

§ 25-2-718. Liquidation or limitation of damages; deposits.

(1) Damages for breach by either party may be liquidated in the agreement but only at an amount which is reasonable in the light of the anticipated or actual harm caused by the breach, the difficulties of proof of loss, and the inconvenience or nonfeasibility of otherwise obtaining an adequate remedy. A term fixing unreasonably large liquidated damages is void as a penalty.

(2) Where the seller justifiably withholds delivery of goods because of the buyer's breach, the buyer is entitled to restitution of any amount by which the sum of his payments exceeds

(a) the amount to which the seller is entitled by virtue of terms liquidating the seller's damages in accordance with subsection (1),

(b) in the absence of such terms, twenty per cent (20%) of the value of the total performance for which the buyer is obligated under the contract or five hundred dollars ($500.00), whichever is smaller, or

(c) at the election of the seller in the case of a layaway contract, the aggregate payments received by seller from buyer under the contract or fifty dollars ($50.00), whichever is smaller.

(3) The buyer's right to restitution under subsection (2) is subject to offset to the extent that the seller establishes

(a) a right to recover damages under the provisions of this article other than subsection (1), and

(b) the amount or value of any benefits received by the buyer directly or indirectly by reason of the contract.

(4) Where a seller has received payment in goods their reasonable value or the proceeds of their resale shall be treated as payments for the purposes of subsection (2); but if the seller has notice of the buyer's breach before reselling goods received in part performance, his resale is subject to the conditions laid down in this article on resale by an aggrieved seller (G.S. 25-2-706). (1965, c. 700, s. 1; 1993, c. 340, s. 2.)

§ 25-2-719. Contractual modification or limitation of remedy.

(1) Subject to the provisions of subsections (2) and (3) of this section and of the preceding section [G.S. 25-2-718] on liquidation and limitation of damages,

(a) the agreement may provide for remedies in addition to or in substitution for those provided in this article and may limit or alter the measure of damages recoverable under this article, as by limiting the buyer's remedies to return of the goods and repayment of the price or to repair and replacement of nonconforming goods or parts; and

(b)   resort to a remedy as provided is optional unless the remedy is expressly agreed to be exclusive, in which case it is the sole remedy.

(2)   Where circumstances cause an exclusive or limited remedy to fail of its essential purpose, remedy may be had as provided in this chapter.

(3)   Consequential damages may be limited or excluded unless the limitation or exclusion is unconscionable. Limitation of consequential damages for injury to the person in the case of consumer goods is prima facie unconscionable but limitation of damages where the loss is commercial is not. (1965, c. 700, s. 1.)

§ 25-2-720. Effect of "cancellation" or "rescission" on claims for antecedent breach.

Unless the contrary intention clearly appears, expressions of "cancellation" or "rescission" of the contract or the like shall not be construed as a renunciation or discharge of any claim in damages for an antecedent breach. (1965, c. 700, s. 1.)

§ 25-2-721. Remedies for fraud.

Remedies for material misrepresentation or fraud include all remedies available under this article for nonfraudulent breach. Neither rescission or a claim for rescission of the contract for sale nor rejection or return of the goods shall bar or be deemed inconsistent with a claim for damages or other remedy. (1965, c. 700, s. 1.)

§ 25-2-722. Who can sue third parties for injury to goods.

Where a third party so deals with goods which have been identified to a contract for sale as to cause actionable injury to a party to that contract

(a) a right of action against the third party is in either party to the contract for sale who has title to or a security interest or a special property or an insurable interest in the goods; and if the goods have been destroyed or converted a right of action is also in the party who either bore the risk of loss under the contract for sale or has since the injury assumed that risk as against the other;

(b) if at the time of the injury the party plaintiff did not bear the risk of loss as against the other party to the contract for sale and there is no arrangement between them for disposition of the recovery, his suit or settlement is, subject to his own interest, as a fiduciary for the other party to the contract;

(c) either party may with the consent of the other sue for the benefit of whom it may concern. (1965, c. 700, s. 1.)

§ 25-2-723. Proof of market price; time and place.

(1) If an action based on anticipatory repudiation comes to trial before the time for performance with respect to some or all of the goods, any damages based on market price (G.S. 25-2-708 or G.S. 25-2-713) shall be determined according to the price of such goods prevailing at the time when the aggrieved party learned of the repudiation.

(2) If evidence of a price prevailing at the times or places described in this article is not readily available the price prevailing within any reasonable time before or after the time described or at any other place which in commercial judgment or under usage of trade would serve as a reasonable substitute for the one described may be used, making any proper allowance for the cost of transporting the goods to or from such other place.

(3) Evidence of a relevant price prevailing at a time or place other than the one described in this article offered by one party is not admissible unless and until he has given the other party such notice as the court finds sufficient to prevent unfair surprise. (1965, c. 700, s. 1; 1967, c. 562, s. 1.)

§ 25-2-724. Admissibility of market quotations.

Whenever the prevailing price or value of any goods regularly bought and sold in any established commodity market is in issue, reports in official publications or trade journals or in newspapers or periodicals of general circulation published as the reports of such market shall be admissible in evidence. The circumstances of the preparation of such a report may be shown to affect its weight but not its admissibility. (1965, c. 700, s. 1.)

§ 25-2-725. Statute of limitations in contracts for sale.

(1) An action for breach of any contract for sale must be commenced within four years after the cause of action has accrued. By the original agreement the parties may reduce the period of limitation to not less than one year but may not extend it.

(2) A cause of action accrues when the breach occurs, regardless of the aggrieved party's lack of knowledge of the breach. A breach of warranty occurs when tender of delivery is made, except that where a warranty explicitly extends to future performance of the goods and discovery of the breach must await the time of such performance the cause of action accrues when the breach is or should have been discovered.

(3) Where an action commenced within the time limited by subsection (1) is so terminated as to leave available a remedy by another action for the same breach such other action may be commenced after the expiration of the time limited and within twelve months after the termination of the first action.

(4) This section does not alter the law on tolling of the statute of limitations nor does it apply to causes of action which have accrued before this chapter becomes effective. (1965, c. 700, s. 1; 1967, c. 562, s. 1.)

Article 2A.

Leases.

Part 1.

GENERAL PROVISIONS.

§ 25-2A-101. Short title.

This Article shall be known and may be cited as the Uniform Commercial Code - Leases. (1993, c. 463, s. 1.)

§ 25-2A-102. Scope.

This Article applies to any transaction, regardless of form, that creates a lease. (1993, c. 463, s. 1.)

Article 2A.

Leases.

PART 1.

GENERAL PROVISIONS.

§ 25-2A-103. Definitions and index of definitions.

(1)   In this Article unless the context otherwise requires:

(a)   "Buyer in ordinary course of business" means a person who, in good faith and without knowledge that the sale to him is in violation of the ownership rights or security interest or leasehold interest of a third party in the goods, buys in ordinary course from a person in the business of selling goods of that kind but does not include a pawnbroker. "Buying" may be for cash or by exchange of other property or on secured or unsecured credit and includes acquiring goods or documents of title under a preexisting contract for sale but does not include a transfer in bulk or as security for or in total or partial satisfaction of a money debt.

(b)   "Cancellation" occurs when either party puts an end to the lease contract for default by the other party.

(c)   "Commercial unit" means such a unit of goods as by commercial usage is a single whole for purposes of lease and division of which materially impairs its character or value on the market or in use. A commercial unit may be a single article, as a machine, or a set of articles, as a suite of furniture or a line of machinery, or a quantity, as a gross or carload, or any other unit treated in use or in the relevant market as a single whole.

(d)   "Conforming" goods or performance under a lease contract means goods or performance that are in accordance with the obligations under the lease contract.

(e)   "Consumer lease" means a lease that a lessor regularly engaged in the business of leasing or selling makes to a lessee who is an individual and who takes under the lease primarily for a personal, family, or household purpose, if the total payments to be made under the lease contract, excluding payments for options to renew or buy, do not exceed twenty-five thousand dollars ($25,000).

(f)   "Fault" means wrongful act, omission, breach, or default.

(g)   "Finance lease" means a lease with respect to which: (i) the lessor does not select, manufacture, or supply the goods; (ii) the lessor acquires the goods or the right to possession and use of the goods in connection with the lease; and (iii) one of the following occurs:

(A)   the lessee receives a copy of the contract by which the lessor acquired the goods or the right to possession and use of the goods before signing the lease contract;

(B)   the lessee's approval of the contract by which the lessor acquired the goods or the right to possession and use of the goods is a condition to effectiveness of the lease contract;

(C)   the lessee, before signing the lease contract, receives an accurate and complete statement designating the promises and warranties, and any disclaimers of warranties, limitations or modifications of remedies, or liquidated damages, including those of a third party, such as the manufacturer of the goods, provided to the lessor by the person supplying the goods in connection with or as part of the contract by which the lessor acquired the goods or the right to possession and use of the goods; or

(D) if the lease is not a consumer lease, the lessor, before the lessee signs the lease contract, informs the lessee in writing (a) of the identity of the person supplying the goods to the lessor, unless the lessee has selected that person and directed the lessor to acquire the goods or the right to possession and use of the goods from that person, (b) that the lessee is entitled under this Article to the promises and warranties, including those of any third party, provided to the lessor by the person supplying the goods in connection with or as part of the contract by which the lessor acquired the goods or the right to possession and use of the goods, and (c) that the lessee may communicate with the person supplying the goods to the lessor and receive an accurate and complete statement of those promises and warranties, including any disclaimers and limitations of them or of remedies.

(h) "Goods" means all things that are movable at the time of identification to the lease contract, or are fixtures (G.S. 25-2A-309), but the term does not include money, documents, instruments, accounts, chattel paper, general intangibles, or minerals or the like, including oil and gas, before extraction. The term also includes the unborn young of animals.

(i) "Installment lease contract" means a lease contract that authorizes or requires the delivery of goods in separate lots to be separately accepted, even though the lease contract contains a clause "each delivery is a separate lease" or its equivalent.

(j) "Lease" means a transfer of the right to possession and use of goods for a term in return for consideration, but a sale, including a sale on approval or a sale or return, or retention or creation of a security interest is not a lease. Unless the context clearly indicates otherwise, the term includes a sublease. The term includes a motor vehicle operating agreement that is considered a lease under § 7701(h) of the Internal Revenue Code.

(k) "Lease agreement" means the bargain, with respect to the lease, of the lessor and the lessee in fact as found in their language or by implication from other circumstances including course of dealing or usage of trade or course of performance as provided in this Article. Unless the context clearly indicates otherwise, the term includes a sublease agreement.

(l) "Lease contract" means the total legal obligation that results from the lease agreement as affected by this Article and any other applicable rules of law. Unless the context clearly indicates otherwise, the term includes a sublease contract.

(m)   "Leasehold interest" means the interest of the lessor or the lessee under a lease contract.

(n)   "Lessee" means a person who acquires the right to possession and use of goods under a lease. Unless the context clearly indicates otherwise, the term includes a sublessee.

(o)   "Lessee in ordinary course of business" means a person who, in good faith and without knowledge that the lease to him is in violation of the ownership rights or security interest or leasehold interest of a third party in the goods, leases in ordinary course from a person in the business of selling or leasing goods of that kind but does not include a pawnbroker. "Leasing" may be for cash or by exchange of other property or on secured or unsecured credit and includes acquiring goods or documents of title under a preexisting lease contract but does not include a transfer in bulk or as security for or in total or partial satisfaction of a money debt.

(p)   "Lessor" means a person who transfers the right to possession and use of goods under a lease. Unless the context clearly indicates otherwise, the term includes a sublessor.

(q)   "Lessor's residual interest" means the lessor's interest in the goods after expiration, termination, or cancellation of the lease contract.

(r)   "Lien" means a charge against or interest in goods to secure payment of a debt or performance of an obligation, but the term does not include a security interest.

(s)   "Lot" means a parcel or a single article that is the subject matter of a separate lease or delivery, whether or not it is sufficient to perform the lease contract.

(t)   "Merchant lessee" means a lessee that is a merchant with respect to goods of the kind subject to the lease.

(u)   "Present value" means the amount as of a date certain of one or more sums payable in the future, discounted to the date certain. The discount is determined by the interest rate specified by the parties if the rate was not manifestly unreasonable at the time the transaction was entered into; otherwise, the discount is determined by a commercially reasonable rate that takes into account the facts and circumstances of each case at the time the transaction was entered into.

(v)   "Purchase" includes taking by sale, lease, mortgage, security interest, pledge, gift, or any other voluntary transaction creating an interest in goods.

(w)   "Sublease" means a lease of goods the right to possession and use of which was acquired by the lessor as a lessee under an existing lease.

(x)   "Supplier" means a person from whom a lessor buys or leases goods to be leased under a finance lease.

(y)   "Supply contract" means a contract under which a lessor buys or leases goods to be leased.

(z)   "Termination" occurs when either party pursuant to a power created by agreement or law puts an end to the lease contract otherwise than for default.

(2)   Other definitions applying to this Article and the sections in which they appear are:

"Accessions".	G.S. 25-2A-310(1).
"Construction mortgage".	G.S. 25-2A-309(1)(d).
"Encumbrance".	G.S. 25-2A-309(1)(e).
"Fixtures".	G.S. 25-2A-309(1)(a).
"Fixture filing".	G.S. 25-2A-309(1)(b).
"Purchase money lease".	G.S. 25-2A-309(1)(c).

(3)   The following definitions in other Articles apply to this Article:

"Account"	G.S. 25-9-102(a)(2).
"Between merchants"	G.S. 25-2-104(3).
"Buyer"	G.S. 25-2-103(1)(a).

"Chattel paper"	G.S. 25-9-102(a)(11).
"Consumer goods"	G.S. 25-9-102(a)(23).
"Document"	G.S. 25-9-102(a)(30).
"Entrusting"	G.S. 25-2-403(3).
"General intangible"	G.S. 25-9-102(a)(42).
"Instrument"	G.S. 25-9-102(a)(47).
"Merchant"	G.S. 25-2-104(1).
"Mortgage"	G.S. 25-9-102(a)(55).
"Pursuant to commitment"	G.S. 25-9-102(a)(68).
"Receipt"	G.S. 25-2-103(1)(c).
"Sale"	G.S. 25-2-106(1).
"Sale on approval"	G.S. 25-2-326.
"Sale or return"	G.S. 25-2-326.
"Seller"	G.S. 25-2-103(1)(d).

(4) In addition, Article 1 contains general definitions and principles of construction and interpretation applicable throughout this Article. (1993, c. 463, s. 1; 1993 (Reg. Sess., 1994), c. 756, s. 1; 1995, c. 509, s. 21; 2000-169, s. 13; 2006-112, ss. 5, 38.)

§ 25-2A-104. Leases subject to other law.

(1) A lease, although subject to this Article, is also subject to any applicable:

(a) certificate of title statute of this State (G.S. 20-50, G.S. 75A-32 et seq.);

(b) certificate of title statute of another jurisdiction (G.S. 25-2A-105); or

(c) consumer protection statute of this State, or final consumer protection decision of a court of this State existing on the effective date of this Article.

(2) In case of conflict between this Article, other than G.S. 2A-105, 2A-304(3), and 2A-305(3), and a statute or decision referred to in subsection (1) of this section, the statute or decision controls.

(3) Failure to comply with an applicable law has only the effect specified therein. (1993, c. 463, s. 1.)

§ 25-2A-105. Territorial application of Article to goods covered by certificate of title.

Subject to the provisions of G.S. 25-2A-304(3) and G.S. 25-2A-305(3), with respect to goods covered by a certificate of title issued under a statute of this State or of another jurisdiction, compliance and the effect of compliance or noncompliance with a certificate of title statute are governed by the law (including the conflict of laws rules) of the jurisdiction issuing the certificate until the earlier of (a) surrender of the certificate, or (b) four months after the goods are removed from that jurisdiction and thereafter until a new certificate of title is issued by another jurisdiction. (1993, c. 463, s. 1.)

§ 25-2A-106. Limitation on power of parties to consumer lease to choose applicable law and judicial forum.

(1) If the law chosen by the parties to a consumer lease is that of a jurisdiction other than a jurisdiction in which the lessee resides at the time the lease agreement becomes enforceable or within 30 days thereafter or in which the goods are to be used, that choice of law is not enforceable.

(2) If the judicial forum chosen by the parties to a consumer lease is a forum that would not otherwise have jurisdiction over the lessee, that choice of forum is not enforceable. (1993, c. 463, s. 1.)

§ 25-2A-107. Waiver or renunciation of claim or right after default.

Any claim or right arising out of an alleged default or breach of warranty may be discharged in whole or in part without consideration by a written waiver or renunciation signed and delivered by the aggrieved party. (1993, c. 463, s. 1.)

§ 25-2A-108. Unconscionability.

(1) If the court as a matter of law finds a lease contract or any clause of a lease contract to have been unconscionable at the time it was made, the court may refuse to enforce the lease contract, or it may enforce the remainder of the lease contract without the unconscionable clause, or it may so limit the application of any unconscionable clause as to avoid any unconscionable result.

(2) With respect to a consumer lease, if the court as a matter of law finds that a lease contract or any clause of a lease contract has been induced by unconscionable conduct or that unconscionable conduct has occurred in the collection of a claim arising from a lease contract, the court may grant appropriate relief.

(3) Before making a finding of unconscionability under subsection (1) or (2) of this section, the court, on its own motion or that of a party, shall afford the parties a reasonable opportunity to present evidence as to the setting, purpose, and effect of the lease contract or clause thereof, or of the conduct.

(4) In an action in which the lessee claims unconscionability with respect to a consumer lease:

(a) if the court finds unconscionability under subsection (1) or (2) of this section, the court shall award reasonable attorneys' fees to the lessee.

(b) if the court does not find unconscionability and the lessee claiming unconscionability has brought or maintained an action he knew to be groundless, the court shall award reasonable attorneys' fees to the party against whom the claim is made.

(c) in determining attorneys' fees, the amount of the recovery on behalf of the claimant under subsections (1) and (2) of this section is not controlling. (1993, c. 463, s. 1.)

§ 25-2A-109. Option to accelerate at will.

(1)   A term providing that one party or his successor in interest may accelerate payment or performance or require collateral or additional collateral "at will" or "when he deems himself insecure" or in words of similar import must be construed to mean that he has power to do so only if he in good faith believes that the prospect of payment or performance is impaired.

(2)   With respect to a consumer lease, the burden of establishing good faith under subsection (1) of this section is on the party who exercised the power; otherwise, the burden of establishing lack of good faith is on the party against whom the power has been exercised. (1993, c. 463, s. 1.)

Part 2.

FORMATION AND CONSTRUCTION OF LEASE CONTRACT.

§ 25-2A-201. Statute of frauds.

(1)   A lease contract is not enforceable by way of action or defense unless:

(a)   the total payments to be made under the lease contract, excluding payments for options to renew or buy, are less than one thousand dollars ($1,000); or

(b)   there is a writing, signed by the party against whom enforcement is sought or by that party's authorized agent, sufficient to indicate that a lease contract has been made between the parties and to describe the goods leased and the lease term.

(2)   Any description of leased goods or of the lease term is sufficient and satisfies subsection (1)(b) of this section, whether or not it is specific, if it reasonably identifies what is described.

(3)   A writing is not insufficient because it omits or incorrectly states a term agreed upon, but the lease contract is not enforceable under subsection (1)(b)

of this section beyond the lease term and the quantity of goods shown in the writing.

(4) A lease contract that does not satisfy the requirements of subsection (1) of this section, but which is valid in other respects, is enforceable:

(a) if the goods are to be specially manufactured or obtained for the lessee and are not suitable for lease or sale to others in the ordinary course of the lessor's business, and the lessor, before notice of repudiation is received and under circumstances that reasonably indicate that the goods are for the lessee, has made either a substantial beginning of their manufacture or commitments for their procurement;

(b) if the party against whom enforcement is sought admits in that party's pleading, testimony, or otherwise in court that a lease contract was made, but the lease contract is not enforceable under this provision beyond the quantity of goods admitted; or

(c) with respect to goods that have been received and accepted by the lessee.

(5) The lease term under a lease contract referred to in subsection (4) of this section is:

(a) if there is a writing signed by the party against whom enforcement is sought or by that party's authorized agent specifying the lease term, the term so specified;

(b) if the party against whom enforcement is sought admits in that party's pleading, testimony, or otherwise in court a lease term, the term so admitted;

(c) if there is other evidence of the parties' intent with regard to the lease term, the term so intended; or

(d) in the absence of evidence of the parties' intent, a reasonable lease term. (1993, c. 463, s. 1.)

§ 25-2A-202. Final written expression: parol or extrinsic evidence.

Terms with respect to which the confirmatory memoranda of the parties agree or which are otherwise set forth in a writing intended by the parties as a final expression of their agreement with respect to such terms as are included therein may not be contradicted by evidence of any prior agreement or of a contemporaneous oral agreement but may be explained or supplemented:

(a) by course of dealing or usage of trade or by course of performance; and

(b) by evidence of consistent additional terms unless the court finds the writing to have been intended also as a complete and exclusive statement of the terms of the agreement. (1993, c. 463, s. 1.)

§ 25-2A-203. Seals inoperative.

The affixing of a seal to a writing evidencing a lease contract or an offer to enter into a lease contract does not render the writing a sealed instrument and the law with respect to sealed instruments does not apply to the lease contract or offer. (1993, c. 463, s. 1.)

§ 25-2A-204. Formation in general.

(1) A lease contract may be made in any manner sufficient to show agreement, including conduct by both parties which recognizes the existence of a lease contract.

(2) An agreement sufficient to constitute a lease contract may be found although the moment of its making is undetermined.

(3) Although one or more terms are left open, a lease contract does not fail for indefiniteness if the parties have intended to make a lease contract and there is a reasonably certain basis for giving an appropriate remedy. (1993, c. 463, s. 1.)

§ 25-2A-205. Firm offers.

An offer by a merchant to lease goods to or from another person in a signed writing that by its terms gives assurance it will be held open is not revocable, for lack of consideration, during the time stated or, if no time is stated, for a reasonable time, but in no event may the period of irrevocability exceed three months. Any such term of assurance on a form supplied by the offeree must be separately signed by the offeror. (1993, c. 463, s. 1.)

§ 25-2A-206. Offer and acceptance in formation of lease contract.

(1)   Unless otherwise unambiguously indicated by the language or circumstances, an offer to make a lease contract must be construed as inviting acceptance in any manner and by any medium reasonable in the circumstances.

(2)   If the beginning of a requested performance is a reasonable mode of acceptance, an offeror who is not notified of acceptance within a reasonable time may treat the offer as having lapsed before acceptance. (1993, c. 463, s. 1.)

§ 25-2A-207: Repealed by Session Laws 2006-112, s. 6, effective October 1, 2006.

§ 25-2A-208. Modification, rescission and waiver.

(1)   An agreement modifying a lease contract needs no consideration to be binding.

(2)   A signed lease agreement that excludes modification or rescission except by a signed writing may not be otherwise modified or rescinded, but, except as between merchants, such a requirement on a form supplied by a merchant must be separately signed by the other party.

(3)   Although an attempt at modification or rescission does not satisfy the requirements of subsection (2) of this section, it may operate as a waiver.

(4)   A party who has made a waiver affecting an executory portion of a lease contract may retract the waiver by reasonable notification received by the other party that strict performance will be required of any term waived, unless the retraction would be unjust in view of a material change of position in reliance on the waiver. (1993, c. 463, s. 1.)

§ 25-2A-209. Lessee under finance lease as beneficiary of supply contract.

(1)   The benefit of a supplier's promises to the lessor under the supply contract and of all warranties, whether express or implied, including those of any third party provided in connection with or as part of the supply contract, extends to the lessee to the extent of the lessee's leasehold interest under a finance lease related to the supply contract, but is subject to the terms of the warranty and of the supply contract and all defenses or claims arising therefrom.

(2)   The extension of the benefit of a supplier's promises and of warranties to the lessee (G.S. 25-2A-209(1)) does not: (i) modify the rights and obligations of the parties to the supply contract, whether arising therefrom or otherwise, or (ii) impose any duty or liability under the supply contract on the lessee.

(3)   Any modification or rescission of the supply contract by the supplier and the lessor is effective between the supplier and the lessee unless, before the modification or rescission, the supplier has received notice that the lessee has entered into a finance lease related to the supply contract. If the modification or rescission is effective between the supplier and the lessee, the lessor is deemed to have assumed, in addition to the obligations of the lessor to the lessee under the lease contract, promises of the supplier to the lessor and warranties that were so modified or rescinded as they existed and were available to the lessee before modification or rescission.

(4)   In addition to the extension of the benefit of the supplier's promises and of warranties to the lessee under subsection (1) of this section, the lessee retains all rights that the lessee may have against the supplier which arise from an agreement between the lessee and the supplier or under other law. (1993, c. 463, s. 1.)

§ 25-2A-210. Express warranties.

(1)   Express warranties by the lessor are created as follows:

(a)   any affirmation of fact or promise made by the lessor to the lessee which relates to the goods and becomes part of the basis of the bargain creates an express warranty that the goods will conform to the affirmation or promise.

(b)   any description of the goods which is made part of the basis of the bargain creates an express warranty that the goods will conform to the description.

(c)   any sample or model that is made part of the basis of the bargain creates an express warranty that the whole of the goods will conform to the sample or model.

(2)   It is not necessary to the creation of an express warranty that the lessor use formal words, such as "warrant" or "guarantee", or that the lessor have a specific intention to make a warranty, but an affirmation merely of the value of the goods or a statement purporting to be merely the lessor's opinion or commendation of the goods does not create a warranty. (1993, c. 463, s. 1.)

§ 25-2A-211. Warranties against interference and against infringement; lessee's obligation against infringement.

(1)   There is in a lease contract a warranty that for the lease term no person holds a claim to or interest in the goods that arose from an act or omission of the lessor, other than a claim by way of infringement or the like, which will interfere with the lessee's enjoyment of its leasehold interest.

(2)   Except in a finance lease there is in a lease contract by a lessor who is a merchant regularly dealing in goods of the kind a warranty that the goods are delivered free of the rightful claim of any person by way of infringement or the like.

(3)   A lessee who furnishes specifications to a lessor or a supplier shall hold the lessor and the supplier harmless against any claim by way of infringement of the like that arises out of compliance with the specifications. (1993, c. 463, s. 1.)

§ 25-2A-212. Implied warranty of merchantability.

(1) Except in a finance lease, a warranty that the goods will be merchantable is implied in a lease contract if the lessor is a merchant with respect to goods of that kind.

(2) Goods to be merchantable must be at least such as:

(a) pass without objection in the trade under the description in the lease agreement;

(b) in the case of fungible goods, are of fair average quality within the description;

(c) are fit for the ordinary purposes for which goods of that type are used;

(d) run, within the variation permitted by the lease agreement, of even kind, quality, and quantity within each unit and among all units involved;

(e) are adequately contained, packaged, and labeled as the lease agreement may require; and

(f) conform to any promises or affirmations of fact made on the container or label.

(3) Other implied warranties may arise from course of dealing or usage of trade. (1993, c. 463, s. 1.)

§ 25-2A-213. Implied warranty of fitness for particular purpose.

Except in a finance lease, if the lessor at the time the lease contract is made has reason to know of any particular purpose for which the goods are required and that the lessee is relying on the lessor's skill or judgment to select or furnish suitable goods, there is in the lease contract an implied warranty that the goods will be fit for that purpose. (1993, c. 463, s. 1.)

§ 25-2A-214. Exclusion or modification of warranties.

(1) Words or conduct relevant to the creation of an express warranty and words or conduct tending to negate or limit a warranty must be construed wherever reasonable as consistent with each other; but, subject to the provisions of G.S. 25-2A-202 on parol or extrinsic evidence, negation or limitation is inoperative to the extent that the construction is unreasonable.

(2) Subject to subsection (3) of this section, to exclude or modify the implied warranty of merchantability, or any part of it, the language must mention "merchantability", by a writing, and be conspicuous. Subject to subsection (3) of this section, to exclude or modify any implied warranty of fitness, the exclusion must be by a writing and be conspicuous. Language to exclude all implied warranties of fitness is sufficient if it is in writing, is conspicuous, and states, for example, "There is no warranty that the goods will be fit for a particular purpose."

(3) Notwithstanding subsection (2) of this section, but subject to subsection (4) of this section:

(a) unless the circumstances indicate otherwise, all implied warranties are excluded by expressions like "as is", or "with all faults", or by other language that in common understanding calls the lessee's attention to the exclusion of warranties and makes plain that there is no implied warranty, if in writing and conspicuous;

(b) if the lessee before entering into the lease contract has examined the goods or the sample or model as fully as desired or has refused to examine the goods, there is no implied warranty with regard to defects that an examination ought in the circumstances to have revealed; and

(c) an implied warranty may also be excluded or modified by course of dealing, course of performance, or usage of trade.

(4) To exclude or modify a warranty against interference or against infringement (G.S. 25-2A-211) or any part of it, the language must be specific, be by a writing, and be conspicuous, unless the circumstances, including course of performance, course of dealing, or usage of trade, give the lessee reason to know that the goods are being leased subject to a claim or interest of any person. (1993, c. 463, s. 1.)

§ 25-2A-215. Cumulation and conflict of warranties express or implied.

Warranties, whether express or implied, must be construed as consistent with each other and as cumulative, but if that construction is unreasonable, the intention of the parties determines which warranty is dominant. In ascertaining that intention the following rules apply:

(a) exact or technical specifications displace an inconsistent sample or model or general language of description.

(b) a sample from an existing bulk displaces inconsistent general language of description.

(c) express warranties displace inconsistent implied warranties other than an implied warranty of fitness for a particular purpose. (1993, c. 463, s. 1.)

§ 25-2A-216. Third-party beneficiaries of express and implied warranties.

A warranty to or for the benefit of a lessee under this Article, whether express or implied, extends to any natural person who is in the family or household of the lessee or who is a guest in the lessee's home if it is reasonable to expect that such person may use, consume, or be affected by the goods and who is injured in person by breach of the warranty. This section does not displace principles of law and equity that extend a warranty to or for the benefit of a lessee to other persons. The operation of this section may not be excluded, modified, or limited, but an exclusion, modification, or limitation of the warranty, including any with respect to rights and remedies, effective against the lessee is also effective against any beneficiary designated under this section. (1993, c. 463, s. 1.)

§ 25-2A-217. Identification.

Identification of goods as goods to which a lease contract refers may be made at any time and in any manner explicitly agreed to by the parties. In the absence of explicit agreement, identification occurs:

(a) when the lease contract is made if the lease contract is for a lease of goods that are existing and identified;

(b) when the goods are shipped, marked, or otherwise designated by the lessor as goods to which the lease contract refers, if the lease contract is for a lease of goods that are not existing and identified; or

(c) when the young are conceived, if the lease contract is for a lease of unborn young of animals. (1993, c. 463, s. 1.)

§ 25-2A-218. Insurance and proceeds.

(1) A lessee obtains an insurable interest when existing goods are identified to the lease contract even though the goods identified are nonconforming and the lessee has an option to reject them.

(2) If a lessee has an insurable interest only by reason of the lessor's identification of the goods, the lessor, until default or insolvency or notification to the lessee that identification is final, may substitute other goods for those identified.

(3) Notwithstanding a lessee's insurable interest under subsections (1) and (2) of this section, the lessor retains an insurable interest until an option to buy has been exercised by the lessee and risk of loss has passed to the lessee.

(4) Nothing in this section impairs any insurable interest recognized under any other statute or rule of law.

(5) The parties by agreement may determine that one or more parties have an obligation to obtain and pay for insurance covering the goods and by agreement may determine the beneficiary of the proceeds of the insurance. (1993, c. 463, s. 1.)

§ 25-2A-219. Risk of loss.

(1) Except in the case of a finance lease, risk of loss is retained by the lessor and does not pass to the lessee. In the case of a finance lease, risk of loss passes to the lessee.

(2) Subject to the provisions of this Article on the effect of default on risk of loss (G.S. 25-2A-220), if risk of loss is to pass to the lessee and the time of passage is not stated, the following rules apply:

(a) if the lease contract requires or authorizes the goods to be shipped by carrier (i) and it does not require delivery at a particular destination, the risk of loss passes to the lessee when the goods are duly delivered to the carrier; but (ii) if it does require delivery at a particular destination and the goods are there duly tendered while in the possession of the carrier, the risk of loss passes to the lessee when the goods are there duly so tendered as to enable the lessee to take delivery.

(b) if the goods are held by a bailee to be delivered without being moved, the risk of loss passes to the lessee on acknowledgment by the bailee of the lessee's right to possession of the goods.

(c) in any case not within subdivision (a) or (b) of this section, the risk of loss passes to the lessee on the lessee's receipt of the goods if the lessor, or, in the case of a finance lease, the supplier, is a merchant; otherwise the risk passes to the lessee on tender of delivery. (1993, c. 463, s. 1.)

§ 25-2A-220. Effect of default on risk of loss.

(1) Where risk of loss is to pass to the lessee and the time of passage is not stated:

(a) if a tender or delivery of goods so fails to conform to the lease contract as to give a right of rejection, the risk of their loss remains with the lessor, or, in the case of a finance lease, the supplier, until cure or acceptance.

(b) if the lessee rightfully revokes acceptance, he, to the extent of any deficiency in his effective insurance coverage, may treat the risk of loss as having remained with the lessor from the beginning.

(2) Whether or not risk of loss is to pass to the lessee, if the lessee as to conforming goods already identified to a lease contract repudiates or is otherwise in default under the lease contract, the lessor, or, in the case of a finance lease, the supplier, to the extent of any deficiency in his effective insurance coverage may treat the risk of loss as resting on the lessee for a commercially reasonable time. (1993, c. 463, s. 1.)

§ 25-2A-221. Casualty to identified goods.

If a lease contract requires goods identified when the lease contract is made, and the goods suffer casualty without fault of the lessee, the lessor, or the supplier before delivery, or the goods suffer casualty before risk of loss passes to the lessee pursuant to the lease agreement or G.S. 25-2A-219, then:

(a) if the loss is total, the lease contract is avoided; and

(b) if the loss is partial or the goods have so deteriorated as to no longer conform to the lease contract, the lessee may nevertheless demand inspection and at his option either treat the lease contract as avoided or, except in a finance lease that is not a consumer lease, accept the goods with due allowance from the rent payable for the balance of the lease term for the deterioration or the deficiency in quantity but without further right against the lessor. (1993, c. 463, s. 1.)

Part 3.

EFFECT OF LEASE CONTRACT.

§ 25-2A-301. Enforceability of lease contract.

Except as otherwise provided in this Article, a lease contract is effective and enforceable according to its terms between the parties, against purchasers of the goods, and against creditors of the parties. (1993, c. 463, s. 1.)

§ 25-2A-302. Title to and possession of goods.

Except as otherwise provided in this Article, each provision of this Article applies whether the lessor or a third party has title to the goods, and whether the lessor, the lessee, or a third party has possession of the goods, notwithstanding any statute or rule of law that possession or the absence of possession is fraudulent. (1993, c. 463, s. 1.)

§ 25-2A-303. Alienability of party's interest under lease contract or of lessor's residual interest in goods; delegation of performance; transfer of rights.

(1) As used in this section, "creation of a security interest" includes the sale of a lease contract that is subject to Article 9 of this Chapter, Secured Transactions, by reason of G.S. 25-9-109(a)(3).

(2) Except as provided in subsection (3) of this section and G.S. 25-9-407, a provision in a lease agreement which (i) prohibits the voluntary or involuntary transfer, including a transfer by sale, sublease, creation, or enforcement of a security interest, or attachment, levy, or other judicial process, of an interest of a party under the lease contract or of the lessor's residual interest in the goods; or (ii) makes such a transfer an event of default, gives rise to the rights and remedies provided in subsection (4) of this section, but a transfer that is prohibited or is an event of default under the lease agreement is otherwise effective.

(3) A provision in a lease agreement which (i) prohibits a transfer of a right to damages for default with respect to the whole lease contract or of a right to payment arising out of the transferor's due performance of the transferor's entire obligation, or (ii) makes such a transfer an event of default, is not enforceable, and such a transfer is not a transfer that materially impairs the prospect of obtaining return performance by, materially changes the duty of, or materially increases the burden or risk imposed on, the other party to the lease contract within the purview of subsection (4) of this section.

(4) Subject to subsection (3) of this section and G.S. 25-9-407:

(a) if a transfer is made which is made an event of default under a lease agreement, the party to the lease contract not making the transfer, unless that party waives the default or otherwise agrees, has the rights and remedies described in G.S. 25-2A-501(2);

(b) if paragraph (a) is not applicable and if a transfer is made that (i) is prohibited under a lease agreement or (ii) materially impairs the prospect of obtaining return performance by, materially changes the duty of, or materially increases the burden or risk imposed on, the other party to the lease contract, unless the party not making the transfer agrees at any time to the transfer in the lease contract or otherwise, then, except as limited by contract, (i) the transferor is liable to the party not making the transfer for damages caused by the transfer to the extent that the damages could not reasonably be prevented by the party not making the transfer and (ii) a court having jurisdiction may grant other appropriate relief, including cancellation of the lease contract or an injunction against the transfer.

(5) A transfer of "the lease" or of "all my rights under the lease", or a transfer in similar general terms, is a transfer of rights and, unless the language or the circumstances, as in a transfer for security, indicate the contrary, the transfer is a delegation of duties by the transferor to the transferee. Acceptance by the transferee constitutes a promise by the transferee to perform those duties. The promise is enforceable by either the transferor or the other party to the lease contract.

(6) Unless otherwise agreed by the lessor and the lessee, a delegation of performance does not relieve the transferor as against the other party of any duty to perform or of any liability for default.

(7) In a consumer lease, to prohibit the transfer of an interest of a party under the lease contract or to make a transfer an event of default, the language must be specific, by a writing, and conspicuous. (1993, c. 463, s. 1; 2000-169, s. 14.)

§ 25-2A-304. Subsequent lease of goods by lessor.

(1) Subject to G.S. 25-2A-303, a subsequent lessee from a lessor of goods under an existing lease contract obtains, to the extent of the leasehold interest transferred, the leasehold interest in the goods that the lessor had or had power to transfer, and except as provided in subsection (2) of this section and G.S. 25-2A-527(4), takes subject to the existing lease contract. A lessor with voidable title has power to transfer a good leasehold interest to a good faith subsequent lessee for value, but only to the extent set forth in the preceding sentence. If goods have been delivered under a transaction of purchase, the lessor has that power even though:

(a) the lessor's transferor was deceived as to the identity of the lessor;

(b) the delivery was in exchange for a check which is later dishonored;

(c) it was agreed that the transaction was to be a "cash sale"; or

(d) the delivery was procured through fraud punishable as larcenous under the criminal law.

(2) A subsequent lessee in the ordinary course of business from a lessor who is a merchant dealing in goods of that kind to whom the goods were entrusted by the existing lessee of that lessor before the interest of the subsequent lessee became enforceable against that lessor obtains, to the extent of the leasehold interest transferred, all of that lessor's and the existing lessee's rights to the goods, and takes free of the existing lease contract.

(3) A subsequent lessee from the lessor of goods that are subject to an existing lease contract and are covered by a certificate of title issued under a statute of this State or of another jurisdiction takes no greater rights than those provided both by this section and by the certificate of title statute. (1993, c. 463, s. 1.)

§ 25-2A-305. Sale or sublease of goods by lessee.

(1) Subject to the provisions of G.S. 25-2A-303, a buyer or sublessee from the lessee of goods under an existing lease contract obtains, to the extent of the interest transferred, the leasehold interest in the goods that the lessee had or had power to transfer, and except as provided in subsection (2) of this section and G.S. 25-2A-511(4), takes subject to the existing lease contract. A lessee with a voidable leasehold interest has power to transfer a good leasehold interest to a good faith buyer for value or a good faith sublessee for value, but only to the extent set forth in the preceding sentence. When goods have been delivered under a transaction of lease, the lessee has that power even though:

(a) the lessor was deceived as to the identity of the lessee;

(b) the delivery was in exchange for a check which is later dishonored; or

(c)   the delivery was procured through fraud punishable as larcenous under the criminal law.

(2)   A buyer in the ordinary course of business or a sublessee in the ordinary course of business from a lessee who is a merchant dealing in goods of that kind to whom the goods were entrusted by the lessor obtains, to the extent of the interest transferred, all of the lessor's and lessee's rights to the goods, and takes free of the existing lease contract.

(3)   A buyer or sublessee from the lessee of goods that are subject to an existing lease contract and are covered by a certificate of title issued under a statute of this State or of another jurisdiction takes no greater rights than those provided both by this section and by the certificate of title statute. (1993, c. 463, s. 1; 1995, c. 509, s. 22.)

§ 25-2A-306. Priority of certain liens arising by operation of law.

If a person in the ordinary course of his business furnishes services or materials with respect to goods subject to a lease contract, a lien upon those goods in the possession of that person given by statute or rule of law for those materials or services takes priority over any interest of the lessor or lessee under the lease contract or this Article unless the lien is created by statute and the statute provides otherwise or unless the lien is created by rule of law and the rule of law provides otherwise. (1993, c. 463, s. 1.)

§ 25-2A-307. Priority of liens arising by attachment or levy on, security interests in, and other claims to goods.

(1)   Except as otherwise provided in G.S. 25-2A-306, a creditor of a lessee takes subject to the lease contract.

(2)   Except as otherwise provided in subsection (3) of this section and in G.S. 25-2A-306 and G.S. 25-2A-308, a creditor of a lessor takes subject to the lease contract unless the creditor holds a lien that attached to the goods before the lease contract became enforceable.

(3)   Except as otherwise provided in G.S. 25-9-317, 25-9-321, and 25-9-323, a lessee takes a leasehold interest subject to a security interest held by a creditor of the lessor. (1993, c. 463, s. 1; 2000-169, s. 15.)

§ 25-2A-308. Special rights of creditors.

(1)   A creditor of a lessor in possession of goods subject to a lease contract may treat the lease contract as void if as against the creditor retention of possession by the lessor is fraudulent under any statute or rule of law, but retention of possession in good faith and current course of trade by the lessor for a commercially reasonable time after the lease contract becomes enforceable is not fraudulent.

(2)   Nothing in this Article impairs the rights of creditors of a lessor if the lease contract (a) becomes enforceable, not in current course of trade but in satisfaction of or as security for a preexisting claim for money, security, or the like, and (b) is made under circumstances which under any statute or rule of law apart from this Article would constitute the transaction a fraudulent transfer or voidable preference.

(3)   A creditor of a seller may treat a sale or an identification of goods to a contract for sale as void if as against the creditor retention of possession by the seller is fraudulent under any statute or rule of law, but retention of possession of the goods pursuant to a lease contract entered into by the seller as lessee and the buyer as lessor in connection with the sale or identification of the goods is not fraudulent if the buyer bought for value and in good faith. (1993, c. 463, s. 1.)

§ 25-2A-309. Lessor's and lessee's rights when goods become fixtures.

(1)   In this section:

(a)   goods are "fixtures" when they become so related to particular real estate that an interest in them arises under real estate law;

(b)   a "fixture filing" is the filing, in the office where a record of a mortgage on the real estate would be filed or recorded, of a financing statement covering goods that are or are to become fixtures and conforming to the requirements of G.S. 25-9-502(a) and (b);

(c) a lease is a "purchase money lease" unless the lessee has possession or use of the goods or the right to possession or use of the goods before the lease agreement is enforceable;

(d) a mortgage is a "construction mortgage" to the extent it secures an obligation incurred for the construction of an improvement on land including the acquisition cost of the land, if the recorded writing so indicates; and

(e) "encumbrance" includes real estate mortgages and other liens on real estate and all other rights in real estate that are not ownership interests.

(2) Under this Article a lease may be of goods that are fixtures or may continue in goods that become fixtures, but no lease exists under this Article of ordinary building materials incorporated into an improvement on land.

(3) This Article does not prevent creation of a lease of fixtures pursuant to real estate law.

(4) The perfected interest of a lessor of fixtures has priority over a conflicting interest of an encumbrancer or owner of the real estate if:

(a) the lease is a purchase money lease, the conflicting interest of the encumbrancer or owner arises before the goods become fixtures, the interest of the lessor is perfected by a fixture filing before the goods become fixtures or within 10 days thereafter, and the lessee has an interest of record in the real estate or is in possession of the real estate; or

(b) the interest of the lessor is perfected by a fixture filing before the interest of the encumbrancer or owner is of record, the lessor's interest has priority over any conflicting interest of a predecessor in title of the encumbrancer or owner, and the lessee has an interest of record in the real estate or is in possession of real estate.

(5) The interest of a lessor of fixtures, whether or not perfected, has priority over the conflicting interest of an encumbrancer or owner of the real estate if:

(a) the fixtures are readily removable factory or office machines, readily removable equipment that is not primarily used or leased for use in the operation of the real estate, or readily removable replacements of domestic appliances that are goods subject to a consumer lease, and before the goods become fixtures, the lease contract is enforceable; or

(b) the conflicting interest is a lien on the real estate obtained by legal or equitable proceedings after the lease contract is enforceable; or

(c) the encumbrancer or owner has consented in writing to the lease or has disclaimed an interest in the goods as fixtures; or

(d) the lessee has a right to remove the goods as against the encumbrancer or owner. If the lessee's right to remove terminates, the priority of the interest of the lessor continues for a reasonable time.

(6) Notwithstanding subsection (4)(a) of this section but otherwise subject to subsections (4) and (5) of this section, the interest of a lessor of fixtures, including the lessor's residual interest, is subordinate to the conflicting interest of an encumbrancer of the real estate under a construction mortgage recorded before the goods become fixtures if the goods become fixtures before the completion of the construction. To the extent given to refinance a construction mortgage, the conflicting interest of an encumbrancer of the real estate under a mortgage has this priority to the same extent as the encumbrancer of the real estate under the construction mortgage.

(7) In cases not within the preceding subsections, priority between the interest of a lessor of fixtures, including the lessor's residual interest, and the conflicting interest of an encumbrancer or owner of the real estate who is not the lessee is determined by the priority rules governing conflicting interests in real estate.

(8) If the interest of a lessor of fixtures, including the lessor's residual interest, has priority over all conflicting interests of all owners and encumbrancers of the real estate, the lessor or the lessee may (i) on default, expiration, termination, or cancellation of the lease agreement but subject to the lease agreement and this Article, or (ii) if necessary to enforce other rights and remedies of the lessor or lessee under this Article, remove the goods from the real estate, free and clear of all conflicting interests of all owners and encumbrancers of the real estate, but the lessor or lessee must reimburse any encumbrancer or owner of the real estate who is not the lessee and who has not otherwise agreed for the cost of repair of any physical injury, but not for any diminution in value of the real estate caused by the absence of the goods

removed or by any necessity of replacing them. A person entitled to reimbursement may refuse permission to remove until the party seeking removal gives adequate security for the performance of this obligation.

(9)   Even though the lease agreement does not create a security interest, the interest of a lessor of fixtures, including the lessor's residual interest, is perfected by filing a financing statement as a fixture filing for leased goods that are or are to become fixtures in accordance with the relevant provisions of the Article on Secured Transactions (Article 9). (1993, c. 463, s. 1; 2000-169, s. 16.)

§ 25-2A-310. Lessor's and lessee's rights when goods become accessions.

(1)   Goods are "accessions" when they are installed in or affixed to other goods.

(2)   The interest of a lessor or a lessee under a lease contract entered into before the goods became accessions is superior to all interests in the whole except as stated in subsection (4) of this section.

(3)   The interest of a lessor or a lessee under a lease contract entered into at the time or after the goods became accessions is superior to all subsequently acquired interests in the whole except as stated in subsection (4) of this section but is subordinate to interests in the whole existing at the time the lease contract was made unless the holders of such interests in the whole have in writing consented to the lease or disclaimed an interest in the goods as part of the whole.

(4)   The interest of a lessor or a lessee under a lease contract described in subsection (2) or (3) of this section is subordinate to the interest of:

(a)   a buyer in the ordinary course of business or a lessee in the ordinary course of business of any interest in the whole acquired after the goods became accessions; or

(b)   a creditor with a security interest in the whole perfected before the lease contract was made to the extent that the creditor makes subsequent advances without knowledge of the lease contract.

(5) When under subsections (2) or (3) and (4) of this section, a lessor or a lessee of accessions holds an interest that is superior to all interests in the whole, the lessor or the lessee may:

(a) on default, expiration, termination, or cancellation of the lease contract by the other party but subject to the provisions of the lease contract and this Article; or

(b) if necessary to enforce his other rights and remedies under this Article, remove the goods from the whole, free and clear of all interests in the whole, but he must reimburse any holder of an interest in the whole who is not the lessee and who has not otherwise agreed for the cost of repair of any physical injury but not for any diminution in value of the whole caused by the absence of the goods removed or by any necessity for replacing them. A person entitled to reimbursement may refuse permission to remove until the party seeking removal gives adequate security for the performance of this obligation. (1993, c. 463, s. 1.)

Part 4.

PERFORMANCE OF LEASE CONTRACT: REPUDIATED, SUBSTITUTED, AND EXCUSED.

§ 25-2A-401. Insecurity: adequate assurance of performance.

(1) A lease contract imposes an obligation on each party that the other's expectation of receiving due performance will not be impaired.

(2) If reasonable grounds for insecurity arise with respect to the performance of either party, the insecure party may demand in writing adequate assurance of due performance. Until the insecure party receives that assurance, if commercially reasonable, the insecure party may suspend any performance for which he has not already received the agreed return.

(3) A repudiation of the lease contract occurs if assurance of due performance adequate under the circumstances of the particular case is not provided to the insecure party within a reasonable time, not to exceed 30 days after receipt of a demand by the other party.

(4) Between merchants, the reasonableness of grounds for insecurity and the adequacy of any assurance offered must be determined according to commercial standards.

(5) Acceptance of any nonconforming delivery or payment does not prejudice the aggrieved party's right to demand adequate assurance of future performance. (1993, c. 463, s. 1.)

§ 25-2A-402. Anticipatory repudiation.

If either party repudiates a lease contract with respect to a performance not yet due under the lease contract, the loss of which performance will substantially impair the value of the lease contract to the other, the aggrieved party may:

(a) for a commercially reasonable time, await retraction of repudiation and performance by the repudiating party;

(b) make demand pursuant to G.S. 25-2A-401 and await assurance of future performance adequate under the circumstances of the particular case; or

(c) resort to any right or remedy upon default under the lease contract or this Article, even though the aggrieved party has notified the repudiating party that the aggrieved party would await the repudiating party's performance and assurance and has urged retraction. In addition, whether or not the aggrieved party is pursuing one of the foregoing remedies, the aggrieved party may suspend performance or, if the aggrieved party is the lessor, proceed in accordance with the provisions of this Article on the lessor's right to identify goods to the lease contract notwithstanding default or to salvage unfinished goods (G.S. 25-2A-524). (1993, c. 463, s. 1.)

§ 25-2A-403. Retraction of anticipatory repudiation.

(1) Until the repudiating party's next performance is due, the repudiating party can retract the repudiation unless, since the repudiation, the aggrieved party has cancelled the lease contract or materially changed the aggrieved party's position or otherwise indicated that the aggrieved party considers the repudiation final.

(2) Retraction may be by any method that clearly indicates to the aggrieved party that the repudiating party intends to perform under the lease contract and includes any assurance demanded under G.S. 25-2A-401.

(3) Retraction reinstates a repudiating party's rights under a lease contract with due excuse and allowance to the aggrieved party for any delay occasioned by the repudiation. (1993, c. 463, s. 1.)

§ 25-2A-404. Substituted performance.

(1) If without fault of the lessee, the lessor and the supplier, the agreed berthing, loading, or unloading facilities fail, or the agreed type of carrier becomes unavailable or the agreed manner of delivery otherwise becomes commercially impracticable, but a commercially reasonable substitute is available, the substitute performance shall be tendered and accepted.

(2) If the agreed means or manner of payment fails because of domestic or foreign governmental regulation:

(a) the lessor may withhold or stop delivery or cause the supplier to withhold or stop delivery unless the lessee provides a means or manner of payment that is commercially a substantial equivalent; and

(b) if delivery has already been taken, payment by the means or in the manner provided by the regulation discharges the lessee's obligation unless the regulation is discriminatory, oppressive, or predatory. (1993, c. 463, s. 1.)

§ 25-2A-405. Excused performance.

Subject to G.S 25-2A-404 on substituted performance, the following rules apply:

(a) delay in delivery or nondelivery in whole or in part by a lessor or a supplier who complies with paragraphs (b) and (c) is not a default under the lease contract if performance as agreed has been made impracticable by the occurrence of a contingency, the nonoccurrence of which was a basic assumption on which the lease contract was made, or by compliance in good faith with any applicable foreign or domestic governmental regulation or order, whether or not the regulation or order later proves to be invalid.

(b)   if the causes mentioned in paragraph (a) affect only part of the lessor's or the supplier's capacity to perform, he shall allocate production and deliveries among his customers but at his option may include regular customers not then under contract for sale or lease as well as his own requirements for further manufacture. He may so allocate in any manner that is fair and reasonable.

(c)   the lessor seasonably shall notify the lessee and in the case of a finance lease the supplier seasonably shall notify the lessor and the lessee, if known, that there will be delay or nondelivery and, if allocation is required under paragraph (b), of the estimated quota thus made available for the lessee. (1993, c. 463, s. 1.)

§ 25-2A-406. Procedure on excused performance.

(1)   If the lessee receives notification of a material or indefinite delay or an allocation justified under G.S. 25-2A-405, the lessee may, by written notification to the lessor as to any goods involved, and with respect to all of the goods if under an installment lease contract, the value of the whole lease contract is substantially impaired (G.S. 25-2A-510):

(a)   terminate the lease contract (G.S. 25-2A-505(2)); or

(b)   except in a finance lease that is not a consumer lease, modify the lease contract by accepting the available quota in substitution, with due allowance from the rent payable for the balance of the lease term for the deficiency but without further right against the lessor.

(2)   If, after receipt of a notification from the lessor under G.S. 25-2A-405, the lessee fails so to modify the lease agreement within a reasonable time not exceeding 30 days, the lease contract lapses with respect to any deliveries affected. (1993, c. 463, s. 1.)

§ 25-2A-407. Irrevocable promises: finance leases.

(1)   In the case of a finance lease that is not a consumer lease, the lessee's promises under the lease contract become irrevocable and independent upon the lessee's acceptance of the goods.

(2)   A promise that has become irrevocable and independent under subsection (1) of this section:

(a)   is effective and enforceable between the parties, and by or against third parties including assignees of the parties; and

(b)   is not subject to cancellation, termination, modification, repudiation, excuse, or substitution without the consent of the party to whom the promise runs.

(3)   This section does not affect the validity under any other law of a covenant in any lease contract making the lessee's promises irrevocable and independent upon the lessee's acceptance of the goods. (1993, c. 463, s. 1.)

PART 5.

DEFAULT.

SUBPART A. In General.

§ 25-2A-501. Default: procedure.

(1)   Whether the lessor or the lessee is in default under a lease contract is determined by the lease agreement and this Article.

(2)   If the lessor or the lessee is in default under the lease contract, the party seeking enforcement has rights and remedies as provided in this Article and, except as limited by this Article, as provided in the lease agreement.

(3)   If the lessor or the lessee is in default under the lease contract, the party seeking enforcement may reduce the party's claim to judgment, or otherwise enforce the lease contract by self-help or any available judicial procedure or nonjudicial procedure, including administrative proceeding, arbitration, or the like, in accordance with this Article.

(4) Except as otherwise provided in G.S. 25-1-305(a) or this Article or the lease agreement, the rights and remedies referred to in subsections (2) and (3) of this section are cumulative.

(5) If the lease agreement covers both real property and goods, the party seeking enforcement may proceed under this Part as to the goods, or under other applicable law as to both the real property and the goods in accordance with that party's rights and remedies in respect of the real property, in which case this Part does not apply. (1993, c. 463, s. 1; 2006-112, s. 7.)

§ 25-2A-502. Notice after default.

Except as otherwise provided in this Article or the lease agreement, the lessor or lessee in default under the lease contract is not entitled to notice of default or notice of enforcement from the other party to the lease agreement. (1993, c. 463, s. 1.)

§ 25-2A-503. Modification or impairment of rights and remedies.

(1) Except as otherwise provided in this Article, the lease agreement may include rights and remedies for default in addition to or in substitution for those provided in this Article and may limit or alter the measure of damages recoverable under this Article.

(2) Resort to a remedy provided under this Article or in the lease agreement is optional unless the remedy is expressly agreed to be exclusive. If circumstances cause an exclusive or limited remedy to fail of its essential purpose, or provision for an exclusive remedy is unconscionable, remedy may be had as provided in this Article.

(3) Consequential damages may be liquidated under G.S. 25-2A-504, or may otherwise be limited, altered, or excluded unless the limitation, alteration, or exclusion is unconscionable. Limitation, alteration, or exclusion of consequential damages for injury to the person in the case of consumer goods is prima facie unconscionable but limitation, alteration, or exclusion of damages where the loss is commercial is not prima facie unconscionable.

(4) Rights and remedies on default by the lessor or the lessee with respect to any obligation or promise collateral or ancillary to the lease contract are not impaired by this Article. (1993, c. 463, s. 1.)

§ 25-2A-504. Liquidation of damages.

(1) Damages payable by either party for default, or any other act or omission, including indemnity for loss or diminution of anticipated tax benefits or loss or damage to lessor's residual interest, may be liquidated in the lease agreement but only at an amount or by a formula that is reasonable in light of the then-anticipated harm caused by the default or other act or omission.

(2) If the lease agreement provides for liquidation of damages, and such provision does not comply with subsection (1) of this section, or such provision is an exclusive or limited remedy that circumstances cause to fail of its essential purpose, remedy may be had as provided in this Article.

(3) If the lessor justifiably withholds or stops delivery of goods because of the lessee's default or insolvency (G.S. 25-2A-525 or G.S. 25-2A-526), the lessee is entitled to restitution of any amount by which the sum of his payments exceeds:

(a) the amount to which the lessor is entitled by virtue of terms liquidating the lessor's damages in accordance with subsection (1) of this section; or

(b) in the absence of those terms, twenty percent (20%) of the then-present value of the total rent the lessee was obligated to pay for the balance of the lease term, or, in the case of a consumer lease, the lesser of such amount or five hundred dollars ($500.00).

(4) A lessee's right to restitution under subsection (3) of this section is subject to offset to the extent the lessor establishes:

(a) a right to recover damages under the provisions of this Article other than subsection (1) of this section; and

(b) the amount or value of any benefits received by the lessee directly or indirectly by reason of the lease contract. (1993, c. 463, s. 1.)

§ 25-2A-505. Cancellation and termination and effect of cancellation, termination, rescission, or fraud on rights and remedies.

(1)   On cancellation of the lease contract, all obligations that are still executory on both sides are discharged, but any right based on prior default or performance survives, and the cancelling party also retains any remedy for default of the whole lease contract or any unperformed balance.

(2)   On termination of the lease contract, all obligations that are still executory on both sides are discharged, but any right based on prior default or performance survives.

(3)   Unless the contrary intention clearly appears, expressions of "cancellation", "rescission", or the like of the lease contract may not be construed as a renunciation or discharge of any claim in damages for an antecedent default.

(4)   Rights and remedies for material misrepresentation or fraud include all rights and remedies available under this Article for default.

(5)   Neither rescission nor a claim for rescission of the lease contract nor rejection or return of the goods may bar or be deemed inconsistent with a claim for damages or other right or remedy. (1993, c. 463, s. 1.)

§ 25-2A-506. Statute of limitations.

(1)   An action for default under a lease contract, including breach of warranty or indemnity, must be commenced within four years after the cause of action accrued. By the original lease contract the parties may reduce the period of limitation to not less than one year.

(2)   A cause of action for default accrues when the act or omission on which the default or breach of warranty is based is or should have been discovered by the aggrieved party, or when the default occurs, whichever is later. A cause of action for indemnity accrues when the act or omission on which the claim for indemnity is based is or should have been discovered by the indemnified party, whichever is later.

(3) If an action commenced within the time limited by subsection (1) of this section is so terminated as to leave available a remedy by another action for the same default or breach of warranty or indemnity, the other action may be commenced after the expiration of the time limited and within six months after the termination of the first action unless the termination resulted from voluntary discontinuance or from dismissal for failure or neglect to prosecute.

(4) This section does not alter the law on tolling of the statute of limitations nor does it apply to causes of action that have accrued before this Article becomes effective. (1993, c. 463, s. 1.)

§ 25-2A-507. Proof of market rent: time and place.

(1) Damages based on market rent (G.S. 25-2A-519 or G.S. 25-2A-528) are determined according to the rent for the use of the goods concerned for a lease term identical to the remaining lease term of the original lease agreement and prevailing at the times specified in G.S. 25-2A-519 and G.S. 25-2A-528.

(2) If evidence of rent for the use of the goods concerned for a lease term identical to the remaining lease term of the original lease agreement and prevailing at the times or places described in this Article is not readily available, the rent prevailing within any reasonable time before or after the time described or at any other place or for a different lease term which in commercial judgment or under usage of trade would serve as a reasonable substitute for the one described may be used, making any proper allowance for the difference, including the cost of transporting the goods to or from the other place.

(3) Evidence of a relevant rent prevailing at a time or place or for a lease term other than the one described in this Article offered by one party is not admissible unless and until he has given the other party notice the court finds sufficient to prevent unfair surprise.

(4) If the prevailing rent or value of any goods regularly leased in any established market is in issue, reports in official publications or trade journals or in newspapers or periodicals of general circulation published as the reports of that market are admissible in evidence. The circumstances of the preparation of the report may be shown to affect its weight but not its admissibility. (1993, c. 463, s. 1.)

B. Default by Lessor.

§ 25-2A-508. Lessee's remedies.

(1)   If a lessor fails to deliver the goods in conformity to the lease contract (G.S. 25-2A-509) or repudiates the lease contract (G.S. 25-2A-402), or a lessee rightfully rejects the goods (G.S. 25-2A-509) or justifiably revokes acceptance of the goods (G.S. 25-2A-517), then with respect to any goods involved, and with respect to all of the goods if under an installment lease contract, the value of the whole lease contract is substantially impaired (G.S. 25-2A-510), the lessor is in default under the lease contract, and the lessee may:

(a)   cancel the lease contract (G.S. 25-2A-505(1));

(b)   recover so much of the rent and security as has been paid and is just under the circumstances;

(c)   cover and recover damages as to all goods affected whether or not they have been identified to the lease contract (G.S. 25-2A-518 and G.S. 25-2A-520), or recover damages for nondelivery (G.S. 25-2A-519 and G.S. 25-2A-520);

(d)   exercise any other rights or pursue any other remedies provided in the lease contract.

(2)   If a lessor fails to deliver the goods in conformity to the lease contract or repudiates the lease contract, the lessee may also:

(a)   if the goods have been identified, recover them (G.S. 25-2A-522); or

(b)   in a proper case, obtain specific performance or replevy the goods (G.S. 25-2A-521).

(3)   If a lessor is otherwise in default under a lease contract, the lessee may exercise the rights and pursue the remedies provided in the lease contract, which may include a right to cancel the lease, and in G.S. 25-2A-519(3).

(4) If a lessor has breached a warranty, whether express or implied, the lessee may recover damages (G.S. 25-2A-519(4)).

(5) On rightful rejection or justifiable revocation of acceptance, a lessee has a security interest in goods in the lessee's possession or control for any rent and security that has been paid and any expenses reasonably incurred in their inspection, receipt, transportation, and care and custody and may hold those goods and dispose of them in good faith and in a commercially reasonable manner, subject to G.S. 25-2A-527(5). A lessee who has rightfully rejected the goods, or justifiably revoked acceptance of the goods, shall account to the lessor for any excess over the amount of the lessee's security interest.

(6) Subject to the provisions of G.S. 25-2A-407, a lessee, on notifying the lessor of the lessee's intention to do so, may deduct all or any part of the damages resulting from any default under the lease contract from any part of the rent still due under the same lease contract. (1993, c. 463, s. 1.)

§ 25-2A-509. Lessee's rights on improper delivery; rightful rejection.

(1) Subject to the provisions of G.S. 25-2A-510 on default in installment lease contracts, if the goods or the tender or delivery fail in any respect to conform to the lease contract, the lessee may reject or accept the goods or accept any commercial unit or units and reject the rest of the goods.

(2) Rejection of goods is ineffective unless it is within a reasonable time after tender or delivery of the goods and the lessee seasonably notifies the lessor. (1993, c. 463, s. 1.)

§ 25-2A-510. Installment lease contracts; rejection and default.

(1) Under an installment lease contract a lessee may reject any delivery that is nonconforming if the nonconformity substantially impairs the value of that delivery and cannot be cured or the nonconformity is a defect in the required documents; but if the nonconformity does not fall within subsection (2) of this section and the lessor or the supplier gives adequate assurance of its cure, the lessee must accept that delivery.

(2) Whenever nonconformity or default with respect to one or more deliveries substantially impairs the value of the installment lease contract as a whole, there is a default with respect to the whole. But, the aggrieved party reinstates the installment lease contract as a whole if the aggrieved party accepts a nonconforming delivery without seasonably notifying of cancellation or brings an action with respect only to past deliveries or demands performance as to future deliveries. (1993, c. 463, s. 1.)

§ 25-2A-511. Merchant lessee's duties as to rightfully rejected goods.

(1) Subject to any security interest of a lessee (G.S. 25-2A-508(5)), if a lessor or a supplier has no agent or place of business at the market of rejection, a merchant lessee, after rejection of goods in his possession or control, shall follow any reasonable instructions received from the lessor or the supplier with respect to the goods. In the absence of those instructions, a merchant lessee shall make reasonable efforts to sell, lease, or otherwise dispose of the goods for the lessor's account if they threaten to decline in value speedily. Instructions are not reasonable if, on demand, indemnity for expenses is not forthcoming.

(2) If a merchant lessee (subsection (1) of this section) or any other lessee (G.S. 25-2A-512) disposes of goods, he is entitled to reimbursement either from the lessor or the supplier or out of the proceeds for reasonable expenses of caring for and disposing of the goods and, if the expenses include no disposition commission, to such commission as is usual in the trade, or if there is none, to a reasonable sum not exceeding ten percent (10%) of the gross proceeds.

(3) In complying with this section or G.S. 25-2A-512, the lessee is held only to good faith. Good faith conduct hereunder is neither acceptance or conversion nor the basis of an action for damages.

(4) A purchaser who purchases in good faith from a lessee pursuant to this section or G.S. 25-2A-512 takes the goods free of any rights of the lessor and the supplier even though the lessee fails to comply with one or more of the requirements of this Article. (1993, c. 463, s. 1.)

§ 25-2A-512. Lessee's duties as to rightfully rejected goods.

(1) Except as otherwise provided with respect to goods that threaten to decline in value speedily (G.S. 25-2A-511) and subject to any security interest of a lessee (G.S. 25-2A-508(5)):

(a) the lessee, after rejection of goods in the lessee's possession, shall hold them with reasonable care at the lessor's or the supplier's disposition for a reasonable time after the lessee's seasonable notification of rejection;

(b) if the lessor or the supplier gives no instructions within a reasonable time after notification of rejection, the lessee may store the rejected goods for the lessor's or the supplier's account or ship them to the lessor or the supplier or dispose of them for the lessor's or the supplier's account with reimbursement in the manner provided in G.S. 25-2A-511; but

(c) the lessee has no further obligations with regard to goods rightfully rejected.

(2) Action by the lessee pursuant to subsection (1) of this section is not acceptance or conversion. (1993, c. 463, s. 1.)

§ 25-2A-513. Cure by lessor of improper tender or delivery; replacement.

(1) If any tender or delivery by the lessor or the supplier is rejected because nonconforming and the time for performance has not yet expired, the lessor or the supplier may seasonably notify the lessee of the lessor's or the supplier's intention to cure and may then make a conforming delivery within the time provided in the lease contract.

(2) If the lessee rejects a nonconforming tender that the lessor or the supplier had reasonable grounds to believe would be acceptable with or without money allowance, the lessor or the supplier may have a further reasonable time to substitute a conforming tender if he seasonably notifies the lessee. (1993, c. 463, s. 1.)

§ 25-2A-514. Waiver of lessee's objections.

(1) In rejecting goods, a lessee's failure to state a particular defect that is ascertainable by reasonable inspection precludes the lessee from relying on the defect to justify rejection or to establish default:

(a) if, stated seasonably, the lessor or the supplier could have cured it (G.S. 25-2A-513); or

(b) between merchants if the lessor or the supplier after rejection has made a request in writing for a full and final written statement of all defects on which the lessee proposes to rely.

(2) A lessee's failure to reserve rights when paying rent or other consideration against documents precludes recovery of the payment for defects apparent in the documents. (1993, c. 463, s. 1; 2006-112, s. 39.)

§ 25-2A-515. Acceptance of goods.

(1) Acceptance of goods occurs after the lessee has had a reasonable opportunity to inspect the goods and:

(a) the lessee signifies or acts with respect to the goods in a manner that signifies to the lessor or the supplier that the goods are conforming or that the lessee will take or retain them in spite of their nonconformity; or

(b) the lessee fails to make an effective rejection of the goods (G.S. 25-2A-509(2)).

(2) Acceptance of a part of any commercial unit is acceptance of that entire unit. (1993, c. 463, s. 1.)

§ 25-2A-516. Effect of acceptance of goods; notice of default; burden of establishing default after acceptance; notice of claim or litigation to person answerable over.

(1) A lessee must pay rent for any goods accepted in accordance with the lease contract, with due allowance for goods rightfully rejected or not delivered.

(2) A lessee's acceptance of goods precludes rejection of the goods accepted. In the case of a finance lease, if made with knowledge of a nonconformity, acceptance cannot be revoked because of it. In any other case, if made with knowledge of a nonconformity, acceptance cannot be revoked because of it unless the acceptance was on the reasonable assumption that the nonconformity would be seasonably cured. Acceptance does not of itself impair any other remedy provided by this Article or the lease agreement for nonconformity.

(3) If a tender has been accepted:

(a) within a reasonable time after the lessee discovers or should have discovered any default, the lessee shall notify the lessor and the supplier, if any, or be barred from any remedy against the party not notified;

(b) except in the case of a consumer lease, within a reasonable time after the lessee receives notice of litigation for infringement or the like (G.S. 25-2A-211) the lessee shall notify the lessor or be barred from any remedy over for liability established by the litigation; and

(c) the burden is on the lessee to establish any default.

(4) If a lessee is sued for breach of a warranty or other obligation for which a lessor or a supplier is answerable over the following apply:

(a) the lessee may give the lessor or the supplier, or both, written notice of the litigation. If the notice states that the person notified may come in and defend and that if the person notified does not do so, that person will be bound in any action against that person by the lessee by any determination of fact common to the two litigations, then, unless the person notified after seasonable receipt of the notice does come in and defend, that person is so bound.

(b) the lessor or the supplier may demand in writing that the lessee turn over control of the litigation, including settlement, if the claim is one for infringement or the like (G.S. 25-2A-211) or else be barred from any remedy over. If the demand states that the lessor or the supplier agrees to bear all expense and to satisfy any adverse judgment, then, unless the lessee after seasonable receipt of the demand does turn over control, the lessee is so barred.

(5) Subsections (3) and (4) of this section apply to any obligation of a lessee to hold the lessor or the supplier harmless against infringement or the like (G.S. 25-2A-211). (1993, c. 463, s. 1.)

§ 25-2A-517. Revocation of acceptance of goods.

(1) A lessee may revoke acceptance of a lot or commercial unit whose nonconformity substantially impairs its value to the lessee if the lessee has accepted it:

(a) except in the case of a finance lease, on the reasonable assumption that its nonconformity would be cured and it has not been seasonably cured; or

(b) without discovery of the nonconformity if the lessee's acceptance was reasonably induced either by the lessor's assurances or, except in the case of a finance lease, by the difficulty of discovery before acceptance.

(2) Except in the case of a finance lease that is not a consumer lease, a lessee may revoke acceptance of a lot or commercial unit if the lessor defaults under the lease contract and the default substantially impairs the value of that lot or commercial unit to the lessee.

(3) If the lease agreement so provides, the lessee may revoke acceptance of a lot or commercial unit because of other defaults by the lessor.

(4) Revocation of acceptance must occur within a reasonable time after the lessee discovers or should have discovered the ground for it and before any substantial change in condition of the goods which is not caused by the nonconformity. Revocation is not effective until the lessee notifies the lessor.

(5) A lessee who so revokes has the same rights and duties with regard to the goods involved as if the lessee had rejected them. (1993, c. 463, s. 1.)

§ 25-2A-518. Cover; substitute goods.

(1) After a default by a lessor under the lease contract of the type described in G.S. 25-2A-508(1), or, if agreed, after other default by the lessor, the lessee

may cover by making any purchase or lease of or contract to purchase or lease goods in substitution for those due from the lessor.

(2) Except as otherwise provided with respect to damages liquidated in the lease agreement (G.S. 25-2A-504) or otherwise determined pursuant to agreement of the parties (G.S. 25-1-302 and G.S. 25-2A-503), if a lessee's cover is by a lease agreement substantially similar to the original lease agreement and the new lease agreement is made in good faith and in a commercially reasonable manner, the lessee may recover from the lessor as damages (i) the present value, as of the date of the commencement of the term of the new lease agreement, of the rent under the new lease agreement applicable to that period of the new lease term which is comparable to the then remaining term of the original lease agreement minus the present value as of the same date of the total rent for the then remaining lease term of the original lease agreement, and (ii) any incidental or consequential damages, less expenses saved in consequence of the lessor's default.

(3) If a lessee's cover is by lease agreement that for any reason does not qualify for treatment under subsection (2) of this section, or is by purchase or otherwise, the lessee may recover from the lessor as if the lessee had elected not to cover and G.S. 25-2A-519 governs. (1993, c. 463, s. 1; 2006-112, s. 8.)

§ 25-2A-519. Lessee's damages for nondelivery, repudiation, default, and breach of warranty in regard to accepted goods.

(1) Except as otherwise provided with respect to damages liquidated in the lease agreement (G.S. 25-2A-504) or otherwise determined pursuant to agreement of the parties (G.S. 25-1-302 and G.S. 25-2A-503), if a lessee elects not to cover or a lessee elects to cover and the cover is by lease agreement that for any reason does not qualify for treatment under G.S. 25-2A-518(2), or is by purchase or otherwise, the measure of damages for nondelivery or repudiation by the lessor or for rejection or revocation of acceptance by the lessee is the present value, as of the date of the default, of the then market rent minus the present value as of the same date of the original rent, computed for the remaining lease term of the original lease agreement, together with incidental and consequential damages, less expenses saved in consequence of the lessor's default.

(2) Market rent is to be determined as of the place for tender or, in cases of rejection after arrival or revocation of acceptance, as of the place of arrival.

(3) Except as otherwise agreed, if the lessee has accepted goods and given notification (G.S. 25-2A-516(3)), the measure of damages for nonconforming tender or delivery or other default by a lessor is the loss resulting in the ordinary course of events from the lessor's default as determined in any manner that is reasonable together with incidental and consequential damages, less expenses saved in consequence of the lessor's default.

(4) Except as otherwise agreed, the measure of damages for breach of warranty is the present value at the time and place of acceptance of the difference between the value of the use of the goods accepted and the value if they had been as warranted for the lease term, unless special circumstances show proximate damages of a different amount, together with incidental and consequential damages, less expenses saved in consequence of the lessor's default or breach of warranty. (1993, c. 463, s. 1; 2006-112, s. 9.)

§ 25-2A-520. Lessee's incidental and consequential damages.

(1) Incidental damages resulting from a lessor's default include expenses reasonably incurred in inspection, receipt, transportation, and care and custody of goods rightfully rejected or goods the acceptance of which is justifiably revoked, any commercially reasonable charges, expenses or commissions in connection with effecting cover, and any other reasonable expense incident to the default.

(2) Consequential damages resulting from a lessor's default include:

(a) any loss resulting from general or particular requirements and needs of which the lessor at the time of contracting had reason to know and which could not reasonably be prevented by cover or otherwise; and

(b) injury to person or property proximately resulting from any breach of warranty. (1993, c. 463, s. 1.)

§ 25-2A-521. Lessee's right to specific performance or replevin.

(1) Specific performance may be decreed if the goods are unique or in other proper circumstances.

(2) A decree for specific performance may include any terms and conditions as to payment of the rent, damages, or other relief that the court deems just.

(3) A lessee has a right of replevin, detinue, sequestration, claim and delivery, or the like for goods identified to the lease contract if after reasonable effort the lessee is unable to effect recovery for those goods or the circumstances reasonably indicate that the effort will be unavailing. (1993, c. 463, s. 1.)

§ 25-2A-522. Lessee's right to goods on lessor's insolvency.

(1) Subject to subsection (2) of this section and even though the goods have not been shipped, a lessee who has paid a part or all of the rent and security for goods identified to a lease contract (G.S. 25-2A-217) on making and keeping good a tender of any unpaid portion of the rent and security due under the lease contract may recover the goods identified from the lessor if the lessor becomes insolvent within 10 days after receipt of the first installment of rent and security.

(2) A lessee acquires the right to recover goods identified to a lease contract only if they conform to the lease contract. (1993, c. 463, s. 1.)

C. Default by Lessee.

§ 25-2A-523. Lessor's remedies.

(1) If a lessee wrongfully rejects or revokes acceptance of goods or fails to make a payment when due or repudiates with respect to a part or the whole, then, with respect to any goods involved, and with respect to all of the goods if under an installment lease contract the value of the whole lease contract is substantially impaired (G.S. 25-2A-510), the lessee is in default under the lease contract and the lessor may:

(a) cancel the lease contract (G.S. 25-2A-505(1));

(b) proceed respecting goods not identified to the lease contract (G.S. 25-2A-524);

(c) withhold delivery of the goods and take possession of goods previously delivered (G.S. 25-2A-525);

(d) stop delivery of the goods by any bailee (G.S. 25-2A-526);

(e) dispose of the goods and recover damages (G.S. 25-2A-527), or retain the goods and recover damages (G.S. 25-2A-528), or in a proper case recover rent (G.S. 25-2A-529);

(f) exercise any other rights or pursue any other remedies provided in the lease contract.

(2) If a lessor does not fully exercise a right or obtain a remedy to which the lessor is entitled under subsection (1) of this section, the lessor may recover the loss resulting in the ordinary course of events from the lessee's default as determined in any reasonable manner, together with incidental damages, less expenses saved in consequence of the lessee's default.

(3) If a lessee is otherwise in default under a lease contract, the lessor may exercise the rights and pursue the remedies provided in the lease contract, which may include a right to cancel the lease. In addition, unless otherwise provided in the lease contract:

(a) if the default substantially impairs the value of the lease contract to the lessor, the lessor may exercise the rights and pursue the remedies provided in subsections (1) or (2) of this section; or

(b) if the default does not substantially impair the value of the lease contract to the lessor, the lessor may recover as provided in subsection (2) of this section. (1993, c. 463, s. 1.)

§ 25-2A-524. Lessor's right to identify goods to lease contract.

(1) After default by the lessee under the lease contract of the type described in G.S. 25-2A-523(1) or G.S. 25-2A-523(3)(a) or, if agreed, after other default by the lessee, the lessor may:

(a) identify to the lease contract conforming goods not already identified if at the time the lessor learned of the default they were in the lessor's or the supplier's possession or control; and

(b) dispose of goods (G.S. 25-2A-527(1)) that demonstrably have been intended for the particular lease contract even though those goods are unfinished.

(2) If the goods are unfinished, in the exercise of reasonable commercial judgment for the purposes of avoiding loss and of effective realization, an aggrieved lessor or the supplier may either complete manufacture and wholly identify the goods to the lease contract or cease manufacture and lease, sell, or otherwise dispose of the goods for scrap or salvage value or proceed in any other reasonable manner. (1993, c. 463, s. 1.)

§ 25-2A-525. Lessor's right to possession of goods.

(1) If a lessor discovers the lessee to be insolvent, the lessor may refuse to deliver the goods.

(2) After a default by the lessee under the lease contract of the type described in G.S. 25-2A-523(1) or G.S. 25-2A-523(3)(a) or, if agreed, after other default by the lessee, the lessor has the right to take possession of the goods. If the lease contract so provides, the lessor may require the lessee to assemble the goods and make them available to the lessor at a place to be designated by the lessor which is reasonably convenient to both parties. Without removal, the lessor may render unusable any goods employed in trade or business, and may dispose of goods on the lessee's premises (G.S. 25-2A-527).

(3) The lessor may proceed under subsection (2) of this section without judicial process if it can be done without breach of the peace or the lessor may proceed by action. (1993, c. 463, s. 1.)

§ 25-2A-526. Lessor's stoppage of delivery in transit or otherwise.

(1)   A lessor may stop delivery of goods in the possession of a carrier or other bailee if the lessor discovers the lessee to be insolvent and may stop delivery of carload, truckload, planeload, or larger shipments of express or freight if the lessee repudiates or fails to make a payment due before delivery, whether for rent, security, or otherwise under the lease contract, or for any other reason the lessor has a right to withhold or take possession of the goods.

(2)   In pursuing its remedies under subsection (1) of this section, the lessor may stop delivery until

(a)   receipt of the goods by the lessee;

(b)   acknowledgment to the lessee by any bailee of the goods, except a carrier, that the bailee holds the goods for the lessee; or

(c)   such an acknowledgment to the lessee by a carrier via reshipment or as a warehouse.

(3)   (a)   To stop delivery, a lessor shall so notify as to enable the bailee by reasonable diligence to prevent delivery of the goods.

(b)   After notification, the bailee shall hold and deliver the goods according to the directions of the lessor, but the lessor is liable to the bailee for any ensuing charges or damages.

(c)   A carrier who has issued a nonnegotiable bill of lading is not obliged to obey a notification to stop received from a person other than the consignor. (1993, c. 463, s. 1; 1995, c. 509, s. 23; 2006-112, s. 40.)

§ 25-2A-527. Lessor's rights to dispose of goods.

(1)   After a default by a lessee under the lease contract of the type described in G.S. 25-2A-523(1) or G.S. 25-2A-523(3)(a) or after the lessor refuses to deliver or takes possession of goods (G.S. 25-2A-525 or G.S. 25-2A-526), or, if agreed, after other default by a lessee, the lessor may dispose of the goods concerned or the undelivered balance thereof by lease, sale, or otherwise.

(2) Except as otherwise provided with respect to damages liquidated in the lease agreement (G.S. 25-2A-504) or otherwise determined pursuant to agreement of the parties (G.S. 25-1-302 and G.S. 25-2A-503), if the disposition is by lease agreement substantially similar to the original lease agreement and the new lease agreement is made in good faith and in a commercially reasonable manner, the lessor may recover from the lessee as damages (i) accrued and unpaid rent as of the date of the commencement of the term of the new lease agreement, (ii) the present value, as of the same date, of the total rent for the then remaining lease term of the original lease agreement minus the present value, as of the same date, of the rent under the new lease agreement applicable to that period of the new lease term which is comparable to the then remaining term of the original lease agreement, and (iii) any incidental damages allowed under G.S. 25-2A-530, less expenses saved in consequence of the lessee's default.

(3) If the lessor's disposition is by lease agreement that for any reason does not qualify for treatment under subsection (2) of this section, or is by sale or otherwise, the lessor may recover from the lessee as if the lessor had elected not to dispose of the goods and G.S. 25-2A-528 governs.

(4) A subsequent buyer or lessee who buys or leases from the lessor in good faith for value as a result of a disposition under this section takes the goods free of the original lease contract and any rights of the original lessee even though the lessor fails to comply with one or more of the requirements of this Article.

(5) The lessor is not accountable to the lessee for any profit made on any disposition. A lessee who has rightfully rejected or justifiably revoked acceptance shall account to the lessor for any excess over the amount of the lessee's security interest (G.S. 25-2A-508(5)). (1993, c. 463, s. 1; 2006-112, s. 10.)

§ 25-2A-528. Lessor's damages for nonacceptance, failure to pay, repudiation, or other default.

(1) Except as otherwise provided with respect to damages liquidated in the lease agreement (G.S. 25-2A-504) or otherwise determined pursuant to agreement of the parties (G.S. 25-1-302 and G.S. 25-2A-503), if a lessor elects

to retain the goods or a lessor elects to dispose of the goods and the disposition is by lease agreement that for any reason does not qualify for treatment under G.S. 25-2A-527(2), or is by sale or otherwise, the lessor may recover from the lessee as damages for a default of the type described in G.S. 25-2A-523(1) or G.S. 25-2A-523(3)(a), or if agreed, for other default of the lessee, (i) accrued and unpaid rent as of the date of default if the lessee has never taken possession of the goods, or, if the lessee has taken possession of the goods, as of the date the lessor repossesses the goods or an earlier date on which the lessee makes a tender of the goods to the lessor, (ii) the present value as of the date determined under clause (i) of the total rent for the then remaining lease term of the original lease agreement minus the present value as of the same date of the market rent at the place where the goods are located computed for the same lease term, and (iii) any incidental damages allowed under G.S. 25-2A-530, less expenses saved in consequence of the lessee's default.

(2) If the measure of damages provided in subsection (1) of this section, is inadequate to put a lessor in as good a position as performance would have, the measure of damages is the present value of the profit, including reasonable overhead, the lessor would have made from full performance by the lessee, together with any incidental damages allowed under G.S. 25-2A-530, due allowance for costs reasonably incurred and due credit for payments or proceeds of disposition. (1993, c. 463, s. 1; 2006-112, s. 11.)

§ 25-2A-529. Lessor's action for the rent.

(1) After default by the lessee under the lease contract of the type described in G.S. 25-2A-523(1) or G.S. 25-2A-523(3)(a) or, if agreed, after other default by the lessee, if the lessor complies with subsection (2) of this section, the lessor may recover from the lessee as damages:

(a) for goods accepted by the lessee and not repossessed by or tendered to the lessor, and for conforming goods lost or damaged within a commercially reasonable time after risk of loss passes to the lessee (G.S. 25-2A-219), (i) accrued and unpaid rent as of the date of entry of judgment in favor of the lessor, (ii) the present value as of the same date of the rent for the then remaining lease term of the lease agreement, and (iii) any incidental damages allowed under G.S. 25-2A-530, less expenses saved in consequence of the lessee's default; and

(b) for goods identified to the lease contract if the lessor is unable after reasonable effort to dispose of them at a reasonable price or the circumstances reasonably indicate that effort will be unavailing, (i) accrued and unpaid rent as of the date of entry of judgment in favor of the lessor, (ii) the present value as of the same date of the rent for the then remaining lease term of the lease agreement, and (iii) any incidental damages allowed under G.S. 25-2A-530, less expenses saved in consequence of the lessee's default.

(2) Except as provided in subsection (3) of this section, the lessor shall hold for the lessee for the remaining lease term of the lease agreement any goods that have been identified to the lease contract and are in the lessor's control.

(3) The lessor may dispose of the goods at any time before collection of the judgment for damages obtained pursuant to subsection (1) of this section. If the disposition is before the end of the remaining lease term of the lease agreement, the lessor's recovery against the lessee for damages is governed by G.S. 25-2A-527 or G.S. 25-2A-528, and the lessor will cause an appropriate credit to be provided against a judgment for damages to the extent that the amount of the judgment exceeds the recovery available pursuant to G.S. 25-2A-527 or G.S. 25-2A-528.

(4) Payment of the judgment for damages obtained pursuant to subsection (1) of this section, entitles the lessee to the use and possession of the goods not then disposed of for the remaining lease term of and in accordance with the lease agreement.

(5) After a default by the lessee under the lease contract of the type described in G.S. 25-2A-523(1) or G.S. 25-2A-523(3)(a) or, if agreed, after other default by the lessee, a lessor who is held not entitled to rent under this section must nevertheless be awarded damages for nonacceptance under G.S. 25-2A-527 or G.S. 25-2A-528. (1993, c. 463, s. 1.)

§ 25-2A-530. Lessor's incidental damages.

Incidental damages to an aggrieved lessor include any commercially reasonable charges, expenses, or commissions incurred in stopping delivery, in the transportation, care, and custody of goods after the lessee's default, in connection with return or disposition of the goods, or otherwise resulting from the default. (1993, c. 463, s. 1.)

§ 25-2A-531. Standing to sue third parties for injury to goods.

(1) If a third party so deals with goods that have been identified to a lease contract as to cause actionable injury to a party to the lease contract then (a) the lessor has a right of action against the third party, and (b) the lessee also has a right of action against the third party if the lessee:

(i) has a security interest in the goods;

(ii) has an insurable interest in the goods; or

(iii) bears the risk of loss under the lease contract or has since the injury assumed that risk as against the lessor and the goods have been converted or destroyed.

(2) If at the time of the injury the party plaintiff did not bear the risk of loss as against the other party to the lease contract and there is no arrangement between them for disposition of the recovery, his suit or settlement, subject to his own interest, is as a fiduciary for the other party to the lease contract.

(3) Either party, with the consent of the other, may sue for the benefit of whom it may concern. (1993, c. 463, s. 1.)

§ 25-2A-532. Lessor's rights to residual interest.

In addition to any other recovery permitted by this Article or other law, the lessor may recover from the lessee an amount that will fully compensate the lessor for any loss of or damage to the lessor's residual interest in the goods caused by the default of the lessee. (1993, c. 463, s. 1.)

Article 3.

Negotiable Instruments.

(Revised)

Part 1.

GENERAL PROVISIONS AND DEFINITIONS.

§ 25-3-101. Short title.

This Article may be cited as Uniform Commercial Code - Negotiable Instruments. (1899, c. 733, ss. 128, 191; Rev., ss. 2278, 2340; C.S., ss. 2976, 3110; 1965, c. 700, s. 1; 1995, c. 232, s. 1.)

§ 25-3-102. Subject matter.

(a) This Article applies to negotiable instruments. It does not apply to money, to payment orders governed by Article 4A, or to securities governed by Article 8.

(b) If there is conflict between this Article and Article 4 or 9, Articles 4 and 9 govern.

(c) Regulations of the Board of Governors of the Federal Reserve System and operating circulars of the Federal Reserve Banks supersede any inconsistent provision of this Article to the extent of the inconsistency. (1965, c. 700, s. 1; 1995, c. 232, s. 1.)

Article 3.

Negotiable Instruments.

PART 1.

GENERAL PROVISIONS AND DEFINITIONS.

§ 25-3-103. Definitions.

(a) In this Article:

(1) "Acceptor" means a drawee who has accepted a draft.

(2) "Drawee" means a person ordered in a draft to make payment.

(3) "Drawer" means a person who signs or is identified in a draft as a person ordering payment.

(4) Repealed by Session Laws 2006-112, s. 12, effective October 1, 2006.

(5) "Maker" means a person who signs or is identified in a note as a person undertaking to pay.

(6) "Order" means a written instruction to pay money signed by the person giving the instruction. The instruction may be addressed to any person, including the person giving the instruction, or to one or more persons jointly or in the alternative but not in succession. An authorization to pay is not an order unless the person authorized to pay is also instructed to pay.

(7) "Ordinary care" in the case of a person engaged in business means observance of reasonable commercial standards, prevailing in the area in which the person is located, with respect to the business in which the person is engaged. In the case of a bank that takes an instrument for processing for collection or payment by automated means, reasonable commercial standards do not require the bank to examine the instrument if the failure to examine does not violate the bank's prescribed procedures and the bank's procedures do not vary unreasonably from general banking usage not disapproved by this Article or Article 4.

(8) "Party" means a party to an instrument.

(9) "Promise" means a written undertaking to pay money signed by the person undertaking to pay. An acknowledgment of an obligation by the obligor is not a promise unless the obligor also undertakes to pay the obligation.

(10) "Prove" with respect to a fact means to meet the burden of establishing the fact (G.S. 25-1-201(b)(8)).

(11) "Remitter" means a person who purchases an instrument from its issuer if the instrument is payable to an identified person other than the purchaser.

(b) Other definitions applying to this Article and the sections in which they appear are:

"Acceptance"	G.S. 25-3-409.
"Accommodated party"	G.S. 25-3-419.
"Accommodation party"	G.S. 25-3-419.
"Alteration"	G.S. 25-3-407.
"Anomalous indorsement"	G.S. 25-3-205.
"Blank indorsement"	G.S. 25-3-205.
"Cashier's check"	G.S. 25-3-104.
"Certificate of deposit"	G.S. 25-3-104.
"Certified check"	G.S. 25-3-409.
"Check"	G.S. 25-3-104.
"Consideration"	G.S. 25-3-303.
"Draft"	G.S. 25-3-104.
"Holder in due course"	G.S. 25-3-302.
"Incomplete instrument"	G.S. 25-3-115.
"Indorsement"	G.S. 25-3-204.
"Indorser"	G.S. 25-3-204.
"Instrument"	G.S. 25-3-104.
"Issue"	G.S. 25-3-105.
"Issuer"	G.S. 25-3-105.

"Negotiable instrument"	G.S. 25-3-104.
"Negotiation"	G.S. 25-3-201.
"Note"	G.S. 25-3-104.
"Payable at a definite time"	G.S. 25-3-108.
"Payable on demand"	G.S. 25-3-108.
"Payable to bearer"	G.S. 25-3-109.
"Payable to order"	G.S. 25-3-109.
"Payment"	G.S. 25-3-602.
"Person entitled to enforce"	G.S. 25-3-301.
"Presentment"	G.S. 25-3-501.
"Reacquisition"	G.S. 25-3-207.
"Special indorsement"	G.S. 25-3-205.
"Teller's check"	G.S. 25-3-104.
"Transfer of instrument"	G.S. 25-3-203.
"Traveler's check"	G.S. 25-3-104.
"Value"	G.S. 25-3-303.

(c) The following definitions in other Articles apply to this Article:

"Bank"	G.S. 25-4-105.
"Banking day"	G.S. 25-4-104.
"Clearing house"	G.S. 25-4-104.
"Collecting bank"	G.S. 25-4-105.

"Depositary bank"	G.S. 25-4-105.
"Documentary draft"	G.S. 25-4-104.
"Intermediary bank"	G.S. 25-4-105.
"Item"	G.S. 25-4-104.
"Payor bank"	G.S. 25-4-105.
"Suspends payments"	G.S. 25-4-104.

(d) In addition, Article 1 contains general definitions and principles of construction and interpretation applicable throughout this Article. (1899, c. 733, ss. 17, 68; Rev., ss. 1952, 2217, 2341; C.S., ss. 2998, 3049; 1965, c. 700, s. 1; 1995, c. 232, s. 1; 2006-112, ss. 12, 13.)

§ 25-3-104. Negotiable instrument.

(a) Except as provided in subsections (c) and (d) of this section, "negotiable instrument" means an unconditional promise or order to pay a fixed amount of money, with or without interest or other charges described in the promise or order, if it:

(1) Is payable to bearer or to order at the time it is issued or first comes into possession of a holder;

(2) Is payable on demand or at a definite time; and

(3) Does not state any other undertaking or instruction by the person promising or ordering payment to do any act in addition to the payment of money, but the promise or order may contain (i) an undertaking or power to give, maintain, or protect collateral to secure payment, (ii) an authorization or power to the holder to confess judgment or realize on or dispose of collateral, or (iii) a waiver of the benefit of any law intended for the advantage or protection of an obligor.

(b) "Instrument" means a negotiable instrument.

(c) An order that meets all of the requirements of subsection (a) of this section, except subdivision (1), and otherwise falls within the definition of "check" in subsection (f) is a negotiable instrument and a check.

(d) A promise or order other than a check is not an instrument if, at the time it is issued or first comes into possession of a holder, it contains a conspicuous statement, however expressed, to the effect that the promise or order is not negotiable or is not an instrument governed by this Article.

(e) An instrument is a "note" if it is a promise and is a "draft" if it is an order. If an instrument falls within the definition of both "note" and "draft", a person entitled to enforce the instrument may treat it as either.

(f) "Check" means (i) a draft, other than a documentary draft, payable on demand and drawn on a bank or (ii) a cashier's check or teller's check. An instrument may be a check even though it is described on its face by another term, such as "money order".

(g) "Cashier's check" means a draft with respect to which the drawer and drawee are the same bank or branches of the same bank.

(h) "Teller's check" means a draft drawn by a bank (i) on another bank, or (ii) payable at or through a bank.

(i) "Traveler's check" means an instrument that (i) is payable on demand, (ii) is drawn on or payable at or through a bank, (iii) is designated by the term "traveler's check" or by a substantially similar term, and (iv) requires, as a condition to payment, a countersignature by a person whose specimen signature appears on the instrument.

(j) "Certificate of deposit" means an instrument containing an acknowledgment by a bank that a sum of money has been received by the bank and a promise by the bank to repay the sum of money. A certificate of deposit is a note of the bank. (1899, c. 733, ss. 1, 2, 5, 6, 10, 17, 86, 126, 184, 185, 197; 1905, c. 327; Rev., ss. 1952, 2151, 2152, 2154, 2155, 2160, 2217, 2276, 2334, 2335, 2341, 2346; C.S., ss. 2982, 2983, 2986, 2987, 2991, 2998, 3049, 3108, 3166, 3167; 1965, c. 700, s. 1; 1995, c. 232, s. 1.)

§ 25-3-105. Issue of instrument.

(a) "Issue" means the first delivery of an instrument by the maker or drawer, whether to a holder or nonholder, for the purpose of giving rights on the instrument to any person.

(b) An unissued instrument, or an unissued incomplete instrument that is completed, is binding on the maker or drawer, but nonissuance is a defense. An instrument that is conditionally issued or is issued for a special purpose is binding on the maker or drawer, but failure of the condition or special purpose to be fulfilled is a defense.

(c) "Issuer" applies to issued and unissued instruments and means a maker or drawer of an instrument. (1899, c. 733, ss. 16, 28, 58, 59; Rev., ss. 2166, 2176, 2207, 2208; C.S., ss. 2997, 3008, 3039, 3040; 1965, c. 700, s. 1; 1995, c. 232, s. 1.)

§ 25-3-106. Unconditional promise or order.

(a) Except as provided in this section, for the purposes of G.S. 25-3-104(a), a promise or order is unconditional unless it states (i) an express condition to payment, (ii) that the promise or order is subject to or governed by another writing, or (iii) that rights or obligations with respect to the promise or order are stated in another writing. A reference to another writing does not of itself make the promise or order conditional.

(b) A promise or order is not made conditional (i) by a reference to another writing for a statement of rights with respect to collateral, prepayment, or acceleration, or (ii) because payment is limited to resort to a particular fund or source.

(c) If a promise or order requires, as a condition to payment, a countersignature by a person whose specimen signature appears on the promise or order, the condition does not make the promise or order conditional for the purposes of G.S. 25-3-104(a). If the person whose specimen signature appears on an instrument fails to countersign the instrument, the failure to countersign is a defense to the obligation of the issuer, but the failure does not prevent a transferee of the instrument from becoming a holder of the instrument.

(d) If a promise or order at the time it is issued or first comes into possession of a holder contains a statement, required by applicable statutory or administrative law, to the effect that the rights of a holder or transferee are subject to claims or defenses that the issuer could assert against the original payee, the promise or order is not thereby made conditional for the purposes of G.S. 25-3-104(a); but if the promise or order is an instrument, there cannot be a holder in due course of the instrument. (1899, c. 733, s. 3; Rev., s. 2153; C.S., s. 2984; 1965, c. 700, s. 1; 1995, c. 232, s. 1.)

§ 25-3-107. Instrument payable in foreign money.

Unless the instrument otherwise provides, an instrument that states the amount payable in foreign money may be paid in the foreign money or in an equivalent amount in dollars calculated by using the current bank-offered spot rate at the place of payment for the purchase of dollars on the day on which the instrument is paid. (1899, c. 733, s. 6; Rev., s. 2155; C.S., s. 2987; 1965, c. 700, s. 1; 1995, c. 232, s. 1.)

§ 25-3-108. Payable on demand or at definite time.

(a) A promise or order is "payable on demand" if it (i) states that it is payable on demand or at sight, or otherwise indicates that it is payable at the will of the holder, or (ii) does not state any time of payment.

(b) A promise or order is "payable at a definite time" if it is payable on elapse of a definite period of time after sight or acceptance or at a fixed date or dates or at a time or times readily ascertainable at the time the promise or order is issued, subject to rights of (i) prepayment, (ii) acceleration, (iii) extension at the option of the holder, or (iv) extension to a further definite time at the option of the maker or acceptor or automatically upon or after a specified act or event.

(c) If an instrument, payable at a fixed date, is also payable upon demand made before the fixed date, the instrument is payable on demand until the fixed date and, if demand for payment is not made before that date, becomes payable at a definite time on the fixed date. (1899, c. 733, ss. 4, 7; Rev., ss. 2156, 2157; C.S., ss. 2985, 2988; 1923, c. 72; 1965, c. 700, s. 1; 1995, c. 232, s. 1.)

§ 25-3-109. Payable to bearer or to order.

(a) A promise or order is payable to bearer if it:

(1) States that it is payable to bearer or to the order of bearer or otherwise indicates that the person in possession of the promise or order is entitled to payment;

(2) Does not state a payee; or

(3) States that it is payable to or to the order of cash or otherwise indicates that it is not payable to an identified person.

(b) A promise or order that is not payable to bearer is payable to order if it is payable (i) to the order of an identified person or (ii) to an identified person or order. A promise or order that is payable to order is payable to the identified person.

(c) An instrument payable to bearer may become payable to an identified person if it is specially indorsed pursuant to G.S. 25-3-205(a). An instrument payable to an identified person may become payable to bearer if it is indorsed in blank pursuant to G.S. 25-3-205(b). (1899, c. 733, ss. 8, 9; Rev., ss. 2158, 2159; C.S., ss. 2989, 2990; 1949, c. 953; 1965, c. 700, s. 1; 1995, c. 232, s. 1.)

§ 25-3-110. Identification of person to whom instrument is payable.

(a) The person to whom an instrument is initially payable is determined by the intent of the person, whether or not authorized, signing as, or in the name or behalf of, the issuer of the instrument. The instrument is payable to the person intended by the signer even if that person is identified in the instrument by a name or other identification that is not that of the intended person. If more than one person signs in the name or behalf of the issuer of an instrument and all the signers do not intend the same person as payee, the instrument is payable to any person intended by one or more of the signers.

(b) If the signature of the issuer of an instrument is made by automated means, such as a check-writing machine, the payee of the instrument is determined by the intent of the person who supplied the name or identification of the payee, whether or not authorized to do so.

(c) A person to whom an instrument is payable may be identified in any way, including by name, identifying number, office, or account number. For the purpose of determining the holder of an instrument, the following rules apply:

(1) If an instrument is payable to an account and the account is identified only by number, the instrument is payable to the person to whom the account is payable. If an instrument is payable to an account identified by number and by the name of a person, the instrument is payable to the named person, whether or not that person is the owner of the account identified by number.

(2) If an instrument is payable to (i) a trust, an estate, or a person described as trustee or representative of a trust or estate, the instrument is payable to the trustee, the representative, or a successor of either, whether or not the beneficiary or estate is also named, (ii) a person described as agent or similar representative of a named or identified person, the instrument is payable to the represented person, the representative, or a successor of the representative, (iii) a fund or organization that is not a legal entity, the instrument is payable to a representative of the members of the fund or organization, or (iv) an office or to a person described as holding an office, the instrument is payable to the named person, the incumbent of the office, or a successor to the incumbent.

(d) If an instrument is payable to two or more persons alternatively, it is payable to any of them and may be negotiated, discharged, or enforced by any or all of them in possession of the instrument. If an instrument is payable to two or more persons not alternatively, it is payable to all of them and may be negotiated, discharged, or enforced only by all of them. If an instrument payable to two or more persons is ambiguous as to whether it is payable to the persons alternatively, the instrument is payable to the persons alternatively. (1899, c. 733, ss. 8, 41, 42; Rev., ss. 2158, 2190, 2191; C.S., ss. 2989, 3022, 3023; 1965, c. 700, s. 1; 1995, c. 232, s. 1.)

§ 25-3-111. Place of payment.

Except as otherwise provided for items in Article 4, an instrument is payable at the place of payment stated in the instrument. If no place of payment is stated, an instrument is payable at the address of the drawee or maker stated in the instrument. If no address is stated, the place of payment is the place of business of the drawee or maker. If a drawee or maker has more than one place of business, the place of payment is any place of business of the drawee or maker chosen by the person entitled to enforce the instrument. If the drawee or maker has no place of business, the place of payment is the residence of the drawee or maker. (1899, c. 733, ss. 72, 73, 77, 78, 145; Rev., ss. 2221, 2222, 2226, 2227, 2295; C.S., ss. 3053, 3054, 3058, 3059, 3127; 1963, c. 242; 1965, c. 700, s. 1; 1995, c. 232, s. 1.)

§ 25-3-112. Interest.

(a) Unless otherwise provided in the instrument, (i) an instrument is not payable with interest, and (ii) interest on an interest-bearing instrument is payable from the date of the instrument.

(b) Interest may be stated in an instrument as a fixed or variable amount of money or it may be expressed as a fixed or variable rate or rates. The amount or rate of interest may be stated or described in the instrument in any manner and may require reference to information not contained in the instrument. If an instrument provides for interest, but the amount of interest payable cannot be ascertained from the description, interest is payable at the judgment rate in effect at the place of payment of the instrument and at the time interest first accrues. (1899, c. 733, ss. 17, 68; Rev., ss. 1952, 2217, 2341; C.S., ss. 2998, 3049; 1965, c. 700, s. 1; 1995, c. 232, s. 1.)

§ 25-3-113. Date of instrument.

(a) An instrument may be antedated or postdated. The date stated determines the time of payment if the instrument is payable at a fixed period after date. Except as provided in G.S. 25-4-401(c), an instrument payable on demand is not payable before the date of the instrument.

(b) If an instrument is undated, its date is the date of its issue or, in the case of an unissued instrument, the date it first comes into possession of a holder. (1899, c. 733, ss. 6, 11, 12, 17; Rev., ss. 1952, 2155, 2161, 2162, 2341; C.S., ss. 2987, 2992, 2993, 2998; 1965, c. 700, s. 1; 1995, c. 232, s. 1.)

§ 25-3-114. Contradictory terms of instrument.

If an instrument contains contradictory terms, typewritten terms prevail over printed terms, handwritten terms prevail over both, and words prevail over numbers. (1899, c. 733, ss. 17, 68; Rev., ss. 1952, 2217, 2341; C.S., ss. 2998, 3049; 1965, c. 700, s. 1; 1995, c. 232, s. 1.)

§ 25-3-115. Incomplete instrument.

(a)   "Incomplete instrument" means a signed writing, whether or not issued by the signer, the contents of which show at the time of signing that it is incomplete but that the signer intended it to be completed by the addition of words or numbers.

(b)   Subject to subsection (c) of this section, if an incomplete instrument is an instrument under G.S. 25-3-104, it may be enforced according to its terms if it is not completed, or according to its terms as augmented by completion. If an incomplete instrument is not an instrument under G.S. 25-3-104, but, after completion, the requirements of G.S. 25-3-104 are met, the instrument may be enforced according to its terms as augmented by completion.

(c)   If words or numbers are added to an incomplete instrument without authority of the signer, there is an alteration of the incomplete instrument under G.S. 25-3-407.

(d)   The burden of establishing that words or numbers were added to an incomplete instrument without authority of the signer is on the person asserting the lack of authority. (1899, c. 733, ss. 13 to 15; Rev., ss. 2163 to 2165; C.S., ss. 2994 to 2996; 1965, c. 700, s. 1; 1995, c. 232, s. 1.)

§ 25-3-116. Joint and several liability; contribution.

(a)   Except as otherwise provided in the instrument, two or more persons who have the same liability on an instrument as makers, drawers, acceptors, indorsers who indorse as joint payees, or anomalous indorsers are jointly and severally liable in the capacity in which they sign.

(b) Except as provided in G.S. 25-3-419(e) or by agreement of the affected parties, a party having joint and several liability who pays the instrument is entitled to receive from any party having the same joint and several liability contribution in accordance with applicable law.

(c) Discharge of one party having joint and several liability by a person entitled to enforce the instrument does not affect the right under subsection (b) of this section of a party having the same joint and several liability to receive contribution from the party discharged. (1899, c. 733, ss. 17, 68; Rev., ss. 1952, 2217, 2341; C.S., ss. 2998, 3049; 1965, c. 700, s. 1; 1995, c. 232, s. 1.)

§ 25-3-117. Other agreements affecting instrument.

Subject to applicable law regarding exclusion of proof of contemporaneous or previous agreements, the obligation of a party to an instrument to pay the instrument may be modified, supplemented, or nullified by a separate agreement of the obligor and a person entitled to enforce the instrument, if the instrument is issued or the obligation is incurred in reliance on the agreement or as part of the same transaction giving rise to the agreement. To the extent an obligation is modified, supplemented, or nullified by an agreement under this section, the agreement is a defense to the obligation. (1965, c. 700, s. 1; 1995, c. 232, s. 1.)

§ 25-3-118. Statute of limitations.

(a) Except as provided in subsection (e) of this section, an action to enforce the obligation of a party to pay a note payable at a definite time must be commenced within six years after the due date or dates stated in the note or, if a due date is accelerated, within six years after the accelerated due date.

(b) Except as provided in subsection (d) or (e) of this section, if demand for payment is made to the maker of a note payable on demand, an action to enforce the obligation of a party to pay the note must be commenced within six years after the demand. If no demand for payment is made to the maker, an action to enforce the note is barred if neither principal nor interest on the note has been paid for a continuous period of 10 years.

(c)   Except as provided in subsection (d) of this section, an action to enforce the obligation of a party to an unaccepted draft to pay the draft must be commenced within three years after dishonor of the draft or 10 years after the date of the draft, whichever period expires first.

(d)   An action to enforce the obligation of the acceptor of a certified check or the issuer of a teller's check, cashier's check, or traveler's check must be commenced within three years after demand for payment is made to the acceptor or issuer, as the case may be.

(e)   An action to enforce the obligation of a party to a certificate of deposit to pay the instrument must be commenced within six years after demand for payment is made to the maker, but if the instrument states a due date and the maker is not required to pay before that date, the six-year period begins when a demand for payment is in effect and the due date has passed.

(f)   An action to enforce the obligation of a party to pay an accepted draft, other than a certified check, must be commenced (i) within six years after the due date or dates stated in the draft or acceptance if the obligation of the acceptor is payable at a definite time, or (ii) within six years after the date of the acceptance if the obligation of the acceptor is payable on demand.

(g)   Unless governed by other law regarding claims for indemnity or contribution, an action (i) for conversion of an instrument, for money had and received, or like action based on conversion, (ii) for breach of warranty, or (iii) to enforce an obligation, duty, or right arising under this Article and not governed by this section must be commenced within three years after the cause of action accrues.

(h)   A sealed instrument otherwise subject to this Article is governed by the time limits of G.S. 1-47(2). (1995, c. 232, s. 1; 2002-159, s. 7.)

§ 25-3-119. Notice of right to defend action.

In an action for breach of an obligation for which a third person is answerable over pursuant to this Article or Article 4, the defendant may give the third person written notice of the litigation, and the person notified may then give similar notice to any other person who is answerable over. If the notice states (i) that the person notified may come in and defend and (ii) that failure to do so will bind the person notified in an action later brought by the person giving the notice as to any determination of fact common to the two litigations, the person notified is so bound unless, after seasonable receipt of the notice, the person notified does come in and defend. (1965, c. 700, s. 1; 1995, c. 232, s. 1.)

Part 2.

NEGOTIATION, TRANSFER, AND INDORSEMENT.

§ 25-3-201. Negotiation.

(a) "Negotiation" means a transfer of possession, whether voluntary or involuntary, of an instrument by a person other than the issuer to a person who thereby becomes its holder.

(b) Except for negotiation by a remitter, if an instrument is payable to an identified person, negotiation requires transfer of possession of the instrument and its indorsement by the holder. If an instrument is payable to bearer, it may be negotiated by transfer of possession alone. ((1899, c. 733, ss. 30-32; Rev., ss. 2178, 2179, 2181; C.S., ss. 3010, 3011, 3013; 1965, c. 700, s. 1; 1995, c. 232, s. 1.)

§ 25-3-202. Negotiation subject to rescission.

(a) Negotiation is effective even if obtained (i) from an infant, a corporation exceeding its powers, or a person without capacity, (ii) by fraud, duress, or mistake, or (iii) in breach of duty or as part of an illegal transaction.

(b) To the extent permitted by other law, negotiation may be rescinded or may be subject to other remedies, but those remedies may not be asserted against a subsequent holder in due course or a person paying the instrument in good faith and without knowledge of facts that are a basis for rescission or other remedy. (1899, c. 733, ss. 22, 58, 59; Rev., ss. 2180, 2207, 2208; C.S., ss. 3012, 3039, 3040; 1965, c. 700, s. 1; 1995, c. 232, s. 1.)

§ 25-3-203. Transfer of instrument; rights acquired by transfer.

(a)   An instrument is transferred when it is delivered by a person other than its issuer for the purpose of giving to the person receiving delivery the right to enforce the instrument.

(b)   Transfer of an instrument, whether or not the transfer is a negotiation, vests in the transferee any right of the transferor to enforce the instrument, including any right as a holder in due course, but the transferee cannot acquire rights of a holder in due course by a transfer, directly or indirectly, from a holder in due course if the transferee engaged in fraud or illegality affecting the instrument.

(c)   Unless otherwise agreed, if an instrument is transferred for value and the transferee does not become a holder because of lack of indorsement by the transferor, the transferee has a specifically enforceable right to the unqualified indorsement of the transferor, but negotiation of the instrument does not occur until the indorsement is made.

(d)   If a transferor purports to transfer less than the entire instrument, negotiation of the instrument does not occur. The transferee obtains no rights under this Article and has only the rights of a partial assignee. (1899, c. 733, ss. 27, 30-32, 49, 58; Rev., ss. 2175, 2178, 2179, 2181, 2198, 2207; C.S., ss. 3007, 3010, 3011, 3013, 3030, 3039; 1965, c. 700, s. 1; 1995, c. 232, s. 1.)

§ 25-3-204. Indorsement.

(a)   "Indorsement" means a signature, other than that of a signer as maker, drawer, or acceptor, that alone or accompanied by other words is made on an instrument for the purpose of (i) negotiating the instrument, (ii) restricting payment of the instrument, or (iii) incurring indorser's liability on the instrument, but regardless of the intent of the signer, a signature and its accompanying words is an indorsement unless the accompanying words, terms of the instrument, place of the signature, or other circumstances unambiguously indicate that the signature was made for a purpose other than indorsement. For the purpose of determining whether a signature is made on an instrument, a paper affixed to the instrument is a part of the instrument.

(b) "Indorser" means a person who makes an indorsement.

(c) For the purpose of determining whether the transferee of an instrument is a holder, an indorsement that transfers a security interest in the instrument is effective as an unqualified indorsement of the instrument.

(d) If an instrument is payable to a holder under a name that is not the name of the holder, indorsement may be made by the holder in the name stated in the instrument or in the holder's name or both, but signature in both names may be required by a person paying or taking the instrument for value or collection. (1899, c. 733, ss. 17, 27, 30-32, 43, 49, 58, 63; Rev., ss. 1952, 2175, 2178, 2179, 2181, 2192, 2198, 2207, 2212, 2341; C.S., ss. 2998, 3007, 3010, 3011, 3013, 3024, 3030, 3039, 3044; 1965, c. 700, s. 1; 1995, c. 232, s. 1.)

§ 25-3-205. Special indorsement; blank indorsement; anomalous indorsement.

(a) If an indorsement is made by the holder of an instrument, whether payable to an identified person or payable to bearer, and the indorsement identifies a person to whom it makes the instrument payable, it is a "special indorsement". When specially indorsed, an instrument becomes payable to the identified person and may be negotiated only by the indorsement of that person. The principles stated in G.S. 25-3-110 apply to special indorsements.

(b) If an indorsement is made by the holder of an instrument and it is not a special indorsement, it is a "blank indorsement". When indorsed in blank, an instrument becomes payable to bearer and may be negotiated by transfer of possession alone until specially indorsed.

(c) The holder may convert a blank indorsement that consists only of a signature into a special indorsement by writing, above the signature of the indorser, words identifying the person to whom the instrument is made payable.

(d) "Anomalous indorsement" means an indorsement made by a person who is not the holder of the instrument. An anomalous indorsement does not affect the manner in which the instrument may be negotiated. (1899, c. 733, ss. 9, 33 to 36, 40; Rev., ss. 2159, 2182 to 2185, 2189; C.S., ss. 2990, 3014 to 3017, 3021; 1949, c. 953; 1965, c. 700, s. 1; 1995, c. 232, s. 1.)

§ 25-3-206. Restrictive indorsement.

(a)   An indorsement limiting payment to a particular person or otherwise prohibiting further transfer or negotiation of the instrument is not effective to prevent further transfer or negotiation of the instrument.

(b)   An indorsement stating a condition to the right of the indorsee to receive payment does not affect the right of the indorsee to enforce the instrument. A person paying the instrument or taking it for value or collection may disregard the condition, and the rights and liabilities of that person are not affected by whether the condition has been fulfilled.

(c)   If an instrument bears an indorsement (i) described in G.S. 25-4-201(b), or (ii) in blank or to a particular bank using the words "for deposit", "for collection", or other words indicating a purpose of having the instrument collected by a bank for the indorser or for a particular account, the following rules apply:

(1)   A person, other than a bank, who purchases the instrument when so indorsed converts the instrument unless the amount paid for the instrument is received by the indorser or applied consistently with the indorsement.

(2)   A depositary bank that purchases the instrument or takes it for collection when so indorsed converts the instrument unless the amount paid by the bank with respect to the instrument is received by the indorser or applied consistently with the indorsement.

(3)   A payor bank that is also the depositary bank or that takes the instrument for immediate payment over the counter from a person other than a collecting bank converts the instrument unless the proceeds of the instrument are received by the indorser or applied consistently with the indorsement.

(4)   Except as otherwise provided in subdivision (3), a payor bank or intermediary bank may disregard the indorsement and is not liable if the proceeds of the instrument are not received by the indorser or applied consistently with the indorsement.

(d) Except for an indorsement covered by subsection (c) of this section, if an instrument bears an indorsement using words to the effect that payment is to be made to the indorsee as agent, trustee, or other fiduciary for the benefit of the indorser or another person, the following rules apply:

(1) Unless there is notice of breach of fiduciary duty as provided in G.S. 25-3-307, a person who purchases the instrument from the indorsee or takes the instrument from the indorsee for collection or payment may pay the proceeds of payment or the value given for the instrument to the indorsee without regard to whether the indorsee violates a fiduciary duty to the indorser.

(2) A subsequent transferee of the instrument or person who pays the instrument is neither given notice nor otherwise affected by the restriction in the indorsement unless the transferee or payor knows that the fiduciary dealt with the instrument or its proceeds in breach of fiduciary duty.

(e) The presence on an instrument of an indorsement to which this section applies does not prevent a purchaser of the instrument from becoming a holder in due course of the instrument unless the purchaser is a converter under subsection (c) of this section or has notice or knowledge of breach of fiduciary duty as stated in subsection (d) of this section.

(f) In an action to enforce the obligation of a party to pay the instrument, the obligor has a defense if payment would violate an indorsement to which this section applies and the payment is not permitted by this section. (1899, c. 733, ss. 36, 37, 39, 47, 137; Rev., ss. 2185, 2186, 2188, 2196, 2287; C.S., ss. 3017, 3018, 3020, 3028, 3119; 1949, c. 954; 1965, c. 700, s. 1; 1995, c. 232, s. 1.)

§ 25-3-207. Reacquisition.

Reacquisition of an instrument occurs if it is transferred to a former holder by negotiation or otherwise. A former holder who reacquires the instrument may cancel indorsements made after the reacquirer first became a holder of the instrument. If the cancellation causes the instrument to be payable to the reacquirer or to bearer, the reacquirer may negotiate the instrument. An indorser whose indorsement is canceled is discharged, and the discharge is effective against any subsequent holder. (1889, c. 733, ss. 22, 48, 50, 121; Rev., ss.

2197, 2199, 2271; C.S., ss. 3029, 3031, 3103; 1965, c. 700, s. 1; 1995, c. 232, s. 1.)

Part 3.

ENFORCEMENT OF INSTRUMENTS.

§ 25-3-301. Person entitled to enforce instrument.

"Person entitled to enforce" an instrument means (i) the holder of the instrument, (ii) a nonholder in possession of the instrument who has the rights of a holder, or (iii) a person not in possession of the instrument who is entitled to enforce the instrument pursuant to G.S. 25-3-309 or G.S. 25-3-418(d). A person may be a person entitled to enforce the instrument even though the person is not the owner of the instrument or is in wrongful possession of the instrument. (1995, c. 232, s. 1.)

§ 25-3-302. Holder in due course.

(a) Subject to subsection (c) of this section and G.S. 25-3-106(d), "holder in due course" means the holder of an instrument if:

(1) The instrument when issued or negotiated to the holder does not bear such apparent evidence of forgery or alteration or is not otherwise so irregular or incomplete as to call into question its authenticity; and

(2) The holder took the instrument (i) for value, (ii) in good faith, (iii) without notice that the instrument is overdue or has been dishonored or that there is an uncured default with respect to payment of another instrument issued as part of the same series, (iv) without notice that the instrument contains an unauthorized signature or has been altered, (v) without notice of any claim to the instrument described in G.S. 25-3-306, and (vi) without notice that any party has a defense or claim in recoupment described in G.S. 25-3-305(a).

(b) Notice of discharge of a party, other than discharge in an insolvency proceeding, is not notice of a defense under subsection (a) of this section, but discharge is effective against a person who became a holder in due course with notice of the discharge. Public filing or recording of a document does not of itself constitute notice of a defense, claim in recoupment, or claim to the instrument.

(c)   Except to the extent a transferor or predecessor in interest has rights as a holder in due course, a person does not acquire rights of a holder in due course of an instrument taken (i) by legal process or by purchase in an execution, bankruptcy, or creditor's sale or similar proceeding, (ii) by purchase as part of a bulk transaction not in ordinary course of business of the transferor, or (iii) as the successor in interest to an estate or other organization.

(d)   If, under G.S. 25-3-303(a)(1), the promise of performance that is the consideration for an instrument has been partially performed, the holder may assert rights as a holder in due course of the instrument only to the fraction of the amount payable under the instrument equal to the value of the partial performance divided by the value of the promised performance.

(e)   If (i) the person entitled to enforce an instrument has only a security interest in the instrument and (ii) the person obliged to pay the instrument has a defense, claim in recoupment, or claim to the instrument that may be asserted against the person who granted the security interest, the person entitled to enforce the instrument may assert rights as a holder in due course only to an amount payable under the instrument which, at the time of enforcement of the instrument, does not exceed the amount of the unpaid obligation secured.

(f)   To be effective, notice must be received at a time and in a manner that gives a reasonable opportunity to act on it.

(g)   This section is subject to any law limiting status as a holder in due course in particular classes of transactions. (1899, c. 733, ss. 45, 52, 53, 55, 56; Rev., ss. 2194, 2201, 2202, 2204, 2205; C.S., ss. 3026, 3033, 3034, 3036, 3037; 1965, c. 700, s. 1; 1995, c. 232, s. 1.)

§ 25-3-303. Value and consideration.

(a)   An instrument is issued or transferred for value if:

(1)   The instrument is issued or transferred for a promise of performance, to the extent the promise has been performed;

(2)   The transferee acquires a security interest or other lien in the instrument other than a lien obtained by judicial proceeding;

(3) The instrument is issued or transferred as payment of, or as security for, an antecedent claim against any person, whether or not the claim is due;

(4) The instrument is issued or transferred in exchange for a negotiable instrument; or

(5) The instrument is issued or transferred in exchange for the incurring of an irrevocable obligation to a third party by the person taking the instrument.

(b) "Consideration" means any consideration sufficient to support a simple contract. The drawer or maker of an instrument has a defense if the instrument is issued without consideration. If an instrument is issued for a promise of performance, the issuer has a defense to the extent performance of the promise is due, and the promise has not been performed. If an instrument is issued for value as stated in subsection (a) of this section, the instrument is also issued for consideration. (1899, c. 733, ss. 16, 24, 25 to 27, 28, 54, 58, 59; Rev., ss. 2166, 2172, 2173 to 2175, 2176, 2203, 2207, 2208; C.S., ss. 2297, 3004, 3005 to 3007, 3008, 3035, 3039, 3040; 1965, c. 700, s. 1; 1995, c. 232, s. 1.)

§ 25-3-304. Overdue instrument.

(a) An instrument payable on demand becomes overdue at the earliest of the following times:

(1) On the day after the day demand for payment is duly made;

(2) If the instrument is a check, 90 days after its date; or

(3) If the instrument is not a check, when the instrument has been outstanding for a period of time after its date which is unreasonably long under the circumstances of the particular case in light of the nature of the instrument and usage of the trade.

(b) With respect to an instrument payable at a definite time the following rules apply:

(1) If the principal is payable in installments and a due date has not been accelerated, the instrument becomes overdue upon default under the instrument

for nonpayment of an installment, and the instrument remains overdue until the default is cured.

(2) If the principal is not payable in installments and the due date has not been accelerated, the instrument becomes overdue on the day after the due date.

(3) If a due date with respect to principal has been accelerated, the instrument becomes overdue on the day after the accelerated due date.

(c) Unless the due date of principal has been accelerated, an instrument does not become overdue if there is default in payment of interest but no default in payment of principal. (1899, c. 733, ss. 45, 52, 53, 55, 56; Rev., ss. 2194, 2201, 2202, 2204, 2205; C.S., ss. 3026, 3033, 3034, 3036, 3037; 1965, c. 700, s. 1; 1995, c. 232, s. 1.)

§ 25-3-305. Defenses and claims in recoupment.

(a) Except as stated in subsection (b) of this section, the right to enforce the obligation of a party to pay an instrument is subject to the following:

(1) A defense of the obligor based on (i) infancy of the obligor to the extent it is a defense to a simple contract, (ii) duress, lack of legal capacity, or illegality of the transaction which, under other law, nullifies the obligation of the obligor, (iii) fraud that induced the obligor to sign the instrument with neither knowledge nor reasonable opportunity to learn of its character or its essential terms, or (iv) discharge of the obligor in insolvency proceedings;

(2) A defense of the obligor stated in another section of this Article or a defense of the obligor that would be available if the person entitled to enforce the instrument were enforcing a right to payment under a simple contract; and

(3) A claim in recoupment of the obligor against the original payee of the instrument if the claim arose from the transaction that gave rise to the instrument; but the claim of the obligor may be asserted against a transferee of the instrument only to reduce the amount owing on the instrument at the time the action is brought.

(b) The right of a holder in due course to enforce the obligation of a party to pay the instrument is subject to defenses of the obligor stated in subsection (a)(1) of this section, but is not subject to defenses of the obligor stated in subsection (a)(2) of this section or claims in recoupment stated in subsection (a)(3) of this section against a person other than the holder.

(c) Except as stated in subsection (d) of this section, in an action to enforce the obligation of a party to pay the instrument, the obligor may not assert against the person entitled to enforce the instrument a defense, claim in recoupment, or claim to the instrument (G.S. 25-3-306) of another person, but the other person's claim to the instrument may be asserted by the obligor if the other person is joined in the action and personally asserts the claim against the person entitled to enforce the instrument. An obligor is not obliged to pay the instrument if the person seeking enforcement of the instrument does not have rights of a holder in due course and the obligor proves that the instrument is a lost or stolen instrument.

(d) In an action to enforce the obligation of an accommodation party to pay an instrument, the accommodation party may assert against the person entitled to enforce the instrument any defense or claim in recoupment under subsection (a) of this section that the accommodated party could assert against the person entitled to enforce the instrument, except the defenses of discharge in insolvency proceedings, infancy, and lack of legal capacity. (1899, c. 733, s. 15, 16, 28, 57, 58, 59; Rev., ss. 2165, 2166, 2176, 2206, 2207, 2208; C.S., ss. 2297, 2996, 2997, 3008, 3038, 3039, 3040; 1965, c. 700, s. 1; 1995, c. 232, s. 1.)

§ 25-3-306. Claims to an instrument.

A person taking an instrument, other than a person having rights of a holder in due course, is subject to a claim of a property or possessory right in the instrument or its proceeds, including a claim to rescind a negotiation and to recover the instrument or its proceeds. A person having rights of a holder in due course takes free of the claim to the instrument. (1899, c. 733, ss. 15, 16, 28, 57, 58, 59; Rev., ss. 2165, 2166, 2176, 2206, 2207, 2208; C.S., ss. 2297, 2996, 2997, 3008, 3038, 3039, 3040; 1965, c. 700, s. 1; 1995, c. 232, s. 1.)

§ 25-3-307. Notice of breach of fiduciary duty.

(a) In this section:

(1) "Fiduciary" means an agent, trustee, partner, corporate officer or director, or other representative owing a fiduciary duty with respect to an instrument.

(2) "Represented person" means the principal, beneficiary, partnership, corporation, or other person to whom the duty stated in subdivision (1) is owed.

(b) If (i) an instrument is taken from a fiduciary for payment or collection or for value, (ii) the taker has knowledge of the fiduciary status of the fiduciary, and (iii) the represented person makes a claim to the instrument or its proceeds on the basis that the transaction of the fiduciary is a breach of fiduciary duty, the following rules apply:

(1) Notice of breach of fiduciary duty by the fiduciary is notice of the claim of the represented person.

(2) In the case of an instrument payable to the represented person or the fiduciary as such, the taker has notice of the breach of fiduciary duty if the instrument is (i) taken in payment of or as security for a debt known by the taker to be the personal debt of the fiduciary, (ii) taken in a transaction known by the taker to be for the personal benefit of the fiduciary, or (iii) deposited to an account other than an account of the fiduciary, as such, or an account of the represented person.

(3) If an instrument is issued by the represented person or the fiduciary as such, and made payable to the fiduciary personally, the taker does not have notice of the breach of fiduciary duty unless the taker knows of the breach of fiduciary duty or knows such facts that his action in taking the instrument is not in good faith.

(4) If an instrument is issued by the represented person or the fiduciary as such, to the taker as payee, the taker has notice of the breach of fiduciary duty if the instrument is (i) taken in payment of or as security for a debt known by the taker to be the personal debt of the fiduciary, (ii) taken in a transaction known by the taker to be for the personal benefit of the fiduciary, or (iii) deposited to an account other than an account of the fiduciary, as such, or an account of the represented person. (1899, c. 733, s. 45, 52, 53, 55, 56; Rev., ss. 2194, 2201,

2202, 2204, 2205; C.S., ss. 3026, 3033, 3034, 3036, 3037; 1965, c. 700, s. 1; 1995, c. 232, s. 1.)

§ 25-3-308. Proof of signatures and status as holder in due course.

(a) In an action with respect to an instrument, the authenticity of, and authority to make, each signature on the instrument is admitted unless specifically denied in the pleadings. If the validity of a signature is denied in the pleadings, the burden of establishing validity is on the person claiming validity, but the signature is presumed to be authentic and authorized unless the action is to enforce the liability of the purported signer and the signer is dead or incompetent at the time of trial of the issue of validity of the signature. If an action to enforce the instrument is brought against a person as the undisclosed principal of a person who signed the instrument as a party to the instrument, the plaintiff has the burden of establishing that the defendant is liable on the instrument as a represented person under G.S. 25-3-402(a).

(b) If the validity of signatures is admitted or proved and there is compliance with subsection (a) of this section, a plaintiff producing the instrument is entitled to payment if the plaintiff proves entitlement to enforce the instrument under G.S. 25-3-301, unless the defendant proves a defense or claim in recoupment. If a defense or claim in recoupment is proved, the right to payment of the plaintiff is subject to the defense or claim, except to the extent the plaintiff proves that the plaintiff has rights of a holder in due course which are not subject to the defense or claim. (1899, c. 733, s. 59; Rev., s. 2208; C.S., s. 3040; 1965, c. 700, s. 1; 1995, c. 232, s. 1.)

§ 25-3-309. Enforcement of lost, destroyed, or stolen instrument.

(a) A person not in possession of an instrument is entitled to enforce the instrument if (i) the person was in possession of the instrument and entitled to enforce it when loss of possession occurred, (ii) the loss of possession was not the result of a transfer by the person or a lawful seizure, and (iii) the person cannot reasonably obtain possession of the instrument because the instrument was destroyed, its whereabouts cannot be determined, or it is in the wrongful possession of an unknown person or a person that cannot be found or is not amenable to service of process.

(b) A person seeking enforcement of an instrument under subsection (a) of this section must prove the terms of the instrument and the person's right to enforce the instrument. If that proof is made, G.S. 25-3-308 applies to the case as if the person seeking enforcement had produced the instrument. The court may not enter judgment in favor of the person seeking enforcement unless it finds that the person required to pay the instrument is adequately protected against loss that might occur by reason of a claim by another person to enforce the instrument. Adequate protection may be provided by any reasonable means. (1965, c. 700, s. 1; 1995, c. 232, s. 1.)

§ 25-3-310. Effect of instrument on obligation for which taken.

(a) Unless otherwise agreed, if a certified check, cashier's check, or teller's check is taken for an obligation, the obligation is discharged to the same extent discharge would result if an amount of money equal to the amount of the instrument were taken in payment of the obligation. Discharge of the obligation does not affect any liability that the obligor may have as an indorser of the instrument.

(b) Unless otherwise agreed and except as provided in subsection (a) of this section, if a note or an uncertified check is taken for an obligation, the obligation is suspended to the same extent the obligation would be discharged if an amount of money equal to the amount of the instrument were taken, and the following rules apply:

(1) In the case of an uncertified check, suspension of the obligation continues until dishonor of the check or until it is paid or certified. Payment or certification of the check results in discharge of the obligation to the extent of the amount of the check.

(2) In the case of a note, suspension of the obligation continues until dishonor of the note or until it is paid. Payment of the note results in discharge of the obligation to the extent of the payment.

(3) Except as provided in subdivision (4), if the check or note is dishonored and the obligee of the obligation for which the instrument was taken is the person entitled to enforce the instrument, the obligee may enforce either the instrument or the obligation. In the case of an instrument of a third person which

is negotiated to the obligee by the obligor, discharge of the obligor on the instrument also discharges the obligation.

(4) If the person entitled to enforce the instrument taken for an obligation is a person other than the obligee, the obligee may not enforce the obligation to the extent the obligation is suspended. If the obligee is the person entitled to enforce the instrument but no longer has possession of it because it was lost, stolen, or destroyed, the obligation may not be enforced to the extent of the amount payable on the instrument, and to that extent the obligee's rights against the obligor are limited to enforcement of the instrument.

(c) If an instrument other than one described in subsection (a) or (b) of this section is taken for an obligation, the effect is (i) that stated in subsection (a) of this section if the instrument is one on which a bank is liable as maker or acceptor, or (ii) that stated in subsection (b) of this section in any other case. (1965, c. 700, s. 1; 1967, c. 562, s. 1; 1995, c. 232, s. 1.)

§ 25-3-311. Accord and satisfaction by use of instrument.

(a) If a person against whom a claim is asserted proves that (i) that person in good faith tendered an instrument to the claimant as full satisfaction of the claim, (ii) the amount of the claim was unliquidated or subject to a bona fide dispute, and (iii) the claimant obtained payment of the instrument, the following subsections apply.

(b) Unless subsection (c) of this section applies, the claim is discharged if the person against whom the claim is asserted proves that the instrument or an accompanying written communication contained a conspicuous statement to the effect that the instrument was tendered as full satisfaction of the claim.

(c) Subject to subsection (d) of this section, a claim is not discharged under subsection (b) of this section when the claimant, if an organization, proves that (i) within a reasonable time before the tender, the claimant sent a conspicuous statement to the person against whom the claim is asserted that communications concerning disputed debts, including an instrument tendered as full satisfaction of a debt, are to be sent to a designated person, office, or place, and (ii) the instrument or accompanying communication was not received by that designated person, office, or place.

(d) A claim is discharged if the person against whom the claim is asserted proves that within a reasonable time before collection of the instrument was initiated, the claimant, or an agent of the claimant having direct responsibility with respect to the disputed obligation, knew that the instrument was tendered in full satisfaction of the claim. (1899, c. 733, ss. 5, 6, 197; 1905, c. 327; Rev., ss. 2154, 2155, 2346; C.S., ss. 2986, 2987; 1965, c. 700, s. 1; 1995, c. 232, s. 1.)

§ 25-3-312. Lost, destroyed, or stolen cashier's check, teller's check, or certified check.

(a) In this section:

(1) "Check" means a cashier's check, teller's check, or certified check.

(2) "Claimant" means a person who claims the right to receive the amount of a cashier's check, teller's check, or certified check that was lost, destroyed, or stolen.

(3) "Declaration of loss" means a written statement, made under penalty of perjury, to the effect that (i) the declarer lost possession of a check, (ii) the declarer is the drawer or payee of the check, in the case of a certified check, or the remitter or payee of the check, in the case of a cashier's check or teller's check, (iii) the loss of possession was not the result of a transfer by the declarer or a lawful seizure, and (iv) the declarer cannot reasonably obtain possession of the check because the check was destroyed, its whereabouts cannot be determined, or it is in the wrongful possession of an unknown person or a person that cannot be found or is not amenable to service of process.

(4) "Obligated bank" means the issuer of a cashier's check or teller's check or the acceptor of a certified check.

(b) A claimant may assert a claim to the amount of a check by a communication to the obligated bank describing the check with reasonable certainty and requesting payment of the amount of the check, if (i) the claimant is the drawer or payee of a certified check or the remitter or payee of a cashier's check or teller's check, (ii) the communication contains or is accompanied by a declaration of loss of the claimant with respect to the check, (iii) the communication is received at a time and in a manner affording the bank a reasonable time to act on it before the check is paid, and (iv) the claimant provides reasonable identification if requested by the obligated bank. Delivery of a declaration of loss is a warranty of the truth of the statements made in the declaration. If a claim is asserted in compliance with this subsection, the following rules apply:

(1) The claim becomes enforceable at the later of (i) the time the claim is asserted, or (ii) the 90th day following the date of the check, in the case of a cashier's check or teller's check, or the 90th day following the date of the acceptance, in the case of a certified check.

(2) Until the claim becomes enforceable, it has no legal effect and the obligated bank may pay the check or, in the case of a teller's check, may permit the drawee to pay the check. Payment to a person entitled to enforce the check discharges all liability of the obligated bank with respect to the check.

(3) If the claim becomes enforceable before the check is presented for payment, the obligated bank is not obliged to pay the check.

(4) When the claim becomes enforceable, the obligated bank becomes obliged to pay the amount of the check to the claimant if payment of the check has not been made to a person entitled to enforce the check. Subject to G.S. 25-4-302(a)(1), payment to the claimant discharges all liability of the obligated bank with respect to the check.

(c) If the obligated bank pays the amount of a check to a claimant under subsection (b)(4) of this section and the check is presented for payment by a person having rights of a holder in due course, the claimant is obliged to (i) refund the payment to the obligated bank if the check is paid, or (ii) pay the amount of the check to the person having rights of a holder in due course if the check is dishonored.

(d) If a claimant has the right to assert a claim under subsection (b) of this section and is also a person entitled to enforce a cashier's check, teller's check, or certified check which is lost, destroyed, or stolen, the claimant may assert rights with respect to the check either under this section or G.S. 25-3-309. (1995, c. 232, s. 1.)

Part 4.

LIABILITY OF PARTIES.

§ 25-3-401. Signature.

(a)   A person is not liable on an instrument unless (i) the person signed the instrument, or (ii) the person is represented by an agent or representative who signed the instrument and the signature is binding on the represented person under G.S. 25-3-402.

(b)   A signature may be made (i) manually or by means of a device or machine, and (ii) by the use of any name, including a trade or assumed name, or by a word, mark, or symbol executed or adopted by a person with present intention to authenticate a writing. (1899, c. 733, s. 18; Rev., s. 2167; C.S., s. 2999; 1965, c. 700, s. 1; 1995, c. 232, s. 1.)

§ 25-3-402. Signature by representative.

(a)   If a person acting, or purporting to act, as a representative signs an instrument by signing either the name of the represented person or the name of the signer, the represented person is bound by the signature to the same extent the represented person would be bound if the signature were on a simple contract. If the represented person is bound, the signature of the representative is the "authorized signature of the represented person" and the represented person is liable on the instrument, whether or not identified in the instrument.

(b)   If a representative signs the name of the representative to an instrument and the signature is an authorized signature of the represented person, the following rules apply:

(1)   If the form of the signature shows unambiguously that the signature is made on behalf of the represented person who is identified in the instrument, the representative is not liable on the instrument.

(2)   Subject to subsection (c) of this section, if (i) the form of the signature does not show unambiguously that the signature is made in a representative capacity, or (ii) the represented person is not identified in the instrument, the representative is liable on the instrument to a holder in due course that took the instrument without notice that the representative was not intended to be liable on the instrument. With respect to any other person, the representative is liable

on the instrument unless the representative proves that the original parties did not intend the representative to be liable on the instrument.

(c) If a representative signs the name of the representative as drawer of a check without indication of the representative status and the check is payable from an account of the represented person who is identified on the check, the signer is not liable on the check if the signature is an authorized signature of the represented person. (1899, c. 733, ss. 19 to 21; Rev., ss. 2168 to 2170; C.S., ss. 3000 to 3002; 1965, c. 700, s. 1; 1995, c. 232, s. 1.)

§ 25-3-403. Unauthorized signature.

(a) Unless otherwise provided in this Article or Article 4, an unauthorized signature is ineffective except as the signature of the unauthorized signer in favor of a person who in good faith pays the instrument or takes it for value. An unauthorized signature may be ratified for all purposes of this Article.

(b) If the signature of more than one person is required to constitute the authorized signature of an organization, the signature of the organization is unauthorized if one of the required signatures is lacking.

(c) The civil or criminal liability of a person who makes an unauthorized signature is not affected by any provision of this Article which makes the unauthorized signature effective for the purposes of this Article. (1899, c. 733, ss. 9, 23; Rev., ss. 2159, 2171; C.S., ss. 2990, 3003; 1949, c. 953; 1965, c. 700, s. 1; 1995, c. 232, s. 1.)

§ 25-3-404. Impostors; fictitious payees.

(a) If an impostor, by use of the mails or otherwise, induces the issuer of an instrument to issue the instrument to the impostor, or to a person acting in concert with the impostor, by impersonating the payee of the instrument or a person authorized to act for the payee, an indorsement of the instrument by any person in the name of the payee is effective as the indorsement of the payee in favor of a person who, in good faith, pays the instrument or takes it for value or for collection.

(b) If (i) a person whose intent determines to whom an instrument is payable (G.S. 25-3-110(a) or (b)) does not intend the person identified as payee to have any interest in the instrument, or (ii) the person identified as payee of an instrument is a fictitious person, the following rules apply until the instrument is negotiated by special indorsement:

(1) Any person in possession of the instrument is its holder.

(2) An indorsement by any person in the name of the payee stated in the instrument is effective as the indorsement of the payee in favor of a person who, in good faith, pays the instrument or takes it for value or for collection.

(c) Under subsection (a) or (b) of this section, an indorsement is made in the name of a payee if (i) it is made in a name substantially similar to that of the payee or (ii) the instrument, whether or not indorsed, is deposited in a depositary bank to an account in a name substantially similar to that of the payee.

(d) With respect to an instrument to which subsection (a) or (b) of this section applies, if a person paying the instrument or taking it for value or for collection fails to exercise ordinary care in paying or taking the instrument and that failure substantially contributes to loss resulting from payment of the instrument, the person bearing the loss may recover from the person failing to exercise ordinary care to the extent the failure to exercise ordinary care contributed to the loss. (1899, c. 733, s. 9; Rev., s. 2159; C.S., s. 2990; 1949, c. 953; 1965, c. 700, s. 1; 1995, c. 232, s. 1.)

§ 25-3-405. Employer's responsibility for fraudulent indorsement by employee.

(a) In this section:

(1) "Employee" includes an independent contractor and employee of an independent contractor retained by the employer.

(2) "Fraudulent indorsement" means (i) in the case of an instrument payable to the employer, a forged indorsement purporting to be that of the employer, or (ii) in the case of an instrument with respect to which the employer is the issuer, a forged indorsement purporting to be that of the person identified as payee.

(3) "Responsibility" with respect to instruments means authority (i) to sign or indorse instruments on behalf of the employer, (ii) to process instruments received by the employer for bookkeeping purposes, for deposit to an account, or for other disposition, (iii) to prepare or process instruments for issue in the name of the employer, (iv) to supply information determining the names or addresses of payees of instruments to be issued in the name of the employer, (v) to control the disposition of instruments to be issued in the name of the employer, or (vi) to act otherwise with respect to instruments in a responsible capacity. "Responsibility" does not include authority that merely allows an employee to have access to instruments or blank or incomplete instrument forms that are being stored or transported or are part of incoming or outgoing mail, or similar access.

(b) For the purpose of determining the rights and liabilities of a person who, in good faith, pays an instrument or takes it for value or for collection, if an employer entrusted an employee with responsibility with respect to the instrument and the employee or a person acting in concert with the employee makes a fraudulent indorsement of the instrument, the indorsement is effective as the indorsement of the person to whom the instrument is payable if it is made in the name of that person. If the person paying the instrument or taking it for value or for collection fails to exercise ordinary care in paying or taking the instrument and that failure substantially contributes to loss resulting from the fraud, the person bearing the loss may recover from the person failing to exercise ordinary care to the extent the failure to exercise ordinary care contributed to the loss.

(c) Under subsection (b) of this section, an indorsement is made in the name of the person to whom an instrument is payable if (i) it is made in a name substantially similar to the name of that person or (ii) the instrument, whether or not indorsed, is deposited in a depositary bank to an account in a name substantially similar to the name of that person. (1899, c. 733, s. 9; Rev., s. 2159; C.S., s. 2990; 1949, c. 953; 1965, c. 700, s. 1; 1995, c. 232, s. 1.)

§ 25-3-406. Negligence contributing to forged signature or alteration of instrument.

(a) A person whose failure to exercise ordinary care substantially contributes to an alteration of an instrument or to the making of a forged signature on an instrument is precluded from asserting the alteration or the forgery against a person who, in good faith, pays the instrument or takes it for value or for collection.

(b)   Under subsection (a) of this section, if the person asserting the preclusion fails to exercise ordinary care in paying or taking the instrument and that failure substantially contributes to loss, the loss is allocated between the person precluded and the person asserting the preclusion according to the extent to which the failure of each to exercise ordinary care contributed to the loss.

(c)   Under subsection (a) of this section, the burden of proving failure to exercise ordinary care is on the person asserting the preclusion. Under subsection (b) of this section, the burden of proving failure to exercise ordinary care is on the person precluded. (1965, c. 700, s. 1; 1995, c. 232, s. 1.)

§ 25-3-407. Alteration.

(a)   "Alteration" means (i) an unauthorized change in an instrument that purports to modify in any respect the obligation of a party, or (ii) an unauthorized addition of words or numbers or other change to an incomplete instrument relating to the obligation of a party.

(b)   Except as provided in subsection (c) of this section, an alteration fraudulently made discharges a party whose obligation is affected by the alteration unless that party assents or is precluded from asserting the alteration. No other alteration discharges a party, and the instrument may be enforced according to its original terms.

(c)   A payor bank or drawee paying a fraudulently altered instrument or a person taking it for value, in good faith and without notice of the alteration, may enforce rights with respect to the instrument (i) according to its original terms, or (ii) in the case of an incomplete instrument altered by unauthorized completion, according to its terms as completed. (1899, c. 733, ss. 14, 15, 124, 125; Rev., ss. 2164, 2165, 2274, 2275; C.S., ss. 2995, 2996, 3106, 3107; 1965, c. 700, s. 1; 1995, c. 232, s. 1.)

§ 25-3-408. Drawee not liable on unaccepted draft.

A check or other draft does not of itself operate as an assignment of funds in the hands of the drawee available for its payment, and the drawee is not liable on the instrument until the drawee accepts it. (1899, c. 733, ss. 127, 189; Rev., ss. 2277, 2339; C.S., ss. 3109, 3171; 1965, c. 700, s. 1; 1995, c. 232, s. 1.)

§ 25-3-409. Acceptance of draft; certified check.

(a) "Acceptance" means the drawee's signed agreement to pay a draft as presented. It must be written on the draft and may consist of the drawee's signature alone. Acceptance may be made at any time and becomes effective when notification pursuant to instructions is given or the accepted draft is delivered for the purpose of giving rights on the acceptance to any person.

(b) A draft may be accepted although it has not been signed by the drawer, is otherwise incomplete, is overdue, or has been dishonored.

(c) If a draft is payable at a fixed period after sight and the acceptor fails to date the acceptance, the holder may complete the acceptance by supplying a date in good faith.

(d) "Certified check" means a check accepted by the bank on which it is drawn. Acceptance may be made as stated in subsection (a) of this section or by a writing on the check which indicates that the check is certified. The drawee of a check has no obligation to certify the check, and refusal to certify is not dishonor of the check. (1899, c. 733, ss. 132 to 138, 161 to 170, 187, 188, 191; Rev., ss. 2282 to 2288, 2311 to 2320, 2337, 2338, 2340; C.S., ss. 2976, 3114 to 3120, 3143 to 3152, 3169, 3170; 1949, c. 954; 1965, c. 700, s. 1; 1995, c. 232, s. 1.)

§ 25-3-410. Acceptance varying draft.

(a) If the terms of a drawee's acceptance vary from the terms of the draft as presented, the holder may refuse the acceptance and treat the draft as dishonored. In that case, the drawee may cancel the acceptance.

(b) The terms of a draft are not varied by an acceptance to pay at a particular bank or place in the United States, unless the acceptance states that the draft is to be paid only at that bank or place.

(c) If the holder assents to an acceptance varying the terms of a draft, the obligation of each drawer and indorser that does not expressly assent to the acceptance is discharged. (1899, c. 733, ss. 139 to 142; Rev., ss. 2289 to 2292; C.S., ss. 3121 to 3124; 1965, c. 700, s. 1; 1995, c. 232, s. 1.)

§ 25-3-411. Refusal to pay cashier's checks, teller's checks, and certified checks.

(a) In this section, "obligated bank" means the acceptor of a certified check or the issuer of a cashier's check or teller's check bought from the issuer.

(b) If the obligated bank wrongfully (i) refuses to pay a cashier's check or certified check, (ii) stops payment of a teller's check, or (iii) refuses to pay a dishonored teller's check, the person asserting the right to enforce the check is entitled to compensation for expenses and loss of interest resulting from the nonpayment and may recover consequential damages if the obligated bank refuses to pay after receiving notice of particular circumstances giving rise to the damages.

(c) Expenses or consequential damages under subsection (b) of this section are not recoverable if the refusal of the obligated bank to pay occurs because (i) the bank suspends payments, (ii) the obligated bank asserts a claim or defense of the bank that it has reasonable grounds to believe is available against the person entitled to enforce the instrument, (iii) the obligated bank has a reasonable doubt whether the person demanding payment is the person entitled to enforce the instrument, or (iv) payment is prohibited by law. (1995, c. 232, s. 1.)

§ 25-3-412. Obligation of issuer of note or cashier's check.

The issuer of a note or cashier's check or other draft drawn on the drawer is obliged to pay the instrument (i) according to its terms at the time it was issued or, if not issued, at the time it first came into possession of a holder, or (ii) if the issuer signed an incomplete instrument, according to its terms when completed, to the extent stated in G.S. 25-3-115 and G.S. 25-3-407. The obligation is owed to a person entitled to enforce the instrument or to an indorser who paid the instrument under G.S. 25-3-415. (1899, c. 733, ss. 60 to 62; Rev., ss. 2209 to 2211; C.S., ss. 3041 to 3043; 1965, c. 700, s. 1; 1995, c. 232, s. 1.)

§ 25-3-413. Obligation of acceptor.

(a) The acceptor of a draft is obliged to pay the draft (i) according to its terms at the time it was accepted, even though the acceptance states that the draft is payable "as originally drawn" or equivalent terms, (ii) if the acceptance varies the terms of the draft, according to the terms of the draft as varied, or (iii) if the acceptance is of a draft that is an incomplete instrument, according to its terms when completed, to the extent stated in G.S. 25-3-115 and G.S. 25-3-407. The obligation is owed to a person entitled to enforce the draft or to the drawer or an indorser who paid the draft under G.S. 25-3-414 or G.S. 25-3-415.

(b) If the certification of a check or other acceptance of a draft states the amount certified or accepted, the obligation of the acceptor is that amount. If (i) the certification or acceptance does not state an amount, (ii) the amount of the instrument is subsequently raised, and (iii) the instrument is then negotiated to a holder in due course, the obligation of the acceptor is the amount of the instrument at the time it was taken by the holder in due course. (1899, c. 733, ss. 60 to 62; Rev., ss. 2209 to 2211; C.S., ss. 3041 to 3043; 1965, c. 700, s. 1; 1995, c. 232, s. 1.)

§ 25-3-414. Obligation of drawer.

(a) This section does not apply to cashier's checks or other drafts drawn on the drawer.

(b) If an unaccepted draft is dishonored, the drawer is obliged to pay the draft (i) according to its terms at the time it was issued or, if not issued, at the time it first came into possession of a holder, or (ii) if the drawer signed an incomplete instrument, according to its terms when completed, to the extent stated in G.S. 25-3-115 and G.S. 25-3-407. The obligation is owed to a person entitled to enforce the draft or to an indorser who paid the draft under G.S. 25-3-415.

(c) If a draft is accepted by a bank, the drawer is discharged, regardless of when or by whom acceptance was obtained.

(d) If a draft is accepted and the acceptor is not a bank, the obligation of the drawer to pay the draft if the draft is dishonored by the acceptor is the same as the obligation of an indorser under G.S. 25-3-415(a) and (c).

(e) If a draft states that it is drawn "without recourse" or otherwise disclaims liability of the drawer to pay the draft, the drawer is not liable under subsection (b) of this section to pay the draft if the draft is not a check. A disclaimer of the liability stated in subsection (b) of this section is not effective if the draft is a check.

(f) If (i) a check is not presented for payment or given to a depositary bank for collection within 30 days after its date, (ii) the drawee suspends payments after expiration of the 30-day period without paying the check, and (iii) because of the suspension of payments, the drawer is deprived of funds maintained with the drawee to cover payment of the check, the drawer to the extent deprived of funds may discharge its obligation to pay the check by assigning to the person entitled to enforce the check the rights of the drawer against the drawee with respect to the funds. (1899, c. 733, ss. 7, 60 to 62, 70, 89, 118, 129, 143, 144, 150 to 153, 158, 186, 187, 188; Rev., ss. 2157, 2209 to 2211, 2219, 2239, 2268, 2279, 2293, 2294, 2300 to 2303, 2308, 2336, 2337, 2338; C.S., ss. 2988, 3041 to 3043, 3051, 3071, 3100, 3111, 3125, 3126, 3132 to 3135, 3140, 3168, 3169, 3170; 1965, c. 700, s. 1; 1967, c. 562, s. 1; 1995, c. 232, s. 1.)

§ 25-3-415. Obligation of indorser.

(a) Subject to subsections (b), (c), (d), and (e) of this section and to G.S. 25-3-419(d), if an instrument is dishonored, an indorser is obliged to pay the amount due on the instrument (i) according to the terms of the instrument at the time it was indorsed, or (ii) if the indorser indorsed an incomplete instrument, according to its terms when completed, to the extent stated in G.S. 25-3-115 and G.S. 25-3-407. The obligation of the indorser is owed to a person entitled to enforce the instrument or to a subsequent indorser who paid the instrument under this section.

(b) If an indorsement states that it is made "without recourse" or otherwise disclaims liability of the indorser, the indorser is not liable under subsection (a) of this section to pay the instrument.

(c) If notice of dishonor of an instrument is required by G.S. 25-3-503 and notice of dishonor complying with that section is not given to an indorser, the liability of the indorser under subsection (a) of this section is discharged.

(d) If a draft is accepted by a bank after an indorsement is made, the liability of the indorser under subsection (a) of this section is discharged.

(e) If an indorser of a check is liable under subsection (a) of this section and the check is not presented for payment, or given to a depositary bank for collection, within 30 days after the day the indorsement was made, the liability of the indorser under subsection (a) of this section is discharged. (1899, c. 733, ss. 7, 28, 29, 38, 44, 64, 66 to 68, 70, 89, 118, 129, 143, 144, 150 to 153, 158, 186; Rev., ss. 2157, 2176, 2177, 2187, 2193, 2213, 2215 to 2217, 2219, 2239, 2268, 2279, 2293, 2294, 2300 to 2303, 2308, 2336; C.S., ss. 2988, 3008, 3009, 3019, 3125, 3045, 3047 to 3049, 3051, 3071, 3100, 3111, 3125, 3126, 3132 to 3135, 3140, 3168; 1965, c. 700, s. 1; 1967, c. 562, s. 1; 1995, c. 232, s. 1.)

§ 25-3-416. Transfer warranties.

(a) A person who transfers an instrument for consideration warrants to the transferee and, if the transfer is by indorsement, to any subsequent transferee that:

(1) The warrantor is a person entitled to enforce the instrument;

(2) All signatures on the instrument are authentic and authorized;

(3) The instrument has not been altered;

(4) The instrument is not subject to a defense or claim in recoupment of any party which can be asserted against the warrantor; and

(5) The warrantor has no knowledge of any insolvency proceeding commenced with respect to the maker or acceptor or, in the case of an unaccepted draft, the drawer.

(b)   A person to whom the warranties under subsection (a) of this section are made and who took the instrument in good faith may recover from the warrantor as damages for breach of warranty an amount equal to the loss suffered as a result of the breach, but not more than the amount of the instrument plus expenses and loss of interest incurred as a result of the breach.

(c)   The warranties stated in subsection (a) of this section cannot be disclaimed with respect to checks. Unless notice of a claim for breach of warranty is given to the warrantor within 30 days after the claimant has reason to know of the breach and the identity of the warrantor, the liability of the warrantor under subsection (b) of this section is discharged to the extent of any loss caused by the delay in giving notice of the claim.

(d)   A cause of action for breach of warranty under this section accrues when the claimant has reason to know of the breach. (1899, c. 733, ss. 65, 69; Rev., ss, 2214, 2218; C.S. ss. 3046, 3050; 1965, c. 700, s. 1; 1995, c. 232, s. 1.)

§ 25-3-417. Presentment warranties.

(a)   If an unaccepted draft is presented to the drawee for payment or acceptance and the drawee pays or accepts the draft, (i) the person obtaining payment or acceptance, at the time of presentment, and (ii) a previous transferor of the draft, at the time of transfer, warrant to the drawee making payment or accepting the draft in good faith that:

(1)   The warrantor is, or was, at the time the warrantor transferred the draft, a person entitled to enforce the draft or authorized to obtain payment or acceptance of the draft on behalf of a person entitled to enforce the draft;

(2)   The draft has not been altered; and

(3)   The warrantor has no knowledge that the signature of the drawer of the draft is unauthorized.

(b)   A drawee making payment may recover from any warrantor damages for breach of warranty equal to the amount paid by the drawee less the amount the drawee received or is entitled to receive from the drawer because of the payment. In addition, the drawee is entitled to compensation for expenses and loss of interest resulting from the breach. The right of the drawee to recover damages under this subsection is not affected by any failure of the drawee to exercise ordinary care in making payment. If the drawee accepts the draft, breach of warranty is a defense to the obligation of the acceptor. If the acceptor makes payment with respect to the draft, the acceptor is entitled to recover from any warrantor for breach of warranty the amounts stated in this subsection.

(c)   If a drawee asserts a claim for breach of warranty under subsection (a) of this section based on an unauthorized indorsement of the draft or an alteration of the draft, the warrantor may defend by proving that the indorsement is effective under G.S. 25-3-404 or G.S. 25-3-405 or the drawer is precluded under G.S. 25-3-406 or G.S. 25-4-406 from asserting against the drawee the unauthorized indorsement or alteration.

(d)   If (i) a dishonored draft is presented for payment to the drawer or an indorser, or (ii) any other instrument is presented for payment to a party obliged to pay the instrument, and (iii) payment is received, the following rules apply:

(1)   The person obtaining payment and a prior transferor of the instrument warrant to the person making payment in good faith that the warrantor is, or was, at the time the warrantor transferred the instrument, a person entitled to enforce the instrument or authorized to obtain payment on behalf of a person entitled to enforce the instrument.

(2)   The person making payment may recover from any warrantor for breach of warranty an amount equal to the amount paid plus expenses and loss of interest resulting from the breach.

(e)   The warranties stated in subsections (a) and (d) of this section cannot be disclaimed with respect to checks. Unless notice of a claim for breach of warranty is given to the warrantor within 30 days after the claimant has reason to know of the breach and the identity of the warrantor, the liability of the warrantor under subsection (b) or (d) of this section is discharged to the extent of any loss caused by the delay in giving notice of the claim.

(f)   A cause of action for breach of warranty under this section accrues when the claimant has reason to know of the breach. (1899, c. 733, ss. 65, 69; Rev., ss. 2214, 2218; C.S., ss. 3046, 3050; 1965, c. 700, s. 1; 1995, c. 232, s. 1.)

§ 25-3-418. Payment or acceptance by mistake.

(a) Except as provided in subsection (c) of this section, if the drawee of a draft pays or accepts the draft and the drawee acted on the mistaken belief that (i) payment of the draft had not been stopped pursuant to G.S. 25-4-403 or (ii) the signature of the drawer of the draft was authorized, the drawee may recover the amount of the draft from the person to whom or for whose benefit payment was made or, in the case of acceptance, may revoke the acceptance. Rights of the drawee under this subsection are not affected by failure of the drawee to exercise ordinary care in paying or accepting the draft.

(b) Except as provided in subsection (c) of this section, if an instrument has been paid or accepted by mistake and the case is not covered by subsection (a) of this section, the person paying or accepting may, to the extent permitted by the law governing mistake and restitution, (i) recover the payment from the person to whom or for whose benefit payment was made or (ii) in the case of acceptance, may revoke the acceptance.

(c) The remedies provided by subsection (a) or (b) of this section may not be asserted against a person who took the instrument in good faith and for value or who in good faith changed position in reliance on the payment or acceptance. This subsection does not limit remedies provided by G.S. 25-3-417, 25-4-208 [25-4-207.1], or 25-4-407.

(d) Notwithstanding G.S. 25-4-215 [25-4-213], if an instrument is paid or accepted by mistake and the payor or acceptor recovers payment or revokes acceptance under subsection (a) or (b) of this section, the instrument is deemed not to have been paid or accepted and is treated as dishonored, and the person from whom payment is recovered has rights as a person entitled to enforce the dishonored instrument. (1899, c. 733, s. 62; Rev., s. 2211; C.S., s. 3043; 1965, c. 700, s. 1; 1995, c. 232, s. 1.)

§ 25-3-419. Instruments signed for accommodation.

(a) If an instrument is issued for value given for the benefit of a party to the instrument, the "accommodated party", and another party to the instrument, the "accommodation party", signs the instrument for the purpose of incurring liability on the instrument without being a direct beneficiary of the value given for the instrument, the instrument is signed by the accommodation party "for accommodation".

(b)   An accommodation party may sign the instrument as maker, drawer, acceptor, or indorser and, subject to subsection (d) of this section, is obliged to pay the instrument in the capacity in which the accommodation party signs. The obligation of an accommodation party may be enforced notwithstanding any statute of frauds and whether or not the accommodation party receives consideration for the accommodation.

(c)   A person signing an instrument is presumed to be an accommodation party and there is notice that the instrument is signed for accommodation if the signature is an anomalous indorsement or is accompanied by words indicating that the signer is acting as surety or guarantor with respect to the obligation of another party to the instrument. Except as provided in G.S. 25-3-605, the obligation of an accommodation party to pay the instrument is not affected by the fact that the person enforcing the obligation had notice when the instrument was taken by that person that the accommodation party signed the instrument for accommodation.

(d)   If the signature of a party to an instrument is accompanied by words indicating unambiguously that the party is guaranteeing collection rather than payment of the obligation of another party to the instrument, the signer is obliged to pay the amount due on the instrument to a person entitled to enforce the instrument only if (i) execution of judgment against the other party has been returned unsatisfied, (ii) the other party is insolvent or in an insolvency proceeding, (iii) the other party cannot be served with process, or (iv) it is otherwise apparent that payment cannot be obtained from the other party.

(e)   An accommodation party who pays the instrument is entitled to reimbursement from the accommodated party and is entitled to enforce the instrument against the accommodated party. An accommodated party who pays the instrument has no right of recourse against, and is not entitled to contribution from, an accommodation party. (1899, c. 733, ss. 28, 29, 64; Rev., ss. 2176, 2177, 2213; C.S., ss. 3008, 3009, 3045; 1965, c. 700, s. 1; 1995, c. 232, s. 1.)

§ 25-3-420. Conversion of instrument.

(a) The law applicable to conversion of personal property applies to instruments. An instrument is also converted if it is taken by transfer, other than a negotiation, from a person not entitled to enforce the instrument or a bank makes or obtains payment with respect to the instrument for a person not entitled to enforce the instrument or receive payment. An action for conversion of an instrument may not be brought by (i) the issuer or acceptor of the instrument, or (ii) a payee or indorsee who did not receive delivery of the instrument either directly or through delivery to an agent or a co-payee.

(b) In an action under subsection (a) of this section, the measure of liability is presumed to be the amount payable on the instrument, but recovery may not exceed the amount of the plaintiff's interest in the instrument.

(c) A representative, other than a depositary bank, who has in good faith dealt with an instrument or its proceeds on behalf of one who was not the person entitled to enforce the instrument is not liable in conversion to that person beyond the amount of any proceeds that it has not paid out. (1899, c. 733, s. 137; Rev., s. 2287; C.S., s. 3119; 1949, c. 954; 1965, c. 700, s. 1; 1995, c. 232, s. 1.)

Part 5.

DISHONOR.

§ 25-3-501. Presentment.

(a) "Presentment" means a demand made by or on behalf of a person entitled to enforce an instrument (i) to pay the instrument made to the drawee or a party obliged to pay the instrument or, in the case of a note or accepted draft payable at a bank, to the bank, or (ii) to accept a draft made to the drawee.

(b) The following rules are subject to Article 4, agreement of the parties, and clearing-house rules and the like:

(1) Presentment may be made at the place of payment of the instrument and must be made at the place of payment if the instrument is payable at a bank in the United States; may be made by any commercially reasonable means, including an oral, written, or electronic communication; is effective when the demand for payment or acceptance is received by the person to whom

presentment is made; and is effective if made to any one of two or more makers, acceptors, drawees, or other payors.

(2) Upon demand of the person to whom presentment is made, the person making presentment must (i) exhibit the instrument, (ii) give reasonable identification and, if presentment is made on behalf of another person, reasonable evidence of authority to do so, and (iii) sign a receipt on the instrument for any payment made or surrender the instrument if full payment is made.

(3) Without dishonoring the instrument, the party to whom presentment is made may (i) return the instrument for lack of a necessary indorsement, or (ii) refuse payment or acceptance for failure of the presentment to comply with the terms of the instrument, an agreement of the parties, or other applicable law or rule.

(4) The party to whom presentment is made may treat presentment as occurring on the next business day after the day of presentment if the party to whom presentment is made has established a cutoff hour not earlier than 2:00 p.m. for the receipt and processing of instruments presented for payment or acceptance and presentment is made after the cutoff hour. (1899, c. 733, ss. 72 to 74, 77, 78, 83, 145, 149; Rev., ss. 2221 to 2223, 2226, 2227, 2232, 2295, 2299; C.S., ss. 3053 to 3055, 3058, 3059, 3064, 3127, 3131; 1963, c. 242; 1965, c. 700, s. 1; 1995, c. 232, s. 1.)

§ 25-3-502. Dishonor.

(a) Dishonor of a note is governed by the following rules:

(1) If the note is payable on demand, the note is dishonored if presentment is duly made to the maker and the note is not paid on the day of presentment.

(2) If the note is not payable on demand and is payable at or through a bank or the terms of the note require presentment, the note is dishonored if presentment is duly made and the note is not paid on the day it becomes payable or the day of presentment, whichever is later.

(3) If the note is not payable on demand and subdivision (2) does not apply, the note is dishonored if it is not paid on the day it becomes payable.

(b) Dishonor of an unaccepted draft other than a documentary draft is governed by the following rules:

(1) If a check is duly presented for payment to the payor bank otherwise than for immediate payment over the counter, the check is dishonored if the payor bank makes timely return of the check or sends timely notice of dishonor or nonpayment under G.S. 25-4-301 or G.S. 25-4-302, or becomes accountable for the amount of the check under G.S. 25-4-302.

(2) If a draft is payable on demand and subdivision (1) does not apply, the draft is dishonored if presentment for payment is duly made to the drawee and the draft is not paid on the day of presentment.

(3) If a draft is payable on a date stated in the draft, the draft is dishonored if (i) presentment for payment is duly made to the drawee and payment is not made on the day the draft becomes payable or the day of presentment, whichever is later, or (ii) presentment for acceptance is duly made before the day the draft becomes payable and the draft is not accepted on the day of presentment.

(4) If a draft is payable on elapse of a period of time after sight or acceptance, the draft is dishonored if presentment for acceptance is duly made and the draft is not accepted on the day of presentment.

(c) Dishonor of an unaccepted documentary draft occurs according to the rules stated in subdivisions (2), (3), and (4) of subsection (b), except that payment or acceptance may be delayed without dishonor until no later than the close of the third business day of the drawee following the day on which payment or acceptance is required by those subdivisions.

(d) Dishonor of an accepted draft is governed by the following rules:

(1) If the draft is payable on demand, the draft is dishonored if presentment for payment is duly made to the acceptor and the draft is not paid on the day of presentment.

(2) If the draft is not payable on demand, the draft is dishonored if presentment for payment is duly made to the acceptor and payment is not made on the day it becomes payable or the day of presentment, whichever is later.

(e) In any case in which presentment is otherwise required for dishonor under this section and presentment is excused under G.S. 25-3-504, dishonor occurs without presentment if the instrument is not duly accepted or paid.

(f) If a draft is dishonored because timely acceptance of the draft was not made and the person entitled to demand acceptance consents to a late acceptance, from the time of acceptance the draft is treated as never having been dishonored. (1899, c. 733, ss. 70, 79 to 82, 83, 89, 109 to 116, 118, 129, 130, 143, 144, 147 to 153, 158, 159, 186; Rev., ss. 2219, 2228 to 2232, 2239, 2259 to 2266, 2268, 2279, 2280, 2293, 2294, 2297 to 2303, 2309, 2336; C.S., ss. 3051, 3060 to 3064, 3071, 3091 to 3098, 3100, 3111, 3112, 3125, 3126, 3129 to 3135, 3140, 3141, 3168; 1965, c. 700, s. 1; 1967, c. 562, s. 1; 1995, c. 232, s. 1.)

§ 25-3-503. Notice of dishonor.

(a) The obligation of an indorser stated in G.S. 25-3-415(a) and the obligation of a drawer stated in G.S. 25-3-414(d) may not be enforced unless (i) the indorser or drawer is given notice of dishonor of the instrument complying with this section or (ii) notice of dishonor is excused under G.S. 25-3-504(b).

(b) Notice of dishonor may be given by any person; may be given by any commercially reasonable means, including an oral, written, or electronic communication; and is sufficient if it reasonably identifies the instrument and indicates that the instrument has been dishonored or has not been paid or accepted. Return of an instrument given to a bank for collection is sufficient notice of dishonor.

(c) Subject to G.S. 25-3-504(c), with respect to an instrument taken for collection by a collecting bank, notice of dishonor must be given (i) by the bank before midnight of the next banking day following the banking day on which the bank receives notice of dishonor of the instrument, or (ii) by any other person within 30 days following the day on which the person receives notice of dishonor. With respect to any other instrument, notice of dishonor must be given within 30 days following the day on which dishonor occurs. (1899, c. 733, ss. 70, 89 to 108, 118, 129, 143, 144, 150 to 153, 158, 186; Rev., ss. 2219, 2239 to 2258, 2268, 2279, 2293, 2294, 2300 to 2303, 2308, 2336; C.S., ss. 3051, 3071 to 3090, 3100, 3111, 3125, 3126, 3132 to 3135, 3140, 3168; 1965, c. 700, s. 1; 1967, c. 562, s. 1; 1995, c. 232, s. 1.)

§ 25-3-504. Excused presentment and notice of dishonor.

(a)   Presentment for payment or acceptance of an instrument is excused if (i) the person entitled to present the instrument cannot with reasonable diligence make presentment, (ii) the maker or acceptor has repudiated an obligation to pay the instrument or is in insolvency proceedings or is dead, (iii) by the terms of the instrument presentment is not necessary to enforce the obligation of indorsers or the drawer, (iv) the drawer or indorser whose obligation is being enforced has waived presentment or otherwise has no reason to expect or right to require that the instrument be paid or accepted, or (v) the drawer instructed the drawee not to pay or accept the draft or the drawee was not obligated to the drawer to pay the draft.

(b)   Notice of dishonor is excused if (i) by the terms of the instrument notice of dishonor is not necessary to enforce the obligation of a party to pay the instrument, or (ii) the party whose obligation is being enforced waived notice of dishonor. A waiver of presentment is also a waiver of notice of dishonor.

(c)   Delay in giving notice of dishonor is excused if the delay was caused by circumstances beyond the control of the person giving the notice and the person giving the notice exercised reasonable diligence after the cause of the delay ceased to operate. (1899, c. 733, ss. 79 to 82, 109 to 116, 130, 147, 148, 151, 159; Rev., ss. 2228 to 2231, 2259 to 2266, 2280, 2297, 2298, 2301, 2309; C.S., ss. 3060 to 3063, 3091 to 3098, 3112, 3129, 3130, 3133, 3141; 1965, c. 700, s. 1; 1995, c. 232, s. 1.)

§ 25-3-505. Evidence of dishonor.

(a)   The following are admissible as evidence and create a presumption of dishonor and of any notice of dishonor stated:

(1)   A document regular in form as provided in subsection (b) of this section which purports to be a protest.

(2)   A purported stamp or writing of the drawee, payor bank, or presenting bank on or accompanying the instrument stating that acceptance or payment

has been refused unless reasons for the refusal are stated and the reasons are not consistent with dishonor.

(3) A book or record of the drawee, payor bank, or collecting bank, kept in the usual course of business which shows dishonor, even if there is no evidence of who made the entry.

(b) A protest is a certificate of dishonor made by a United States consul or vice-consul, or a notary public or other person authorized to administer oaths by the law of the place where dishonor occurs. It may be made upon information satisfactory to that person. The protest must identify the instrument and certify either that presentment has been made or, if not made, the reason why it was not made, and that the instrument has been dishonored by nonacceptance or nonpayment. The protest may also certify that notice of dishonor has been given to some or all parties. (1899, c. 733, ss. 153, 156, 158, 160; Rev., ss. 2303, 2306, 2308, 2310; C.S., ss. 3135, 3138, 3140, 3142; 1965, c. 700, s. 1; 1995, c. 232, s. 1.)

§ 25-3-506. Collection of processing fee for returned checks.

A person who accepts a check in payment for goods or services or his assignee may charge and collect a processing fee, not to exceed twenty-five dollars ($25.00), for a check on which payment has been refused by the payor bank because of insufficient funds or because the drawer did not have an account at that bank.

If a collection agency collects or seeks to collect on behalf of its principal a processing fee as specified in this section in addition to the sum payable of a check, the amount of such processing fee must be separately stated on the collection notice. The collection agency shall not collect or seek to collect from the drawer any sum other than the actual amount of the returned check and the specified processing fee. (1981, c. 781, s. 1; 1983, c. 529; 1987, c. 147; 1991, c. 455, s. 1; 1995, c. 232, s. 1; 1997-334, s. 1; 2000-118, s. 1.)

Part 6.

DISCHARGE AND PAYMENT.

§ 25-3-601. Discharge and effect of discharge.

(a) The obligation of a party to pay the instrument is discharged as stated in this Article or by an act or agreement with the party which would discharge an obligation to pay money under a simple contract.

(b) Discharge of the obligation of a party is not effective against a person acquiring rights of a holder in due course of the instrument without notice of the discharge. (1899, c. 733, ss. 15, 16, 57, 119 to 121; Rev., ss. 2165, 2166, 2206, 2269 to 2271; C.S., ss. 2296, 2297, 3038, 3101 to 3103; 1965, c. 700, s. 1; 1995, c. 232, s. 1.)

§ 25-3-602. Payment.

(a) Subject to subsection (b) of this section, an instrument is paid to the extent payment is made (i) by or on behalf of a party obliged to pay the instrument, and (ii) to a person entitled to enforce the instrument. To the extent of the payment, the obligation of the party obliged to pay the instrument is discharged even though payment is made with knowledge of a claim to the instrument under G.S. 25-3-306 by another person.

(b) The obligation of a party to pay the instrument is not discharged under subsection (a) of this section if:

(1) A claim to the instrument under G.S. 25-3-306 is enforceable against the party receiving payment and (i) payment is made with knowledge by the payor that payment is prohibited by injunction or similar process of a court of competent jurisdiction, or (ii) in the case of an instrument other than a cashier's check, teller's check, or certified check, the party making payment accepted, from the person having a claim to the instrument, indemnity against loss resulting from refusal to pay the person entitled to enforce the instrument; or

(2) The person making payment knows that the instrument is a stolen instrument and pays a person it knows is in wrongful possession of the instrument. (1899, c. 733, ss. 55, 88, 119, 121, 171 to 177; Rev., ss. 2204, 2238, 2269, 2271, 2321 to 2327; C.S., ss. 3036, 3070, 3101, 3103, 3153 to 3159; 1965, c. 700, s. 1; 1995, c. 232, s. 1.)

§ 25-3-603. Tender of payment.

(a)   If tender of payment of an obligation to pay an instrument is made to a person entitled to enforce the instrument, the effect of tender is governed by principles of law applicable to tender of payment under a simple contract.

(b)   If tender of payment of an obligation to pay an instrument is made to a person entitled to enforce the instrument and the tender is refused, there is discharge, to the extent of the amount of the tender, of the obligation of an indorser or accommodation party having a right of recourse with respect to the obligation to which the tender relates.

(c)   If tender of payment of an amount due on an instrument is made to a person entitled to enforce the instrument, the obligation of the obligor to pay interest after the due date on the amount tendered is discharged. If presentment is required with respect to an instrument and the obligor is able and ready to pay on the due date at every place of payment stated in the instrument, the obligor is deemed to have made tender of payment on the due date to the person entitled to enforce the instrument. (1899, c. 733, ss. 70, 120; Rev., ss. 2219, 2270; C.S., ss. 3051, 3102; 1965, c. 700, s. 1; 1995, c. 232, s. 1.)

§ 25-3-604. Discharge by cancellation or renunciation.

(a)   A person entitled to enforce an instrument, with or without consideration, may discharge the obligation of a party to pay the instrument (i) by an intentional voluntary act, such as surrender of the instrument to the party, destruction, mutilation, or cancellation of the instrument, cancellation or striking out of the party's signature, or the addition of words to the instrument indicating discharge, or (ii) by agreeing not to sue or otherwise renouncing rights against the party by a signed writing.

(b)   Cancellation or striking out of an endorsement pursuant to subsection (a) of this section does not affect the status and rights of a party derived from the indorsement. (1899, c. 733, ss. 48, 119, 120, 122, 123; Rev., ss. 2197, 2269, 2270, 2272, 2273; C.S., ss. 3029, 3101, 3102, 3104, 3105; 1965, c. 700, s. 1; 1995, c. 232, s. 1.)

§ 25-3-605. Discharge of indorsers and accommodation parties.

(a)   In this section, the term "indorser" includes a drawer having the obligation described in G.S. 25-3-414(d).

(b)   Discharge, under G.S. 25-3-604, of the obligation of a party to pay an instrument does not discharge the obligation of an indorser or accommodation party having a right of recourse against the discharged party.

(c)   If a person entitled to enforce an instrument agrees, with or without consideration, to an extension of the due date of the obligation of a party to pay the instrument, the extension discharges an indorser or accommodation party having a right of recourse against the party whose obligation is extended to the extent the indorser or accommodation party proves that the extension caused loss to the indorser or accommodation party with respect to the right of recourse.

(d)   If a person entitled to enforce an instrument agrees, with or without consideration, to a material modification of the obligation of a party other than an extension of the due date, the modification discharges the obligation of an indorser or accommodation party having a right of recourse against the person whose obligation is modified to the extent the modification causes loss to the indorser or accommodation party with respect to the right of recourse. The loss suffered by the indorser or accommodation party as a result of the modification is equal to the amount of the right of recourse unless the person enforcing the instrument proves that no loss was caused by the modification or that the loss caused by the modification was an amount less than the amount of the right of recourse.

(e)   If the obligation of a party to pay an instrument is secured by an interest in collateral and a person entitled to enforce the instrument impairs the value of the interest in collateral, the obligation of an indorser or accommodation party having a right of recourse against the obligor is discharged to the extent of the impairment. The value of an interest in collateral is impaired to the extent (i) the value of the interest is reduced to an amount less than the amount of the right of recourse of the party asserting discharge, or (ii) the reduction in value of the interest causes an increase in the amount by which the amount of the right of recourse exceeds the value of the interest. The burden of proving impairment is on the party asserting discharge.

(f) If the obligation of a party is secured by an interest in collateral not provided by an accommodation party and a person entitled to enforce the instrument impairs the value of the interest in collateral, the obligation of any party who is jointly and severally liable with respect to the secured obligation is discharged to the extent the impairment causes the party asserting discharge to pay more than that party would have been obliged to pay, taking into account rights of contribution, if impairment had not occurred. If the party asserting discharge is an accommodation party not entitled to discharge under subsection (e) of this section, the party is deemed to have a right to contribution based on joint and several liability rather than a right to reimbursement. The burden of proving impairment is on the party asserting discharge.

(g) Under subsection (e) or (f) of this section, impairing value of an interest in collateral includes (i) failure to obtain or maintain perfection or recordation of the interest in collateral, (ii) release of collateral without substitution of collateral of equal value, (iii) failure to perform a duty to preserve the value of collateral owed, under Article 9 or other law, to a debtor or surety or other person secondarily liable, or (iv) failure to comply with applicable law in disposing of collateral.

(h) An accommodation party is not discharged under subsection (c), (d), or (e) of this section unless the person entitled to enforce the instrument knows of the accommodation or has notice under G.S. 25-3-419(c) that the instrument was signed for accommodation.

(i) A party is not discharged under this section if (i) the party asserting discharge consents to the event or conduct that is the basis of the discharge, or (ii) the instrument or a separate agreement of the party provides for waiver of discharge under this section either specifically or by general language indicating that parties waive defenses based on suretyship or impairment of collateral. (1899, c. 733, s. 120; Rev., s. 2270; C.S., s. 3102; 1965, c. 700, s. 1; 1995, c. 232, s. 1.)

Article 4.

Bank Deposits and Collections.

Part 1. General Provisions and Definitions.

§ 25-4-101. Short title.

This Article may be cited as Uniform Commercial Code - Bank Deposits and Collections. (1965, c. 700, s. 1; 1995, c. 232, s. 2.)

§ 25-4-102. Applicability.

(a)   To the extent that items within this Article are also within Articles 3 and 8, they are subject to those Articles. If there is conflict, this Article governs Article 3, but Article 8 governs this Article.

(b)   The liability of a bank for action or nonaction with respect to an item handled by it for purposes of presentment, payment, or collection is governed by the law of the place where the bank is located. In the case of action or nonaction by or at a branch or separate office of a bank, its liability is governed by the law of the place where the branch or separate office is located. (1965, c. 700, s. 1; 1995, c. 232, s. 2.)

§ 25-4-103. Variation by agreement; measure of damages; action constituting ordinary care.

(a)   The effect of the provisions of this Article may be varied by agreement, but the parties to the agreement cannot disclaim a bank's responsibility for its lack of good faith or failure to exercise ordinary care or limit the measure of damages for the lack or failure. However, the parties may determine by agreement the standards by which the bank's responsibility is to be measured if those standards are not manifestly unreasonable.

(b)   Federal reserve regulations and operating circulars, clearing-house rules, and the like have the effect of agreements under subsection (a) of this section, whether or not specifically assented to by all parties interested in items handled.

(c)   Action or nonaction approved by this Article or pursuant to federal reserve regulations or operating circulars is the exercise of ordinary care and, in the absence of special instructions, action or nonaction consistent with clearing-house rules and the like or with a general banking usage not disapproved by this Article, is prima facie the exercise of ordinary care.

(d)   The specification or approval of certain procedures by this Article is not disapproval of other procedures that may be reasonable under the circumstances.

(e)   The measure of damages for failure to exercise ordinary care in handling an item is the amount of the item reduced by an amount that could not have been realized by the exercise of ordinary care. If there is also bad faith, it includes any other damages the party suffered as a proximate consequence. (1965, c. 700, s. 1; 1995, c. 232, s. 2.)

§ 25-4-104. Definitions and index of definitions.

(a)   In this Article, unless the context otherwise requires:

(1)   "Account" means any deposit or credit account with a bank, including a demand, time, savings, passbook, share draft, or like account, other than an account evidenced by a certificate of deposit.

(2)   "Afternoon" means the period of a day between noon and midnight.

(3)   "Banking day" means the part of a day on which a bank is open to the public for carrying on substantially all of its banking functions.

(4)   "Clearing house" means an association of banks or other payors regularly clearing items.

(5)   "Customer" means a person having an account with a bank or for whom a bank has agreed to collect items, including a bank that maintains an account at another bank.

(6)   "Documentary draft" means a draft to be presented for acceptance or payment if specified documents, certificated securities (G.S. 25-8-102) or instructions for uncertificated securities (G.S. 25-8-102), or other certificates, statements, or the like are to be received by the drawee or other payor before acceptance or payment of the draft.

(7) "Draft" means a draft as defined in G.S. 25-3-104 or an item, other than an instrument, that is an order.

(8) "Drawee" means a person ordered in a draft to make payment.

(9) "Item" means an instrument or a promise or order to pay money handled by a bank for collection or payment. The term does not include a payment order governed by Article 4A or a credit or debit card slip.

(10) "Midnight deadline" with respect to a bank is midnight on its next banking day following the banking day on which it receives the relevant item or notice or from which the time for taking action commences to run, whichever is later.

(11) "Settle" means to pay in cash, by clearing-house settlement, in a charge or credit, by remittance, or otherwise as agreed. A settlement may be either provisional or final.

(12) "Suspends payments" with respect to a bank means that it has been closed by order of the supervisory authorities, that a public officer has been appointed to take it over, or that it ceases or refuses to make payments in the ordinary course of business.

(b) Other definitions applying to this Article and the sections in which they appear are:

"Agreement for electronic presentment" G.S. 25-4-110.

"Bank" G.S. 25-4-105.

"Collecting bank" G.S. 25-4-105.

"Depositary bank" G.S. 25-4-105.

"Intermediary bank" G.S. 25-4-105.

"Payor bank" G.S. 25-4-105.

"Presenting bank" G.S. 25-4-105.

"Presentment notice" G.S. 25-4-110.

(c) "Control" as provided in G.S. 25-7-106 and the following definitions in other Articles apply to this Article:

"Acceptance" G.S. 25-3-409.

"Alteration" G.S. 25-3-407.

"Cashier's check" G.S. 25-3-104.

"Certificate of deposit" G.S. 25-3-104.

"Certified check" G.S. 25-3-409.

"Check" G.S. 25-3-104.

"Draft" G.S. 25-3-104.

"Holder in due course" G.S. 25-3-302.

"Instrument" G.S. 25-3-104.

"Notice of dishonor" G.S. 25-3-503.

"Order" G.S. 25-3-103.

"Ordinary care" G.S. 25-3-103.

"Person entitled to enforce" G.S. 25-3-301.

"Presentment" G.S. 25-3-501.

"Promise" G.S. 25-3-103.

"Prove" G.S. 25-3-103.

"Teller's check" G.S. 25-3-104.

"Unauthorized signature" G.S. 25-3-403.

(d) In addition Article 1 contains general definitions and principles of construction and interpretation applicable throughout this Article. (1965, c. 700, s. 1; 1995, c. 232, s. 2; 1997-181, s. 19; 2006-112, ss. 14, 41.)

§ 25-4-105. "Bank"; "depositary bank"; "intermediary bank"; "collecting bank"; "payor bank"; "presenting bank".

In this Article:

(1) "Bank" means a person engaged in the business of banking, including a savings bank, savings and loan association, credit union, or trust company.

(2) "Depositary bank" means the first bank to take an item even though it is also the payor bank, unless the item is presented for immediate payment over the counter.

(3) "Payor bank" means a bank that is the drawee of a draft.

(4) "Intermediary bank" means a bank to which an item is transferred in course of collection except the depositary or payor bank.

(5) "Collecting bank" means a bank handling an item for collection except the payor bank.

(6) "Presenting bank" means a bank presenting an item except a payor bank. (1965, c. 700, s. 1; 1995, c. 232, s. 2.)

§ 25-4-105.1. Payable through or payable at bank; collecting bank.

(a) If an item states that it is "payable through" a bank identified in the item, (i) the item designates the bank as a collecting bank and does not by itself authorize the bank to pay the item, and (ii) the item may be presented for payment only by or through the bank.

(b) If an item states that it is "payable at" a bank identified in the item, (i) the item designates the bank as a collecting bank and does not by itself authorize the bank to pay the item, and (ii) the item may be presented for payment only by or through the bank.

(c) If a draft names a nonbank drawee and it is unclear whether a bank named in the draft is a co-drawee or a collecting bank, the bank is a collecting bank. (1995, c. 232, s. 2.)

§ 25-4-106. Separate office of a bank.

A branch or separate office of a bank is a separate bank for the purpose of computing the time within which and determining the place at which action may be taken or to which notices or orders must be given under this Article and under Article 3. (1965, c. 700, s. 1; 1967, c. 562, s. 1; 1995, c. 232, s. 2.)

§ 25-4-107. Time of receipt of items.

(a) For the purpose of allowing time to process items, prove balances, and make the necessary entries on its books to determine its position for the day, a bank may fix an afternoon hour of 2:00 p.m. or later as a cutoff hour for the handling of money and items and the making of entries on its books.

(b) An item or deposit of money received on any day after a cutoff hour so fixed or after the close of the banking day may be treated as being received at the opening of the next banking day. (1965, c. 700, s. 1; 1995, c. 232, s. 2.)

§ 25-4-108. Delays.

(a) Unless otherwise instructed, a collecting bank in a good faith effort to secure payment of a specific item drawn on a payor other than a bank, and with or without the approval of any person involved, may waive, modify, or extend time limits imposed or permitted by this Chapter for a period not exceeding two additional banking days without discharge of drawers or indorsers or liability to its transferor or a prior party.

(b) Delay by a collecting bank or payor bank beyond time limits prescribed or permitted by this Chapter or by instructions is excused if (i) the delay is caused by interruption of communication or computer facilities, suspension of payments by another bank, war, emergency conditions, failure of equipment, or other circumstances beyond the control of the bank, and (ii) the bank exercises such diligence as the circumstances require. (1965, c. 700, s. 1; 1995, c. 232, s. 2.)

§ 25-4-109: Repealed by Session Laws 1995, c. 232, s. 2.

§ 25-4-110. Electronic presentment.

(a) "Agreement for electronic presentment" means an agreement, clearing-house rule, or federal reserve regulation or operating circular, providing that presentment of an item may be made by transmission of an image of the item or information describing the item ("presentment notice") rather than delivery of the item itself. The agreement may provide for procedures governing retention, presentment, payment, dishonor, and other matters concerning items subject to the agreement.

(b) Presentment of an item pursuant to an agreement for presentment is made when the presentment notice is received.

(c) If presentment is made by presentment notice, a reference to "item" or "check" in this Article means the presentment notice unless the context otherwise indicates. (1995, c. 232, s. 2.)

§ 25-4-111. Statute of limitations.

An action to enforce an obligation, duty, or right arising under this Article must be commenced within three years after the cause of action accrues. (1995, c. 232, s. 2.)

Part 2.

COLLECTION OF ITEMS: DEPOSITARY AND COLLECTING BANKS.

§ 25-4-201. Status of collecting bank as agent and provisional status of credits; applicability of Article; item indorsed "pay any bank".

(a) Unless a contrary intent clearly appears and before the time that a settlement given by a collecting bank for an item is or becomes final, the bank, with respect to the item, is an agent or subagent of the owner of the item and any settlement given for the item is provisional. This provision applies regardless of the form of indorsement or lack or indorsement and even though credit given for the item is subject to immediate withdrawal as of right or is in fact withdrawn; but the continuance of ownership of an item by its owner and any rights of the owner to proceeds of the item are subject to rights of a collecting bank, such as those resulting from outstanding advances on the item and rights of recoupment or setoff. If an item is handled by banks for purposes of presentment, payment, collection, or return, the relevant provisions of this Article apply even though action of the parties clearly establishes that a particular bank has purchased the item and is the owner of it.

(b) After an item has been indorsed with the words "pay any bank" or the like, only a bank may acquire the rights of a holder until the item has been:

(1) Returned to the customer initiating collection; or

(2) Specially indorsed by a bank to a person who is not a bank. (1965, c. 700, s. 1; 1995, c. 232, s. 2.)

§ 25-4-202. Responsibility for collection or return; when action timely.

(a) A collecting bank must exercise ordinary care in:

(1) Presenting an item or sending it for presentment;

(2) Sending notice of dishonor or nonpayment or returning an item other than a documentary draft to the bank's transferor after learning that the item has not been paid or accepted, as the case may be;

(3) Settling for an item when the bank receives final settlement; and

(4) Notifying its transferor of any loss of delay in transit within a reasonable time after discovery thereof.

(b) A collecting bank exercises ordinary care under subsection (a) of this section by taking proper action before its midnight deadline following receipt of an item, notice, or settlement. Taking proper action within a longer reasonable time may constitute the exercise of ordinary care, but the bank has the burden of establishing timeliness.

(c) Subject to subsection (a)(1) of this section, a bank is not liable for the insolvency, neglect, misconduct, mistake, or default of another bank or person or for loss or destruction of an item in the possession of others or in transit. (1965, c. 700, s. 1; 1995, c. 232, s. 2.)

§ 25-4-203. Effect of instructions.

Subject to Article 3 concerning conversion of instruments (G.S. 25-3-420) and restrictive indorsements (G.S. 25-3-206), only a collecting bank's transferor can give instructions that affect the bank or constitute notice to it, and a collecting bank is not liable to prior parties for any action taken pursuant to the instructions or in accordance with any agreement with its transferor. (1965, c. 700, s. 1; 1995, c. 232, s. 2.)

§ 25-4-204. Methods of sending and presenting; sending directly to payor.

(a) A collecting bank shall send items by a reasonably prompt method, taking into consideration relevant instructions, the nature of the item, the number of those items on hand, the cost of collection involved, and the method generally used by it or others to present those items.

(b) A collecting bank may send:

(1) An item directly to the payor bank;

(2) An item to a nonbank payor if authorized by its transferor; and

(3) An item other than documentary drafts to a nonbank payor, if authorized by federal reserve regulation or operating circular, clearing-house rule, or the like.

(c) Presentment may be made by a presenting bank at a place where the payor bank or other payor has requested that presentment be made. (1921, c. 4, s. 39; C.S., s. 220(n); 1949, c. 818; 1965, c. 700, s. 1; 1995, c. 232, s. 2.)

§ 25-4-205. Depositary bank holder of unindorsed item.

If a customer delivers an item to a depositary bank for collection:

(1) The depositary bank becomes a holder of the item at the time it receives the item for collection if the customer at the time of delivery was a holder of the item, whether or not the customer indorses the item, and, if the bank satisfies the other requirements of G.S. 25-3-302, it is a holder in due course; and

(2) The depositary bank warrants to collecting banks, the payor bank or other payor, and the drawer that the amount of the item was paid to the customer or deposited to the customer's account. (1965, c. 700, s. 1; 1995, c. 232, s. 2.)

§ 25-4-206. Transfer between banks.

Any agreed method that identifies the transferor bank is sufficient for the item's further transfer to another bank. (1965, c. 700, s. 1; 1995, c. 232, s. 2.)

§ 25-4-207. Transfer warranties.

(a) A customer or collecting bank that transfers an item and receives a settlement or other consideration warrants to the transferee and to any subsequent collecting bank that:

(1) The warrantor is a person entitled to enforce the item;

(2) All signatures on the item are authentic and authorized;

(3) The item has not been altered;

(4) The item is not subject to a defense or claim in recoupment (G.S. 25-3-305(a)) of any party that can be asserted against the warrantor; and

(5) The warrantor has no knowledge of any insolvency proceeding commenced with respect to the maker or acceptor or, in the case of an unaccepted draft, the drawer.

(b) If an item is dishonored, a customer or collecting bank transferring the item and receiving settlement or other consideration is obliged to pay the amount due on the item (i) according to the terms of the item at the time it was transferred, or (ii) if the transfer was of an incomplete item, according to its terms when completed as stated in G.S. 25-3-115 and G.S. 25-3-407. The obligation of a transferor is owed to the transferee and to any subsequent collecting bank that takes the item in good faith. A transferor cannot disclaim its obligation under this subsection by an indorsement stating that it is made "without recourse" or otherwise disclaiming liability.

(c) A person to whom the warranties under subsection (a) of this section are made and who took the item in good faith may recover from the warrantor as damages for breach of warranty an amount equal to the loss suffered as a result of the breach, but not more than the amount of the item plus expenses and loss of interest incurred as a result of the breach.

(d) The warranties stated in subsection (a) of this section cannot be disclaimed with respect to checks. Unless notice of a claim for breach of warranty is given to the warrantor within 30 days after the claimant has reason to know of the breach and the identity of the warrantor, the warrantor is discharged to the extent of any loss caused by the delay in giving notice of the claim.

(e) A cause of action for breach of warranty under this section accrues when the claimant has reason to know of the breach. (1965, c. 700, s. 1; 1995, c. 232, s. 2.)

§ 25-4-207.1. Presentment warranties.

(a) If an unaccepted draft is presented to the drawee for payment or acceptance and the drawee pays or accepts the draft, (i) the person obtaining payment or acceptance, at the time of presentment, and (ii) a previous transferor of the draft, at the time of transfer, warrant to the drawee that pays or accepts the draft in good faith that:

(1) The warrantor is, or was, at the time the warrantor transferred the draft, a person entitled to enforce the draft or authorized to obtain payment or acceptance of the draft on behalf of a person entitled to enforce the draft;

(2) The draft has not been altered; and

(3) The warrantor has no knowledge that the signature of the purported drawer of the draft is unauthorized.

(b) A drawee making payment may recover from a warrantor damages for breach of warranty equal to the amount paid by the drawee less the amount the drawee received or is entitled to receive from the drawer because of the payment. In addition, the drawee is entitled to compensation for expenses and loss of interest resulting from the breach. The right of the drawee to recover damages under this subsection is not affected by any failure of the drawee to exercise ordinary care in making payment. If the drawee accepts the draft (i) breach of warranty is a defense to the obligation of the acceptor, and (ii) if the acceptor makes payment with respect to the draft, the acceptor is entitled to recover from a warrantor for breach of warranty the amounts stated in this subsection.

(c) If a drawee asserts a claim for breach of warranty under subsection (a) of this section based on an unauthorized indorsement of the draft or an alteration of the draft, the warrantor may defend by proving that the indorsement is effective under G.S. 25-3-404 or G.S. 25-3-405 or the drawer is precluded under G.S. 25-3-406 or G.S. 25-4-406 from asserting against the drawee the unauthorized indorsement or alteration.

(d) If (i) a dishonored draft is presented for payment to the drawer or an indorser or (ii) any other item is presented for payment to a party obliged to pay the item, and the item is paid, the person obtaining payment and a prior transferor of the item warrant to the person making payment in good faith that the warrantor is, or was, at the time the warrantor transferred the item, a person entitled to enforce the item or authorized to obtain payment on behalf of a person entitled to enforce the item. The person making payment may recover from any warrantor for breach of warranty an amount equal to the amount paid plus expenses and loss of interest resulting from the breach.

(e) The warranties stated in subsections (a) and (d) of this section cannot be disclaimed with respect to checks. Unless notice of a claim for breach of warranty is given to the warrantor within 30 days after the claimant has reason to know of the breach and the identity of the warrantor, the warrantor is discharged to the extent of any loss caused by the delay in giving notice of the claim.

(f) A cause of action for breach of warranty under this section accrues when the claimant has reason to know of the breach. (1965, c. 700, s. 1; 1995, c. 232, s. 2.)

§ 25-4-207.2. Encoding and retention warranties.

(a) A person who encodes information on or with respect to an item after issue warrants to any subsequent collecting bank and to the payor bank or other payor that the information is correctly encoded. If the customer of a depositary bank encodes, that bank also makes the warranty.

(b) A person who undertakes to retain an item pursuant to an agreement for electronic presentment warrants to any subsequent collecting bank and to the payor bank or other payor that retention and presentment of the item comply with the agreement. If a customer of a depositary bank undertakes to retain an item, that bank also makes this warranty.

(c) A person to whom warranties are made under this section and who took the item in good faith may recover from the warrantor as damages for breach of warranty an amount equal to the loss suffered as a result of the breach, plus expenses and loss of interest incurred as a result of the breach. (1965, c. 700, s. 1; 1995, c. 232, s. 2.)

§ 25-4-208. Security interest of collecting bank in items, accompanying documents and proceeds.

(a) A collecting bank has a security interest in an item and any accompanying documents or the proceeds of either:

(1) In case of an item deposited in an account, to the extent to which credit given for the item has been withdrawn or applied;

(2) In case of an item for which it has given credit available for withdrawal as of right, to the extent of the credit given, whether or not the credit is drawn upon or there is a right of charge-back; or

(3) If it makes an advance on or against the item.

(b) If credit given for several items received at one time or pursuant to a single agreement is withdrawn or applied in part, the security interest remains upon all the items, any accompanying documents or the proceeds of either. For the purpose of this section, credits first given are first withdrawn.

(c) Receipt by a collecting bank of a final settlement for an item is a realization on its security interest in the item, accompanying documents, and proceeds. So long as the bank does not receive final settlement for the item or give up possession of the item or possession or control of the accompanying documents for purposes other than collection, the security interest continues to that extent and is subject to Article 9, but:

(1) No security agreement is necessary to make the security interest enforceable (G.S. 25-9-203(b)(3)a.);

(2) No filing is required to perfect the security interest; and

(3) The security interest has priority over conflicting perfected security interests in the item, accompanying documents, or proceeds. (1965, c. 700, s. 1; 1995, c. 232, s. 2; 2000-169, s. 17; 2006-112, s. 42.)

§ 25-4-209. When bank gives value for purposes of holder in due course.

For purposes of determining its status as a holder in due course, a bank has given value to the extent it has a security interest in an item, if the bank otherwise complies with the requirements of G.S. 25-3-302 on what constitutes a holder in due course. (1899, c. 733, s. 27; Rev., s. 2175; C.S., s. 3007; 1965, c. 700, s. 1; 1995, c. 232, s. 2.)

§ 25-4-210. Presentment by notice of item not payable by, through, or at a bank; liability of drawer or indorser.

(a) Unless otherwise instructed, a collecting bank may present an item not payable by, through or at a bank by sending to the party to accept or pay a written notice that the bank holds the item for acceptance or payment. The notice must be sent in time to be received on or before the day when presentment is due and the bank must meet any requirement of the party to accept or pay under G.S. 25-3-501 by the close of the bank's next banking day after it knows of the requirement.

(b) If presentment is made by notice and payment, acceptance, or request for compliance with a requirement under G.S. 25-3-501 is not received by the close of business on the day after maturity or, in the case of demand items, by the close of business on the third banking day after notice was sent, the presenting bank may treat the item as dishonored and charge any drawer or indorser by sending it notice of the facts. (1965, c. 700, s. 1; 1995, c. 232, s. 2.)

§ 25-4-211. Medium and time of settlement by bank.

(a) With respect to settlement by a bank, the medium and time of settlement may be prescribed by federal reserve regulations or circulars, clearing-house rules, and the like, or agreement. In the absence of such prescription:

(1) The medium of settlement is cash or credit to an account in a Federal Reserve Bank of or specified by the person to receive settlement; and

(2) The time of settlement is:

(i) With respect to tender of settlement by cash, a cashier's check, or teller's check, when the cash or check is sent or delivered;

(ii) With respect to tender of settlement by credit in an account in a Federal Reserve Bank, when the credit is made;

(iii)   With respect to tender of settlement by a credit or debit to an account in a bank, when the credit or debit is made or, in the case of tender of settlement by authority to charge an account, when the authority is sent or delivered; or

(iv)   With respect to tender of settlement by a funds transfer, when payment is made pursuant to G.S. 25-4A-406(a) to the person receiving settlement.

(b)   If the tender of settlement is not by a medium authorized by subsection (a) of this section or the time of settlement is not fixed by subsection (a), no settlement occurs until the tender of settlement is accepted by the person receiving settlement.

(c)   If settlement for an item is made by cashier's check or teller's check and the person receiving settlement, before its midnight deadline:

(1)   Presents or forwards the check for collection, settlement is final when the check is finally paid; or

(2)   Fails to present or forward the check for collection, settlement is final at the midnight deadline of the person receiving settlement.

(d)   If settlement for an item is made by giving authority to charge the account of the bank giving settlement in the bank receiving settlement, settlement is final when the charge is made by the bank receiving settlement if there are funds available in the account for the amount of the item. (1965, c. 700, s. 1; 1995, c. 232, s. 2.)

§ 25-4-212. Right of charge-back or refund; liability of collecting bank; return of item.

(a)   If a collecting bank has made provisional settlement with its customer for an item and itself fails by reason of dishonor, suspension of payments by a bank or otherwise to receive a settlement for the item which is or becomes final, the bank may revoke the settlement given by it, charge back the amount of any credit given for the item to its customer's account, or obtain refund from its customer, whether or not it is able to return the item, if by its midnight deadline or within a longer reasonable time after it learns the facts it returns the item or sends notification of the facts. If the return or notice is delayed beyond the bank's midnight deadline or a longer reasonable time after it learns the facts, the bank may revoke the settlement, charge back the credit, or obtain refund from its customer, but it is liable for any loss resulting from the delay. These rights to revoke, charge back, and obtain refund terminate if and when a settlement for the item received by the bank is or becomes final.

(b)   A collecting bank returns an item when it is sent or delivered to the bank's customer or transferor or pursuant to its instructions.

(c)   A depositary bank that is also the payor may charge back the amount of an item to its customer's account or obtain refund in accordance with the section governing return of an item received by a payor bank for credit on its books (G.S. 25-4-301).

(d)   The right to charge back is not affected by:

(1)   Previous use of a credit given for the item; or

(2)   Failure by any bank to exercise ordinary care with respect to the item, but a bank so failing remains liable.

(e)   A failure to charge back or claim refund does not affect other rights of the bank against the customer or any other party.

(f)   If credit is given in dollars as the equivalent of the value of an item payable in foreign money, the dollar amount of any charge-back or refund must be calculated on the basis of the bank-offered spot rate for the foreign money prevailing on the day when the person entitled to the charge-back or refund learns that it will not receive payment in ordinary course. (1965, c. 700, s. 1; 1995, c. 232, s. 2.)

§ 25-4-213. Final payment of item by payor bank; when provisional debits and credits become final; when certain credits become available for withdrawal.

(a)   An item is finally paid by a payor bank when the bank has first done any of the following:

(1)   Paid the item in cash;

(2) Settled for the item without having a right to revoke the settlement under statute, clearing-house rule, or agreement; or

(3) Made a provisional settlement for the item and failed to revoke the settlement in the time and manner permitted by statute, clearing-house rule, or agreement.

(b) If provisional settlement for an item does not become final, the item is not finally paid.

(c) If provisional settlement for an item between the presenting and payor banks is made through a clearing house or by debits or credits in an account between them, then to the extent that provisional debits or credits for the item are entered in accounts between the presenting and payor banks or between the presenting and successive prior collecting banks seriatim, they become final upon final payment of the item by the payor bank.

(d) If a collecting bank receives a settlement for an item which is or becomes final, the bank is accountable to its customer for the amount of the item and any provisional credit given for the item in an account with its customer becomes final.

(e) Subject to (i) applicable law stating a time for availability of funds, and (ii) any right of the bank to apply the credit to an obligation of the customer, credit given by a bank for an item in a customer's account becomes available for withdrawal as of right:

(1) If the bank has received a provisional settlement for the item, when the settlement becomes final and the bank has had a reasonable time to receive return of the item and the item has not been received within that time.

(2) If the bank is both the depositary bank and the payor bank, and the item is finally paid, - at the opening of the bank's second banking day following receipt of the item.

(f) Subject to applicable law stating a time for availability of funds and any right of a bank to apply a deposit to an obligation of the depositor, a deposit of money becomes available for withdrawal as of right at the opening of the bank's next banking day after receipt of the deposit. (1899, c. 733, s. 137; Rev., s. 2287; C.S., s. 3119; 1949, c. 954; 1965, c. 700, s. 1; 1995, c. 232, s. 2.)

§ 25-4-214. Insolvency and preference.

(a)   If an item is in or comes into the possession of a payor or collecting bank that suspends payment and the item has not been finally paid, the item must be returned by the receiver, trustee or agent in charge of the closed bank to the presenting bank or the closed bank's customer.

(b)   If a payor bank finally pays an item and suspends payments without making a settlement for the item with its customer or the presenting bank which settlement is or becomes final, the owner of the item has a preferred claim against the payor bank.

(c)   If a payor bank gives or a collecting bank gives or receives a provisional settlement for an item and thereafter suspends payments, the suspension does not prevent or interfere with the settlement's becoming final if the finality occurs automatically upon the lapse of certain time or the happening of certain events.

(d)   If a collecting bank receives from subsequent parties settlement for an item, which settlement is or becomes final and the bank suspends payments without making a settlement for the item with its customer which settlement is or becomes final, the owner of the item has a preferred claim against the collecting bank. (1965, c. 700, s. 1; 1995, c. 232, s. 2.)

Part 3.

COLLECTION OF ITEMS: PAYOR BANKS.

§ 25-4-301. Deferred posting; recovery of payment by return of items; time of dishonor; return of items by payor bank.

(a)   If a payor bank settles for a demand item other than a documentary draft presented otherwise than for immediate payment over the counter before midnight of the banking day of receipt, the payor bank may revoke the settlement and recover the settlement if, before it has made final payment and before its midnight deadline, it:

(1)   Returns the item; or

(2) Sends written notice of dishonor or nonpayment if the item is unavailable for return.

(b) If a demand item is received by a payor bank for credit on its books, it may return the item or send notice of dishonor and may revoke any credit given or recover the amount thereof withdrawn by its customer, if it acts within the time limit and in the manner specified in subsection (a) of this section.

(c) Unless previous notice of dishonor has been sent, an item is dishonored at the time when for purposes of dishonor it is returned or notice sent in accordance with this section.

(d) An item is returned:

(1) As to an item presented through a clearing house, when it is delivered to the presenting or last collecting bank or to the clearing house or is sent or delivered in accordance with clearing-house rules; or

(2) In all other cases, when it is sent or delivered to the bank's customer or transferor or pursuant to instructions. (1899, c. 733, s. 137; Rev., s. 2287; C.S., s. 3119; 1949, c. 954; 1965, c. 700, s. 1; 1995, c. 232, s. 2.)

§ 25-4-302. Payor bank's responsibility for late return of item.

(a) If an item is presented to and received by a payor bank, the bank is accountable for the amount of:

(1) A demand item, other than a documentary draft, whether properly payable or not, if the bank, in any case in which it is not also the depositary bank, retains the item beyond midnight of the banking day of receipt without settling for it or, whether or not it is also the depositary bank, does not pay or return the item or send notice of dishonor until after its midnight deadline; or

(2) Any other properly payable item unless within the time allowed for acceptance or payment of that item, the bank either accepts or pays the item or returns it and accompanying documents.

(b) The liability of a payor bank to pay an item pursuant to subsection (a) of this section is subject to defenses based on breach of a presentment warranty (G.S. 25-4-208) [25-4-207.1] or proof that the person seeking enforcement of the liability presented or transferred the item for the purpose of defrauding the payor bank. (1899, c. 733, s. 137; Rev., s. 2287; C.S., s. 3119; 1949, c. 954; 1965, c. 700, s. 1; 1995, c. 232, s. 2.)

§ 25-4-303. When items subject to notice, stop-payment order, legal process, or setoff; order in which items may be charged or certified.

(a) Any knowledge, notice, or stop-payment order received by, legal process served upon, or setoff exercised by a payor bank comes too late to terminate, suspend, or modify the bank's right or duty to pay an item or to charge its customer's account for the item if the knowledge, notice, stop-payment order, or legal process is received or served and a reasonable time for the bank to act thereon expires or the setoff is exercised after the earliest of the following:

(1) The bank accepts or certifies the item;

(2) The bank pays the item in cash;

(3) The bank settles for the item without having a right to revoke the settlement under statute, clearing-house rule, or agreement;

(4) The bank becomes accountable for the amount of the item under G.S. 25-4-302 dealing with the payor bank's responsibility for late return of item; or

(5) With respect to checks, a cutoff hour no earlier than one hour after the opening of the next banking day after the banking day on which the bank received the check and no later than the close of that next banking day or, if no cutoff hour is fixed, the close of the next banking day after the banking day on which the bank received the check.

(b) Subject to subsection (a) of this section, items may be accepted, paid, certified or charged to the indicated account of its customer in any order. (1965, c. 700, s. 1; 1995, c. 232, s. 2.)

Part 4.

RELATIONSHIP BETWEEN PAYOR BANK AND ITS CUSTOMER.

§ 25-4-401. When bank may charge customer's account.

(a) A bank may charge against the account of a customer an item that is properly payable from that account even though the charge creates an overdraft. An item is properly payable if it is authorized by the customer and is in accordance with any agreement between the customer and bank.

(b) A customer is not liable for the amount of an overdraft if the customer neither signed the item nor benefited from the proceeds of the item.

(c) A bank may charge against the account of a customer a check that is otherwise properly payable from the account, even though payment was made before the date of the check, unless the customer has given notice to the bank of the postdating describing the check with reasonable certainty. The notice is effective for the period stated in G.S. 25-4-403(b) for stop-payment orders, and must be received at a time and in a manner that afforded the bank a reasonable opportunity to act on it before the bank takes any action with respect to the check described in G.S. 25-4-303. If a bank charges against the account of a customer a check before the date stated in the notice of postdating, the bank is liable for damages for the loss resulting from its act. The loss may include damages for dishonor of subsequent items under G.S. 25-4-402.

(d) A bank that in good faith makes payment to a holder may charge the indicated account of its customer according to:

(1) The original terms of the altered item; or

(2) The terms of the completed item, even though the bank knows the item has been completed unless the bank has notice that the completion was improper. (1965, c. 700, s. 1; 1995, c. 232, s. 2.)

§ 25-4-402. Bank's liability to customer for wrongful dishonor; time of determining insufficiency of account.

(a) Except as otherwise provided in this Article, a payor bank wrongfully dishonors an item if it dishonors an item that is properly payable, but a bank may dishonor an item that would create an overdraft unless it has agreed to pay the overdraft.

(b) A payor bank is liable to its customer for damages proximately caused by the wrongful dishonor of an item. Liability is limited to actual damages proved and may include damages for an arrest or prosecution of the customer or other consequential damages. Whether any consequential damages are proximately caused by the wrongful dishonor is a question of fact to be determined in each case. This subsection does not preclude noncompensatory damages.

(c) A payor bank's determination of the customer's account balance on which a decision to dishonor for insufficiency of available funds is based may be made at any time between the time the item is received by the payor bank and the time that the payor bank returns the item or gives notice in lieu of return, and no more than one determination need be made. If, at the election of the payor bank, a subsequent balance determination is made for the purpose of reevaluating the bank's decision to dishonor the item, the account balance at that time is determinative of whether a dishonor for insufficiency of available funds is wrongful. (1921, c. 4, s. 38; C.S., s. 220(m); 1965, c. 700, s. 1; 1995, c. 232, s. 2.)

§ 25-4-403. Customer's right to stop payment; burden of proof of loss.

(a) A customer or any person authorized to draw on the account if there is more than one person may stop payment of any item drawn on the customer's account or close the account by an order to the bank describing the item or account with reasonable certainty received at a time and in a manner that affords the bank a reasonable opportunity to act on it before any action by the bank with respect to the item described in G.S. 25-4-303. If the signature of more than one person is required to draw on an account, any of these persons may stop payment or close the account.

(b) A stop-payment order is effective for six months, but it lapses after 14 calendar days if the original order was oral and was not confirmed in writing within that period. A stop-payment order may be renewed for additional six-month periods by a writing given to the bank within a period during which the stop-payment order is effective.

(c) The burden of establishing the fact and amount of loss resulting from the payment of an item contrary to a stop-payment order or order to close an account is on the customer. The loss from payment of an item contrary to a stop-payment order may include damages for dishonor of subsequent items under G.S. 25-4-402. (1929, c. 341, s. 1; 1965, c. 700, s. 1; 1995, c. 232, s. 2.)

§ 25-4-404. Bank not obligated to pay check more than six months old.

A bank is under no obligation to a customer having a checking account to pay a check, other than a certified check, which is presented more than six months after its date, but it may charge its customer's account for a payment made thereafter in good faith. (C. S., s. 3168; 1929, c. 341, s. 3; 1965, c. 700, s. 1.)

§ 25-4-405. Death or incompetence of customer.

(a) A payor or collecting bank's authority to accept, pay, or collect an item or to account for proceeds of its collection, if otherwise effective, is not rendered ineffective by incompetence of a customer of either bank existing at the time the item is issued or its collection is undertaken if the bank does not know of an adjudication of incompetence. Neither death nor incompetence of a customer revokes the authority to accept, pay, collect, or account until the bank knows of the fact of death or of an adjudication of incompetence and has reasonable opportunity to act on it.

(b) Even with knowledge, a bank may for ten days after the date of death pay or certify checks drawn on or before that date unless ordered to stop payment by a person claiming an interest in the account.

(c) A transaction, although subject to this Article, is also subject to G.S. 41-2.1, 53C-6-6, 54-109.58, and 54B-129, and in case of conflict between the provisions of this section and either of those sections, the provisions of those sections control. (1965, c. 700, s. 1; 1967, c. 24, s. 10; c. 562, s. 1; 1995, c. 232, s. 2; 1998-69, s. 10; 2012-56, s. 7.)

§ 25-4-406. Customer's duty to discover and report unauthorized signature or alteration.

(a)   A bank that sends or makes available to a customer a statement of account showing payment of items for the account shall either return or make available to the customer the items paid or provide information in the statement of account sufficient to allow the customer reasonably to identify the items paid. The statement of account provides sufficient information if the item is described by item number, amount, and date of payment.

(b)   If the items are not returned to the customer, the person retaining the items shall either retain the items or, if the items are destroyed, maintain the capacity to furnish legible copies of the items until the expiration of seven years after receipt of the items. A customer may request an item from the bank that paid the item, and that bank must provide in a reasonable time either the item or, if the item has been destroyed or is not otherwise obtainable, a legible copy of the item.

(c)   If a bank sends or makes available a statement of account or items pursuant to subsection (a) of this section, the customer must exercise reasonable promptness in examining the statement or the items to determine whether any payment was not authorized because of an alteration of an item or because a purported signature by or on behalf of the customer was not authorized. If, based on the statement or items provided, the customer should reasonably have discovered the unauthorized payment, the customer must promptly notify the bank of the relevant facts.

(d)   If the bank proves that the customer failed, with respect to an item, to comply with the duties imposed on the customer by subsection (c) of this section, the customer is precluded from asserting against the bank:

(1)   The customer's unauthorized signature or any alteration on the item, if the bank also proves that it suffered a loss by reason of the failure; and

(2)   The customer's unauthorized signature or alteration by the same wrongdoer on any other item paid in good faith by the bank if the payment was made before the bank received notice from the customer of the unauthorized signature or alteration and after the customer had been afforded a reasonable period of time, not exceeding 30 days, in which to examine the item or statement of account and notify the bank.

(e) If subsection (d) of this section applies and the customer proves that the bank failed to exercise ordinary care in paying the item and that the failure substantially contributed to loss, the loss is allocated between the customer precluded and the bank asserting the preclusion according to the extent to which the failure of the customer to comply with subsection (c) of this section and the failure of the bank to exercise ordinary care contributed to the loss. If the customer proves that the bank did not pay the item in good faith, the preclusion under subsection (d) of this section does not apply.

(f) Without regard to care or lack of care of either the customer or the bank, a customer who does not within one year after the statement or items are made available to the customer (subsection (a) of this section) discover and report the customer's unauthorized signature on or any alteration on the item is precluded from asserting against the bank the unauthorized signature or alteration. If there is a preclusion under this subsection, the payor bank may not recover for breach of warranty under G.S. 25-4-208 [25-4-207.1] with respect to the unauthorized signature or alteration to which the preclusion applies. (1965, c. 700, s. 1; 1981, c. 599, s. 19; 1995, c. 232, s. 2.)

§ 25-4-407. Payor bank's right to subrogation on improper payment.

If a payor bank has paid an item over the order of the drawer or maker to stop payment, or after an account has been closed, or otherwise under circumstances giving a basis for objection by the drawer or maker, to prevent unjust enrichment and only to the extent necessary to prevent loss to the bank by reason of its payment of the item, the payor bank is subrogated to the rights:

(1) Of any holder in due course on the item against the drawer or maker;

(2) Of the payee or any other holder of the item against the drawer or maker either on the item or under the transaction out of which the item arose; and

(3) Of the drawer or maker against the payee or any other holder of the item with respect to the transaction out of which the item arose. (1965, c. 700, s. 1; 1995, c. 232, s. 2.)

Part 5.

COLLECTION OF DOCUMENTARY DRAFTS.

§ 25-4-501. Handling of documentary drafts; duty to send for presentment and to notify customer of dishonor.

A bank that takes a documentary draft for collection shall present or send the draft and accompanying documents for presentment, and upon learning that the draft has not been paid or accepted in due course, shall seasonably notify its customer of the fact even though it may have discounted or bought the draft or extended credit available for withdrawal as of right. (1965, c. 700, s. 1; 1995, c. 232, s. 2.)

§ 25-4-502. Presentment of "on arrival" drafts.

If a draft or the relevant instructions require presentment "on arrival," "when goods arrive" or the like, the collecting bank need not present until in its judgment a reasonable time for arrival of the goods has expired. Refusal to pay or accept because the goods have not arrived is not dishonor; the bank must notify its transferor of the refusal but need not present the draft again until it is instructed to do so or learns of the arrival of the goods. (1965, c. 700, s. 1; 1995, c. 232, s. 2.)

§ 25-4-503. Responsibility of presenting bank for documents and goods; report of reasons for dishonor; referee in case of need.

Unless otherwise instructed and except as provided in Article 5, a bank presenting a documentary draft:

(1) Must deliver the documents to the drawee on acceptance of the draft if it is payable more than three days after presentment; otherwise, only on payment; and

(2) Upon dishonor, either in the case of presentment for acceptance or presentment for payment, may seek and follow instructions from any referee in case of need designated in the draft or, if the presenting bank does not choose to utilize the referee's services, it must use diligence and good faith to ascertain

the reason for dishonor, must notify its transferor of the dishonor and of the results of its effort to ascertain the reasons therefor, and must request instructions.

However, the presenting bank is under no obligation with respect to goods represented by the documents except to follow any reasonable instructions seasonably received; it has a right to reimbursement for any expense incurred in following instructions and to prepayment of or indemnity for those expenses. (1899, c. 733, s. 131; Rev., s. 2281; C.S., s. 3113; 1965, c. 700, s. 1; 1995, c. 232, s. 2.)

§ 25-4-504. Privilege of presenting bank to deal with goods; security interest for expenses.

(a) A presenting bank that, following the dishonor of a documentary draft, has seasonably requested instructions but does not receive them within a reasonable time may store, sell, or otherwise deal with the goods in any reasonable manner.

(b) For its reasonable expenses incurred by action under subsection (a) of this section, the presenting bank has a lien upon the goods or their proceeds, which may be foreclosed in the same manner as an unpaid seller's lien. (1965, c. 700, s. 1; 1995, c. 232, s. 2.)

Article 4A.

Funds Transfers.

Part 1.

SUBJECT MATTER AND DEFINITIONS.

§ 25-4A-101. Short title.

This Article may be cited as Uniform Commercial Code-Funds Transfers. (1993, c. 157, s. 1.)

§ 25-4A-102. Subject matter.

Except as otherwise provided in G.S. 25-4A-108, this Article applies to funds transfers defined in G.S. 25-4A-104. (1993, c. 157, s. 1.)

§ 25-4A-103. Payment order - definitions.

(a) In this Article:

(1) "Payment order" means an instruction of a sender to a receiving bank, transmitted orally, electronically, or in writing, to pay, or to cause another bank to pay, a fixed or determinable amount of money to a beneficiary if:

(i) The instruction does not state a condition of payment to the beneficiary other than time of payment,

(ii) The receiving bank is to be reimbursed by debiting an account of, or otherwise receiving payment from, the sender, and

(iii) The instruction is transmitted by the sender directly to the receiving bank or to an agent, funds-transfer system, or communication system for transmittal to the receiving bank.

(2) "Beneficiary" means the person to be paid by the beneficiary's bank.

(3) "Beneficiary's bank" means the bank identified in a payment order in which an account of the beneficiary is to be credited pursuant to the order or which otherwise is to make payment to the beneficiary if the order does not provide for payment to an account.

(4) "Receiving bank" means the bank to which the sender's instruction is addressed.

(5) "Sender" means the person giving the instruction to the receiving bank.

(b) If an instruction complying with subsection (a)(1) is to make more than one payment to a beneficiary, the instruction is a separate payment order with respect to each payment.

(c) A payment order is issued when it is sent to the receiving bank. (1993, c. 157, s. 1.)

§ 25-4A-104. Funds transfer - definitions.

In this Article:

(a) "Funds transfer" means the series of transactions, beginning with the originator's payment order, made for the purpose of making payment to the beneficiary of the order. The term includes any payment order issued by the originator's bank or an intermediary bank intended to carry out the originator's payment order. A funds transfer is completed by acceptance by the beneficiary's bank of a payment order for the benefit of the beneficiary of the originator's payment order.

(b) "Intermediary bank" means a receiving bank other than the originator's bank or the beneficiary's bank.

(c) "Originator" means the sender of the first payment order in a funds transfer.

(d) "Originator's bank" means (i) the receiving bank to which the payment order of the originator is issued if the originator is not a bank, or (ii) the originator if the originator is a bank. (1993, c. 157, s. 1.)

Article 4A.

Funds Transfers

PART 1.

SUBJECT MATTER AND DEFINITIONS.

§ 25-4A-105. Other definitions.

(a)   In this Article:

(1)   "Authorized account" means a deposit account of a customer in a bank designated by the customer as a source of payment of payment orders issued by the customer to the bank. If a customer does not so designate an account, any account of the customer is an authorized account if payment of a payment order from that account is not inconsistent with a restriction on the use of that account.

(2)   "Bank" means a person engaged in the business of banking and includes a savings bank, savings and loan association, credit union, and trust company. A branch or separate office of a bank is a separate bank for purposes of this Article.

(3)   "Customer" means a person, including a bank, having an account with a bank or from whom a bank has agreed to receive payment orders.

(4)   "Funds-transfer business day" of a receiving bank means the part of a day during which the receiving bank is open for the receipt, processing, and transmittal of payment orders and cancellations and amendments of payment orders.

(5)   "Funds-transfer system" means a wire transfer network, automated clearinghouse, or other communication system of a clearinghouse or other association of banks through which a payment order by a bank may be transmitted to the bank to which the order is addressed.

(6)   Repealed by Session Laws 2006-112, s. 15, effective October 1, 2006.

(7)   "Prove" with respect to a fact means to meet the burden of establishing the fact (G.S. 25-1-201(b)(8)).

(b)   Other definitions applying to this Article and the sections in which they appear are:

"Acceptance"   G.S. 25-4A-209

"Beneficiary"   G.S. 25-4A-103

"Beneficiary's bank"   G.S. 25-4A-103

"Executed"   G.S. 25-4A-301

"Execution date"   G.S. 25-4A-301

"Funds transfer"   G.S. 25-4A-104

"Funds-transfer system rule"   G.S. 25-4A-501

"Intermediary bank"   G.S. 25-4A-104

"Originator"   G.S. 25-4A-104

"Originator's bank"   G.S. 25-4A-104

"Payment by beneficiary's bank to beneficiary"   G.S. 25-4A-405

"Payment by originator to beneficiary"   G.S. 25-4A-406

"Payment by sender to receiving bank"   G.S. 25-4A-403

"Payment date"   G.S. 25-4A-401

"Payment order"   G.S. 25-4A-103

"Receiving bank"   G.S. 25-4A-103

"Security procedure"   G.S. 25-4A-201

"Sender"   G.S. 25-4A-103.

(c)   The following definitions in Article 4 apply to this Article:

"Clearing house"   G.S. 25-4-104

"Item"   G.S. 25-4-104

"Suspends payments"   G.S. 25-4-104.

(d)   In addition, Article 1 of this Chapter contains general definitions and principles of construction and interpretation applicable throughout this Article. (1993, c. 157, s. 1; 2006-112, ss. 15, 16.)

§ 25-4A-106. Time payment order is received.

(a)   The time of receipt of a payment order or communication cancelling or amending a payment order is determined by the rules applicable to receipt of a notice stated in G.S. 25-1-202. A receiving bank may fix a cutoff time or times on a funds-transfer business day for the receipt and processing of payment orders and communications cancelling or amending payment orders. Different cutoff times may apply to payment orders, cancellations, or amendments, or to different categories of payment orders, cancellations, or amendments. A cutoff time may apply to senders generally or different cutoff times may apply to different senders or categories of payment orders. If a payment order or communication cancelling or amending a payment order is received after the close of a funds-transfer business day or after the appropriate cutoff time on a funds-transfer business day, the receiving bank may treat the payment order or communication as received at the opening of the next funds-transfer business day.

(b) If this Article refers to an execution date or payment date or states a day on which a receiving bank is required to take action, and the date or day does not fall on a funds-transfer business day, the next day that is a funds-transfer business day is treated as the date or day stated, unless the contrary is stated in this Article. (1993, c. 157, s. 1; 2006-112, s. 17.)

§ 25-4A-107. Federal reserve regulations and operating circulars.

Regulations of the Board of Governors of the Federal Reserve System and operating circulars of the Federal Reserve Banks supersede any inconsistent provision of this Article to the extent of the inconsistency. (1993, c. 157, s. 1.)

§ 25-4A-108. Relationship to Electronic Fund Transfer Act.

(a) Except as provided in subsection (b) of this section, this Article does not apply to a funds transfer any part of which is governed by the Electronic Fund Transfer Act of 1978 (Title XX, Public Law 95-630, 92 Stat. 3728, 15 U.S.C. § 1693, et seq.), as amended from time to time.

(b) This Article applies to a funds transfer that is a remittance transfer as defined in the Electronic Fund Transfer Act (15 U.S.C. § 1693o-1), as amended from time to time, unless the remittance transfer is an electronic fund transfer as defined in the Electronic Fund Transfer Act (15 U.S.C. § 1693a), as amended from time to time.

(c) In a funds transfer to which this Article applies, in the event of an inconsistency between an applicable provision of this Article and an applicable provision of the Electronic Fund Transfer Act, the provision of the Electronic Fund Transfer Act governs to the extent of the inconsistency. (1993, c. 157, s. 1; 2013-14, s. 1.)

Part 2.

ISSUE AND ACCEPTANCE OF PAYMENT ORDER.

§ 25-4A-201. Security procedure.

"Security procedure" means a procedure established by agreement of a customer and a receiving bank for the purpose of (i) verifying that a payment order or communication amending or cancelling a payment order is that of the customer, or (ii) detecting error in the transmission or the content of the payment order or communication. A security procedure may require the use of algorithms or other codes, identifying words or numbers, encryption, call-back procedures, or similar security devices. Comparison of a signature on a payment order or communication with an authorized specimen signature of the customer is not by itself a security procedure. (1993, c. 157, s. 1.)

§ 25-4A-202. Authorized and verified payment orders.

(a)   A payment order received by the receiving bank is the authorized order of the person identified as sender if that person authorized the order or is otherwise bound by it under the law of agency.

(b)   If a bank and its customer have agreed that the authenticity of payment orders issued to the bank in the name of the customer as sender will be verified pursuant to a security procedure, a payment order received by the receiving bank is effective as the order of the customer, whether or not authorized, if (i) the security procedure is a commercially reasonable method of providing security against unauthorized payment orders, and (ii) the bank proves that it accepted the payment order in good faith and in compliance with the security procedure and any written agreement or instruction of the customer restricting acceptance of payment orders issued in the name of the customer. The bank is not required to follow an instruction that violates a written agreement with the customer or notice of which is not received at a time and in a manner affording the bank a reasonable opportunity to act on it before the payment order is accepted.

(c)   Commercial reasonableness of a security procedure is a question of law to be determined by considering the wishes of the customer expressed to the bank, the circumstances of the customer known to the bank, including the size, type, and frequency of payment orders normally issued by the customer to the bank, alternative security procedures offered to the customer, and security procedures in general use by customers and receiving banks similarly situated.

A security procedure is deemed to be commercially reasonable if (i) the security procedure was chosen by the customer after the bank offered, and the customer refused, a security procedure that was commercially reasonable for that customer, and (ii) the customer expressly agreed in writing to be bound by any payment order, whether or not authorized, issued in its name and accepted by the bank in compliance with the security procedure chosen by the customer.

(d) The term "sender" in this Article includes the customer in whose name a payment order is issued if the order is the authorized order of the customer under subsection (a), or it is effective as the order of the customer under subsection (b).

(e) This section applies to amendments and cancellations of payment orders to the same extent it applies to payment orders.

(f) Except as provided in this section and in G.S. 25-4A-203(a)(1), rights and obligations arising under this section or G.S. 25-4A-203 may not be varied by agreement. (1993, c. 157, s. 1.)

§ 25-4A-203. Unenforceability of certain verified payment orders.

(a) If an accepted payment order is not, under G.S. 25-4A-202(a), an authorized order of a customer identified as sender, but is effective as an order of the customer pursuant to G.S. 25-4A-202(b), the following rules apply:

(1) By express written agreement, the receiving bank may limit the extent to which it is entitled to enforce or retain payment of the payment order.

(2) The receiving bank is not entitled to enforce or retain payment of the payment order if the customer proves that the order was not caused, directly or indirectly, by a person (i) entrusted at any time with duties to act for the customer with respect to payment orders or the security procedure, or (ii) who obtained access to transmitting facilities of the customer or who obtained, from a source controlled by the customer and without authority of the receiving bank, information facilitating breach of the security procedure, regardless of how the information was obtained or whether the customer was at fault. Information includes any access device, computer software, or the like.

(b) This section applies to amendments of payment orders to the same extent it applies to payment orders. (1993, c. 157, s. 1.)

PART 2.

ISSUE AND ACCEPTANCE OF PAYMENT ORDER.

§ 25-4A-204. Refund of payment and duty of customer to report with respect to unauthorized payment order.

(a)   If a receiving bank accepts a payment order issued in the name of its customer as sender which is (i) not authorized and not effective as the order of the customer under G.S. 25-4A-202, or (ii) not enforceable, in whole or in part, against the customer under G.S. 25-4A-203, the bank shall refund any payment of the payment order received from the customer to the extent the bank is not entitled to enforce payment and shall pay interest on the refundable amount calculated from the date the bank received payment to the date of the refund. However, the customer is not entitled to interest from the bank on the amount to be refunded if the customer fails to exercise ordinary care to determine that the order was not authorized by the customer and to notify the bank of the relevant facts within a reasonable time not exceeding 90 days after the date the customer received notification from the bank that the order was accepted or that the customer's account was debited with respect to the order. The bank is not entitled to any recovery from the customer on account of a failure by the customer to give notification as stated in this section.

(b)   Reasonable time under subsection (a) of this section may be fixed by agreement as stated in G.S. 25-1-302(b), but the obligation of a receiving bank to refund payment as stated in subsection (a) of this section may not otherwise be varied by agreement. (1993, c. 157, s. 1; 2006-112, s. 18.)

§ 25-4A-205. Erroneous payment orders.

(a)   If an accepted payment order was transmitted pursuant to a security procedure for the detection of error and the payment order (i) erroneously instructed payment to a beneficiary not intended by the sender, (ii) erroneously instructed payment in an amount greater than the amount intended by the sender, or (iii) was an erroneously transmitted duplicate of a payment order previously sent by the sender, the following rules apply:

(1) If the sender proves that the sender or a person acting on behalf of the sender pursuant to G.S. 25-4A-206 complied with the security procedure and that the error would have been detected if the receiving bank had also complied, the sender is not obliged to pay the order to the extent stated in paragraphs (2) and (3).

(2) If the funds transfer is completed on the basis of an erroneous payment order described in clause (i) or (iii) of subsection (a), the sender is not obliged to pay the order and the receiving bank is entitled to recover from the beneficiary any amount paid to the beneficiary to the extent allowed by the law governing mistake and restitution.

(3) If the funds transfer is completed on the basis of a payment order described in clause (ii) of subsection (a), the sender is not obliged to pay the order to the extent the amount received by the beneficiary is greater than the amount intended by the sender. In that case, the receiving bank is entitled to recover from the beneficiary the excess amount received to the extent allowed by the law governing mistake and restitution.

(b) If (i) the sender of an erroneous payment order described in subsection (a) is not obliged to pay all or part of the order, and (ii) the sender receives notification from the receiving bank that the order was accepted by the bank or that the sender's account was debited with respect to the order, the sender has a duty to exercise ordinary care, on the basis of information available to the sender, to discover the error with respect to the order and to advise the bank of the relevant facts within a reasonable time, not exceeding 90 days, after the bank's notification was received by the sender. If the bank proves that the sender failed to perform that duty, the sender is liable to the bank for the loss the bank proves it incurred as a result of the failure, but the liability of the sender may not exceed the amount of the sender's order.

(c) This section applies to amendments to payment orders to the same extent it applies to payment orders. (1993, c. 157, s. 1.)

§ 25-4A-206. Transmission of payment order through funds-transfer or other communication system.

(a) If a payment order addressed to a receiving bank is transmitted to a funds-transfer system or other third-party communication system for transmittal to the bank, the system is deemed to be an agent of the sender for the purpose of transmitting the payment order to the bank. If there is a discrepancy between the terms of the payment order transmitted to the system and the terms of the payment order transmitted by the system to the bank, the terms of the payment order of the sender are those transmitted by the system. This section does not apply to a funds-transfer system of the Federal Reserve Banks.

(b) This section applies to cancellations and amendments of payment orders to the same extent it applies to payment orders. (1993, c. 157, s. 1.)

§ 25-4A-207. Misdescription of beneficiary.

(a) Subject to subsection (b), if, in a payment order received by the beneficiary's bank, the name, bank account number, or other identification of the beneficiary refers to a nonexistent or unidentifiable person or account, no person has rights as a beneficiary of the order and acceptance of the order cannot occur.

(b) If a payment order received by the beneficiary's bank identifies the beneficiary both by name and by an identifying or bank account number and the name and number identify different persons, the following rules apply:

(1) Except as otherwise provided in subsection (c), if the beneficiary's bank does not know that the name and number refer to different persons, it may rely on the number as the proper identification of the beneficiary of the order. The beneficiary's bank need not determine whether the name and number refer to the same person.

(2) If the beneficiary's bank pays the person identified by name or knows that the name and number identify different persons, no person has rights as beneficiary except the person paid by the beneficiary's bank if that person was entitled to receive payment from the originator of the funds transfer. If no person has rights as beneficiary, acceptance of the order cannot occur.

(c) If (i) a payment order described in subsection (b) is accepted, (ii) the originator's payment order described the beneficiary inconsistently by name and number, and (iii) the beneficiary's bank pays the person identified by number as permitted by subsection (b)(1), the following rules apply:

(1) If the originator is a bank, the originator is obliged to pay its order.

(2) If the originator is not a bank and proves that the person identified by number was not entitled to receive payment from the originator, the originator is not obliged to pay its order unless the originator's bank proves that the originator, before acceptance of the originator's order, had notice that payment of a payment order issued by the originator might be made by the beneficiary's bank on the basis of an identifying or bank account number even if it identifies a person different from the named beneficiary. Proof of notice may be made by any admissible evidence. The originator's bank satisfies the burden of proof if it proves that the originator, before the payment order was accepted, signed a writing stating the information to which the notice relates.

(d) In a case governed by subsection (b)(1), if the beneficiary's bank rightfully pays the person identified by number and that person was not entitled to receive payment from the originator, the amount paid may be recovered from that person to the extent allowed by the law governing mistake and restitution as follows:

(1) If the originator is obliged to pay its payment order as stated in subsection (c), the originator has the right to recover.

(2) If the originator is not a bank and is not obliged to pay its payment order, the originator's bank has the right to recover. (1993, c. 157, s. 1.)

§ 25-4A-208. Misdescription of intermediary bank or beneficiary's bank.

(a) This subsection applies to a payment order identifying an intermediary bank or the beneficiary's bank only by an identifying number.

(1) The receiving bank may rely on the number as the proper identification of the intermediary or beneficiary's bank and need not determine whether the number identifies a bank.

(2) The sender is obliged to compensate the receiving bank for any loss and expenses incurred by the receiving bank as a result of its reliance on the number in executing or attempting to execute the order.

(b) This subsection applies to a payment order identifying an intermediary bank or the beneficiary's bank both by name and an identifying number if the name and number identify different persons.

(1) If the sender is a bank, the receiving bank may rely on the number as the proper identification of the intermediary or beneficiary's bank if the receiving bank, when it executes the sender's order, does not know that the name and number identify different persons. The receiving bank need not determine whether the name and number refer to the same person or whether the number refers to a bank. The sender is obliged to compensate the receiving bank for any loss and expenses incurred by the receiving bank as a result of its reliance on the number in executing or attempting to execute the order.

(2) If the sender is not a bank and the receiving bank proves that the sender, before the payment order was accepted, had notice that the receiving bank might rely on the number as the proper identification of the intermediary or beneficiary's bank even if it identifies a person different from the bank identified by name, the rights and obligations of the sender and the receiving bank are governed by subsection (b)(1), as though the sender were a bank. Proof of notice may be made by any admissible evidence. The receiving bank satisfies the burden of proof if it proves that the sender, before the payment order was accepted, signed a writing stating the information to which the notice relates.

(3) Regardless of whether the sender is a bank, the receiving bank may rely on the name as the proper identification of the intermediary or beneficiary's bank if the receiving bank, at the time it executes the sender's order, does not know that the name and number identify different persons. The receiving bank need not determine whether the name and number refer to the same person.

(4) If the receiving bank knows that the name and number identify different persons, reliance on either the name or the number in executing the sender's payment order is a breach of the obligation stated in G.S. 25-4A-302(a)(1). (1993, c. 157, s. 1.)

§ 25-4A-209. Acceptance of payment order.

(a) Subject to subsection (d), a receiving bank other than the beneficiary's bank accepts a payment order when it executes the order.

(b) Subject to subsections (c) and (d), a beneficiary's bank accepts a payment order at the earliest of the following times:

(1) When the bank (i) pays the beneficiary as stated in G.S. 25-4A-405(a) or G.S. 25-4A-405(b), or (ii) notifies the beneficiary of receipt of the order or that the account of the beneficiary has been credited with respect to the order unless the notice indicates that the bank is rejecting the order or that funds with respect to the order may not be withdrawn or used until receipt of payment from the sender of the order;

(2) When the bank receives payment of the entire amount of the sender's order pursuant to G.S. 25-4A-403(a)(1) or G.S. 25-4A-403(a)(2); or

(3) The opening of the next funds-transfer business day of the bank following the payment date of the order if, at that time, the amount of the sender's order is fully covered by a withdrawable credit balance in an authorized account of the sender or the bank has otherwise received full payment from the sender, unless the order was rejected before that time or is rejected within (i) one hour after that time, or (ii) one hour after the opening of the next business day of the sender following the payment date if that time is later. If notice of rejection is received by the sender after the payment date and the authorized account of the sender does not bear interest, the bank is obliged to pay interest to the sender on the amount of the order for the number of days elapsing after the payment date to the day the sender receives notice or learns that the order was not accepted, counting that day as an elapsed day. If the withdrawable credit balance during that period falls below the amount of the order, the amount of interest payable is reduced accordingly.

(c) Acceptance of a payment order cannot occur before the order is received by the receiving bank. Acceptance does not occur under subsection (b)(2) or (b)(3) if the beneficiary of the payment order does not have an account with the receiving bank, the account has been closed, or the receiving bank is not permitted by law to receive credits for the beneficiary's account.

(d) A payment order issued to the originator's bank cannot be accepted until the payment date if the bank is the beneficiary's bank, or the execution date if the bank is not the beneficiary's bank. If the originator's bank executes the originator's payment order before the execution date or pays the beneficiary of the originator's payment order before the payment date and the payment order is subsequently cancelled pursuant to G.S. 25-4A-211(b), the bank may recover from the beneficiary any payment received to the extent allowed by the law governing mistake and restitution. (1993, c. 157, s. 1.)

§ 25-4A-210. Rejection of payment order.

(a) A payment order is rejected by the receiving bank by a notice of rejection transmitted to the sender orally, electronically, or in writing. A notice of rejection need not use any particular words and is sufficient if it indicates that the receiving bank is rejecting the order or will not execute or pay the order. Rejection is effective when the notice is given if transmission is by a means that is reasonable in the circumstances. If notice of rejection is given by a means that is not reasonable, rejection is effective when the notice is received. If an agreement of the sender and receiving bank establishes the means to be used to reject a payment order, (i) any means complying with the agreement is reasonable and (ii) any means not complying is not reasonable unless no significant delay in receipt of the notice resulted from the use of the noncomplying means.

(b) This subsection applies if a receiving bank other than the beneficiary's bank fails to execute a payment order despite the existence on the execution date of a withdrawable credit balance in an authorized account of the sender sufficient to cover the order. If the sender does not receive notice of rejection of the order on the execution date and the authorized account of the sender does not bear interest, the bank is obliged to pay interest to the sender on the amount of the order for the number of days elapsing after the execution date to the earlier of the day the order is cancelled pursuant to G.S. 25-4A-211(d) or the day the sender receives notice or learns that the order was not executed, counting the final day of the period as an elapsed day. If the withdrawable credit balance during that period falls below the amount of the order, the amount of interest is reduced accordingly.

(c) If a receiving bank suspends payments, all unaccepted payment orders issued to it are deemed rejected at the time the bank suspends payments.

(d) Acceptance of a payment order precludes a later rejection of the order. Rejection of a payment order precludes a later acceptance of the order. (1993, c. 157, s. 1.)

§ 25-4A-211. Cancellation and amendment of payment order.

(a) A communication of the sender of a payment order cancelling or amending the order may be transmitted to the receiving bank orally, electronically, or in writing. If a security procedure is in effect between the sender and the receiving bank, the communication is not effective to cancel or amend the order unless the communication is verified pursuant to the security procedure or the bank agrees to the cancellation or amendment.

(b) Subject to subsection (a), a communication by the sender cancelling or amending a payment order is effective to cancel or amend the order if notice of the communication is received at a time and in a manner affording the receiving bank a reasonable opportunity to act on the communication before the bank accepts the payment order.

(c) After a payment order has been accepted, cancellation or amendment of the order is not effective unless the receiving bank agrees or a funds-transfer system rule allows cancellation or amendment without agreement of the bank.

(1) With respect to a payment order accepted by a receiving bank other than the beneficiary's bank, cancellation or amendment is not effective unless a conforming cancellation or amendment of the payment order issued by the receiving bank is also made.

(2) With respect to a payment order accepted by the beneficiary's bank, cancellation or amendment is not effective unless the order was issued in execution of an unauthorized payment order, or because of a mistake by a sender in the funds transfer which resulted in the issuance of a payment order (i) that is a duplicate of a payment order previously issued by the sender, (ii) that orders payment to a beneficiary not entitled to receive payment from the originator, or (iii) that orders payment in an amount greater than the amount the beneficiary was entitled to receive from the originator. If the payment order is cancelled or amended, the beneficiary's bank is entitled to recover from the beneficiary any amount paid to the beneficiary to the extent allowed by the law governing mistake and restitution.

(d) An unaccepted payment order is cancelled by operation of law at the close of the fifth funds-transfer business day of the receiving bank after the execution date or payment date of the order.

(e) A cancelled payment order cannot be accepted. If an accepted payment order is cancelled, the acceptance is nullified and no person has any right or obligation based on the acceptance. Amendment of a payment order is deemed to be cancellation of the original order at the time of amendment and issue of a new payment order in the amended form at the same time.

(f) Unless otherwise provided in an agreement of the parties or in a funds-transfer system rule, if the receiving bank, after accepting a payment order, agrees to cancellation or amendment of the order by the sender or is bound by a funds-transfer system rule allowing cancellation or amendment without the bank's agreement, the sender, whether or not cancellation or amendment is effective, is liable to the bank for any loss and expenses, including reasonable attorneys' fees, incurred by the bank as a result of the cancellation or amendment or attempted cancellation or amendment.

(g) A payment order is not revoked by the death or legal incapacity of the sender unless the receiving bank knows of the death or of an adjudication of incapacity by a court of competent jurisdiction and has reasonable opportunity to act before acceptance of the order.

(h) A funds-transfer system rule is not effective to the extent it conflicts with subsection (c)(2). (1993, c. 157, s. 1.)

§ 25-4A-212. Liability and duty of receiving bank regarding unaccepted payment order.

If a receiving bank fails to accept a payment order that it is obliged by express agreement to accept, the bank is liable for breach of the agreement to the extent provided in the agreement or in this Article, but does not otherwise have any duty to accept a payment order or, before acceptance, to take any action, or refrain from taking action, with respect to the order except as provided in this Article or by express agreement. Liability based on acceptance arises only when acceptance occurs as stated in G.S. 25-4A-209, and liability is limited to that provided in this Article. A receiving bank is not the agent of the sender or beneficiary of the payment order it accepts, or of any other party to the funds transfer, and the bank owes no duty to any party to the funds transfer except as provided in this Article or by express agreement. (1993, c. 157, s. 1.)

Part 3.

EXECUTION OF SENDER'S PAYMENT ORDER BY RECEIVING BANK.

§ 25-4A-301. Execution and execution date.

(a)   A payment order is "executed" by the receiving bank when it issues a payment order intended to carry out the payment order received by the bank. A payment order received by the beneficiary's bank can be accepted but cannot be executed.

(b)   "Execution date" of a payment order means the day on which the receiving bank may properly issue a payment order in execution of the sender's order. The execution date may be determined by instruction of the sender but cannot be earlier than the day the order is received and, unless otherwise determined, is the day the order is received. If the sender's instruction states a payment date, the execution date is the payment date or an earlier date on which execution is reasonably necessary to allow payment to the beneficiary on the payment date. (1993, c. 157, s. 1.)

§ 25-4A-302. Obligations of receiving bank in execution of payment order.

(a)   Except as provided in subsections (b) through (d), if the receiving bank accepts a payment order pursuant to G.S. 25-4A-209(a), the bank has the following obligations in executing the order:

(1)   The receiving bank is obliged to issue, on the execution date, a payment order complying with the sender's order and to follow the sender's instructions concerning (i) any intermediary bank or funds-transfer system to be used in carrying out the funds transfer, or (ii) the means by which payment orders are to be transmitted in the funds transfer. If the originator's bank issues a payment order to an intermediary bank, the originator's bank is obliged to instruct the intermediary bank according to the instruction of the originator. An intermediary bank in the funds transfer is similarly bound by an instruction given to it by the sender of the payment order it accepts.

(2)   If the sender's instruction states that the funds transfer is to be carried out telephonically or by wire transfer or otherwise indicates that the funds

transfer is to be carried out by the most expeditious means, the receiving bank is obliged to transmit its payment order by the most expeditious available means, and to instruct any intermediary bank accordingly. If a sender's instruction states a payment date, the receiving bank is obliged to transmit its payment order at a time and by means reasonably necessary to allow payment to the beneficiary on the payment date or as soon thereafter as is feasible.

(b) Unless otherwise instructed, a receiving bank executing a payment order may (i) use any funds-transfer system if use of that system is reasonable in the circumstances, and (ii) issue a payment order to the beneficiary's bank or to an intermediary bank through which a payment order conforming to the sender's order can expeditiously be issued to the beneficiary's bank if the receiving bank exercises ordinary care in the selection of the intermediary bank. A receiving bank is not required to follow an instruction of the sender designating a funds-transfer system to be used in carrying out the funds transfer if the receiving bank, in good faith, determines that it is not feasible to follow the instruction or that following the instruction would unduly delay completion of the funds transfer.

(c) Unless subsection (a)(2) applies or the receiving bank is otherwise instructed, the bank may execute a payment order by transmitting its payment order by first class mail or by any means reasonable in the circumstances. If the receiving bank is instructed to execute the sender's order by transmitting its payment order by a particular means, the receiving bank may issue its payment order by the means stated or by any means as expeditious as the means stated.

(d) Unless instructed by the sender, (i) the receiving bank may not obtain payment of its charges for services and expenses in connection with the execution of the sender's order by issuing a payment order in an amount equal to the amount of the sender's order less the amount of the charges, and (ii) may not instruct a subsequent receiving bank to obtain payment of its charges in the same manner. (1993, c. 157, s. 1.)

§ 25-4A-303. Erroneous execution of payment order.

(a) A receiving bank that (i) executes the payment order of the sender by issuing a payment order in an amount greater than the amount of the sender's order, or (ii) issues a payment order in execution of the sender's order and then issues a duplicate order, is entitled to payment of the amount of the sender's order under G.S. 25-4A-402(c) if that subsection is otherwise satisfied. The bank is entitled to recover from the beneficiary of the erroneous order the excess payment received to the extent allowed by the law governing mistake and restitution.

(b)   A receiving bank that executes the payment order of the sender by issuing a payment order in an amount less than the amount of the sender's order is entitled to payment of the amount of the sender's order under G.S. 25-4A-402(c) if (i) that subsection is otherwise satisfied and (ii) the bank corrects its mistake by issuing an additional payment order for the benefit of the beneficiary of the sender's order. If the error is not corrected, the issuer of the erroneous order is entitled to receive or retain payment from the sender of the order it accepted only to the extent of the amount of the erroneous order. This subsection does not apply if the receiving bank executes the sender's payment order by issuing a payment order in an amount less than the amount of the sender's order for the purpose of obtaining payment of its charges for services and expenses pursuant to instruction of the sender.

(c)   If a receiving bank executes the payment order of the sender by issuing a payment order to a beneficiary different from the beneficiary of the sender's order and the funds transfer is completed on the basis of that error, the sender of the payment order that was erroneously executed and all previous senders in the funds transfer are not obliged to pay the payment orders they issued. The issuer of the erroneous order is entitled to recover from the beneficiary of the order the payment received to the extent allowed by the law governing mistake and restitution. (1993, c. 157, s. 1.)

§ 25-4A-304. Duty of sender to report erroneously executed payment order.

If the sender of a payment order that is erroneously executed as stated in G.S. 25-4A-303 receives notification from the receiving bank that the order was executed or that the sender's account was debited with respect to the order, the sender has a duty to exercise ordinary care to determine, on the basis of information available to the sender, that the order was erroneously executed and to notify the bank of the relevant facts within a reasonable time not exceeding 90 days after the notification from the bank was received by the sender. If the sender fails to perform that duty, the bank is not obliged to pay interest on any amount refundable to the sender under G.S. 25-4A-402(d) for the period before the bank learns of the execution error. The bank is not entitled to any recovery from the sender on account of a failure by the sender to perform the duty stated in this section. (1993, c. 157, s. 1.)

§ 25-4A-305. Liability for late or improper execution or failure to execute payment order.

(a)　If a funds transfer is completed but execution of a payment order by the receiving bank in breach of G.S. 25-4A-302 results in delay in payment to the beneficiary, the bank is obliged to pay interest to either the originator or the beneficiary of the funds transfer for the period of delay caused by the improper execution. Except as provided in subsection (c), additional damages are not recoverable.

(b)　If execution of a payment order by a receiving bank in breach of G.S. 25-4A-302 results in (i) noncompletion of the funds transfer, (ii) failure to use an intermediary bank designated by the originator, or (iii) issuance of a payment order that does not comply with the terms of the payment order of the originator, the bank is liable to the originator for its expenses in the funds transfer and for incidental expenses and interest losses, to the extent not covered by subsection (a), resulting from the improper execution. Except as provided in subsection (c), additional damages are not recoverable.

(c)　In addition to the amounts payable under subsections (a) and (b), damages, including consequential damages, are recoverable to the extent provided in an express written agreement of the receiving bank.

(d)　If a receiving bank fails to execute a payment order it was obliged by express agreement to execute, the receiving bank is liable to the sender for its expenses in the transaction and for incidental expenses and interest losses resulting from the failure to execute. Additional damages, including consequential damages, are recoverable to the extent provided in an express written agreement of the receiving bank, but are not otherwise recoverable.

(e)　Reasonable attorneys' fees are recoverable if demand for compensation under subsection (a) or (b) is made and refused before an action is brought on the claim. If a claim is made for breach of an agreement under subsection (d) and the agreement does not provide for damages, reasonable attorneys' fees are recoverable if demand for compensation under subsection (d) is made and refused before an action is brought on the claim.

(f) Except as stated in this section, the liability of a receiving bank under subsections (a) and (b) may not be varied by agreement. (1993, c. 157, s. 1.)

Part 4.

PAYMENT.

§ 25-4A-401. Payment date.

"Payment date" of a payment order means the day on which the amount of the order is payable to the beneficiary by the beneficiary's bank. The payment date may be determined by instruction of the sender but cannot be earlier than the day the order is received by the beneficiary's bank and, unless otherwise determined, is the day the order is received by the beneficiary's bank. (1993, c. 157, s. 1.)

§ 25-4A-402. Obligation of sender to pay receiving bank.

(a) This section is subject to G.S. 25-4A-205 and G.S. 25-4A-207.

(b) With respect to a payment order issued to the beneficiary's bank, acceptance of the order by the bank obliges the sender to pay the bank the amount of the order, but payment is not due until the payment date of the order.

(c) This subsection is subject to subsection (e) and to G.S. 25-4A-303. With respect to a payment order issued to a receiving bank other than the beneficiary's bank, acceptance of the order by the receiving bank obliges the sender to pay the bank the amount of the sender's order. Payment by the sender is not due until the execution date of the sender's order. The obligation of that sender to pay its payment order is excused if the funds transfer is not completed by acceptance by the beneficiary's bank of a payment order instructing payment to the beneficiary of that sender's payment order.

(d) If the sender of a payment order pays the order and was not obliged to pay all or part of the amount paid, the bank receiving payment is obliged to refund payment to the extent the sender was not obliged to pay. Except as provided in G.S. 25-4A-204 and G.S. 25-4A-304, interest is payable on the refundable amount from the date of payment.

(e)   If a funds transfer is not completed as stated in subsection (c) and an intermediary bank is obliged to refund payment as stated in subsection (d) but is unable to do so because not permitted by applicable law or because the bank suspends payments, a sender in the funds transfer that executed a payment order in compliance with an instruction, as stated in G.S. 25-4A-302(a)(1), to route the funds transfer through that intermediary bank is entitled to receive or retain payment from the sender of the payment order that it accepted. The first sender in the funds transfer that issued an instruction requiring routing through that intermediary bank is subrogated to the right of the bank that paid the intermediary bank to refund as stated in subsection (d).

(f)   The right of the sender of a payment order to be excused from the obligation to pay the order as stated in subsection (c) or to receive refund under subsection (d) may not be varied by agreement. (1993, c. 157, s. 1.)

§ 25-4A-403. Payment by sender to receiving bank.

(a)   Payment of the sender's obligation under G.S. 25-4A-402 to pay the receiving bank occurs as follows:

(1)   If the sender is a bank, payment occurs when the receiving bank receives final settlement of the obligation through a Federal Reserve Bank or through a funds-transfer system.

(2)   If the sender is a bank and the sender (i) credited an account of the receiving bank with the sender, or (ii) caused an account of the receiving bank in another bank to be credited, payment occurs when the credit is withdrawn or, if not withdrawn, at midnight of the day on which the credit is withdrawable and the receiving bank learns of that fact.

(3)   If the receiving bank debits an account of the sender with the receiving bank, payment occurs when the debit is made to the extent the debit is covered by a withdrawable credit balance in the account.

(b)   If the sender and receiving bank are members of a funds-transfer system that nets obligations multilaterally among participants, the receiving bank receives final settlement when settlement is complete in accordance with the rules of the system. The obligation of the sender to pay the amount of a payment order transmitted through the funds-transfer system may be satisfied, to the extent permitted by the rules of the system, by setting off and applying against the sender's obligation the right of the sender to receive payment from the receiving bank of the amount of any other payment order transmitted to the sender by the receiving bank through the funds-transfer system. The aggregate balance of obligations owed by each sender to each receiving bank in the funds-transfer system may be satisfied, to the extent permitted by the rules of the system, by setting off and applying against that balance the aggregate balance of obligations owed to the sender by other members of the system. The aggregate balance is determined after the right of setoff stated in the second sentence of this subsection has been exercised.

(c) If two banks transmit payment orders to each other under an agreement that settlement of the obligations of each bank to the other under G.S. 25-4A-402 will be made at the end of the day or other period, the total amount owed with respect to all orders transmitted by one bank shall be set off against the total amount owed with respect to all orders transmitted by the other bank. To the extent of the setoff, each bank has made payment to the other.

(d) In a case not covered by subsection (a), the time when payment of the sender's obligation under G.S. 25-4A-402(b) or G.S. 25-4A-402(c) occurs is governed by applicable principles of law that determine when an obligation is satisfied. (1993, c. 157, s. 1.)

§ 25-4A-404. Obligation of beneficiary's bank to pay and give notice to beneficiary.

(a) Subject to G.S. 25-4A-211(e), 25-4A-405(d), and 25-4A-405(e), if a beneficiary's bank accepts a payment order, the bank is obliged to pay the amount of the order to the beneficiary of the order. Payment is due on the payment date of the order, but if acceptance occurs on the payment date after the close of the funds-transfer business day of the bank, payment is due on the next funds-transfer business day. If the bank refuses to pay after demand by the beneficiary and receipt of notice of particular circumstances that will give rise to consequential damages as a result of nonpayment, the beneficiary may recover damages resulting from the refusal to pay to the extent the bank had notice of the damages, unless the bank proves that it did not pay because of a reasonable doubt concerning the right of the beneficiary to payment.

(b)   If a payment order accepted by the beneficiary's bank instructs payment to an account of the beneficiary, the bank is obliged to notify the beneficiary of receipt of the order before midnight of the next funds-transfer business day following the payment date. If the payment order does not instruct payment to an account of the beneficiary, the bank is required to notify the beneficiary only if notice is required by the order. Notice may be given by first-class mail or any other means reasonable in the circumstances. If the bank fails to give the required notice, the bank is obliged to pay interest to the beneficiary on the amount of the payment order from the day notice should have been given until the day the beneficiary learned of receipt of the payment order by the bank. No other damages are recoverable. Reasonable attorneys' fees are also recoverable if demand for interest is made and refused before an action is brought on the claim.

(c)   The right of a beneficiary to receive payment and damages as stated in subsection (a) may not be varied by agreement or a funds-transfer system rule. The right of a beneficiary to be notified as stated in subsection (b) may be varied by agreement of the beneficiary or by a funds-transfer system rule if the beneficiary is notified of the rule before initiation of the funds transfer. (1993, c. 157, s. 1.)

§ 25-4A-405. Payment by beneficiary's bank to beneficiary.

(a)   If the beneficiary's bank credits an account of the beneficiary of a payment order, payment of the bank's obligation under G.S. 25-4A-404(a) occurs when and to the extent (i) the beneficiary is notified of the right to withdraw the credit, (ii) the bank lawfully applies the credit to a debt of the beneficiary, or (iii) funds with respect to the order are otherwise made available to the beneficiary by the bank.

(b)   If the beneficiary's bank does not credit an account of the beneficiary of a payment order, the time when payment of the bank's obligation under G.S. 25-4A-404(a) occurs is governed by principles of law that determine when an obligation is satisfied.

(c) Except as stated in subsections (d) and (e), if the beneficiary's bank pays the beneficiary of a payment order under a condition to payment or agreement of the beneficiary giving the bank the right to recover payment from the beneficiary if the bank does not receive payment of the order, the condition to payment or agreement is not enforceable.

(d) A funds-transfer system rule may provide that payments made to beneficiaries of funds transfers made through the system are provisional until receipt of payment by the beneficiary's bank of the payment order it accepted. A beneficiary's bank that makes a payment that is provisional under the rule is entitled to refund from the beneficiary if (i) the rule requires that both the beneficiary and the originator be given notice of the provisional nature of the payment before the funds transfer is initiated, (ii) the beneficiary, the beneficiary's bank, and the originator's bank agreed to be bound by the rule, and (iii) the beneficiary's bank did not receive payment of the payment order that it accepted. If the beneficiary is obliged to refund payment to the beneficiary's bank, acceptance of the payment order by the beneficiary's bank is nullified and no payment by the originator of the funds transfer to the beneficiary occurs under G.S. 25-4A-406.

(e) This subsection applies to a funds transfer that includes a payment order transmitted over a funds-transfer system that (i) nets obligations multilaterally among participants, and (ii) has in effect a loss-sharing agreement among participants for the purpose of providing funds necessary to complete settlement of the obligations of one or more participants that do not meet their settlement obligations. If the beneficiary's bank in the funds transfer accepts a payment order and the system fails to complete settlement pursuant to its rules with respect to any payment order in the funds transfer, (i) the acceptance by the beneficiary's bank is nullified and no person has any right or obligation based on the acceptance, (ii) the beneficiary's bank is entitled to recover payment from the beneficiary, (iii) no payment by the originator to the beneficiary occurs under G.S. 25-4A-406, and (iv) subject to G.S. 25-4A-402(e), each sender in the funds transfer is excused from its obligation to pay its payment order under G.S. 25-4A-402(c) because the funds transfer has not been completed. (1993, c. 157, s. 1.)

§ 25-4A-406. Payment by originator to beneficiary; discharge of underlying obligation.

(a)   Subject to G.S. 25-4A-211(e), 25-4A-405(d), and 25-4A-405(e), the originator of a funds transfer pays the beneficiary of the originator's payment order (i) at the time a payment order for the benefit of the beneficiary is accepted by the beneficiary's bank in the funds transfer and (ii) in an amount equal to the amount of the order accepted by the beneficiary's bank, but not more than the amount of the originator's order.

(b)   If payment under subsection (a) is made to satisfy an obligation, the obligation is discharged to the same extent discharge would result from payment to the beneficiary of the same amount in money, unless (i) the payment under subsection (a) was made by a means prohibited by the contract of the beneficiary with respect to the obligation, (ii) the beneficiary, within a reasonable time after receiving notice of receipt of the order by the beneficiary's bank, notified the originator of the beneficiary's refusal of the payment, (iii) funds with respect to the order were not withdrawn by the beneficiary or applied to a debt of the beneficiary, and (iv) the beneficiary would suffer a loss that could reasonably have been avoided if payment had been made by a means complying with the contract. If payment by the originator does not result in discharge under this section, the originator is subrogated to the rights of the beneficiary to receive payment from the beneficiary's bank under G.S. 25-4A-404(a).

(c)   For the purpose of determining whether discharge of an obligation occurs under subsection (b), if the beneficiary's bank accepts a payment order in an amount equal to the amount of the originator's payment order less charges of one or more receiving banks in the funds transfer, payment to the beneficiary is deemed to be in the amount of the originator's order unless upon demand by the beneficiary the originator does not pay the beneficiary the amount of the deducted charges.

(d)   Rights of the originator or of the beneficiary of a funds transfer under this section may be varied only by agreement of the originator and the beneficiary. (1993, c. 157, s. 1.)

Part 5.

MISCELLANEOUS PROVISIONS.

§ 25-4A-501. Variation by agreement and effect of funds-transfer system rule.

(a) Except as otherwise provided in this Article, the rights and obligations of a party to a funds transfer may be varied by agreement of the affected party.

(b) "Funds-transfer system rule" means a rule of an association of banks (i) governing transmission of payment orders by means of a funds-transfer system of the association or rights and obligations with respect to those orders, or (ii) to the extent the rule governs rights and obligations between banks that are parties to a funds transfer in which a Federal Reserve Bank, acting as an intermediary bank, sends a payment order to the beneficiary's bank. Except as otherwise provided in this Article, a funds-transfer system rule governing rights and obligations between participating banks using the system may be effective even if the rule conflicts with this Article and indirectly affects another party to the funds transfer who does not consent to the rule. A funds-transfer system rule may also govern rights and obligations of parties other than participating banks using the system to the extent stated in G.S. 25-4A-404(c), 25-4A-405(d), and 25-4A-507(c). (1993, c. 157, s. 1.)

§ 25-4A-502. Creditor process served on receiving bank; setoff by beneficiary's bank.

(a) As used in this section, "creditor process" means levy, attachment, garnishment, notice of lien, sequestration, or similar process issued by or on behalf of a creditor or other claimant with respect to an account.

(b) This subsection applies to creditor process with respect to an authorized account of the sender of a payment order if the creditor process is served on the receiving bank. For the purpose of determining rights with respect to the creditor process, if the receiving bank accepts the payment order the balance in the authorized account is deemed to be reduced by the amount of the payment order to the extent the bank did not otherwise receive payment of the order, unless the creditor process is served at a time and in a manner affording the bank a reasonable opportunity to act on it before the bank accepts the payment order.

(c) If a beneficiary's bank has received a payment order for payment to the beneficiary's account in the bank, the following rules apply:

(1) The bank may credit the beneficiary's account. The amount credited may be set off against an obligation owed by the beneficiary to the bank or may be applied to satisfy creditor process served on the bank with respect to the account.

(2) The bank may credit the beneficiary's account and allow withdrawal of the amount credited unless creditor process with respect to the account is served at a time and in a manner affording the bank a reasonable opportunity to act to prevent withdrawal.

(3) If creditor process with respect to the beneficiary's account has been served and the bank has had a reasonable opportunity to act on it, the bank may not reject the payment order except for a reason unrelated to the service of process.

(d) Creditor process with respect to a payment by the originator to the beneficiary pursuant to a funds transfer may be served only on the beneficiary's bank with respect to the debt owed by that bank to the beneficiary. Any other bank served with the creditor process is not obliged to act with respect to the process. (1993, c. 157, s. 1.)

§ 25-4A-503. Injunction or restraining order with respect to funds transfer.

For proper cause and in compliance with applicable law, a court may restrain (i) a person from issuing a payment order to initiate a funds transfer, (ii) an originator's bank from executing the payment order of the originator, or (iii) the beneficiary's bank from releasing funds to the beneficiary or the beneficiary from withdrawing the funds. A court may not otherwise restrain a person from issuing a payment order, paying or receiving payment of a payment order, or otherwise acting with respect to a funds transfer. (1993, c. 157, s. 1.)

§ 25-4A-504. Order in which items and payment orders may be charged to account; order of withdrawals from account.

(a) If a receiving bank has received more than one payment order of the sender or one or more payment orders and other items that are payable from the sender's account, the bank may charge the sender's account with respect to the various orders and items in any sequence.

(b)   In determining whether a credit to an account has been withdrawn by the holder of the account or applied to a debt of the holder of the account, credits first made to the account are first withdrawn or applied. (1993, c. 157, s. 1.)

§ 25-4A-505. Preclusion of objection to debit of customer's account.

If a receiving bank has received payment from its customer with respect to a payment order issued in the name of the customer as sender and accepted by the bank, and the customer received notification reasonably identifying the order, the customer is precluded from asserting that the bank is not entitled to retain the payment unless the customer notifies the bank of the customer's objection to the payment within one year after the notification was received by the customer. (1993, c. 157, s. 1.)

§ 25-4A-506. Rate of interest.

(a)   If, under this Article, a receiving bank is obliged to pay interest with respect to a payment order issued to the bank, the amount payable may be determined (i) by agreement of the sender and receiving bank, or (ii) by a funds-transfer system rule if the payment order is transmitted through a funds-transfer system.

(b)   If the amount of interest is not determined by an agreement or rule as stated in subsection (a), the amount is calculated by multiplying the applicable federal funds rate by the amount on which interest is payable, and then multiplying the product by the number of days for which interest is payable. The applicable federal funds rate is the average of the federal funds rates published by the Federal Reserve Bank of New York for each of the days for which interest is payable divided by 360. The federal funds rate for any day on which a published rate is not available is the same as the published rate for the next preceding day for which there is a published rate. If a receiving bank that accepted a payment order is required to refund payment to the sender of the order because the funds transfer was not completed, but the failure to complete was not due to any fault by the bank, the interest payable is reduced by a percentage equal to the reserve requirement on deposits of the receiving bank. (1993, c. 157, s. 1.)

§ 25-4A-507. Choice of law.

(a) The following rules apply unless the affected parties otherwise agree or subsection (c) applies:

(1) The rights and obligations between the sender of a payment order and the receiving bank are governed by the law of the jurisdiction in which the receiving bank is located.

(2) The rights and obligations between the beneficiary's bank and the beneficiary are governed by the law of the jurisdiction in which the beneficiary's bank is located.

(3) The issue of when payment is made pursuant to a funds transfer by the originator to the beneficiary is governed by the law of the jurisdiction in which the beneficiary's bank is located.

(b) If the parties described in each paragraph of subsection (a) have made an agreement selecting the law of a particular jurisdiction to govern rights and obligations between each other, the law of that jurisdiction governs those rights and obligations, whether or not the payment order or the funds transfer bears a reasonable relation to that jurisdiction.

(c) A funds-transfer system rule may select the law of a particular jurisdiction to govern (i) rights and obligations between participating banks with respect to payment orders transmitted or processed through the system, or (ii) the rights and obligations of some or all parties to a funds transfer any part of which is carried out by means of the system. A choice of law made pursuant to clause (i) is binding on participating banks. A choice of law made pursuant to clause (ii) is binding on the originator, other sender, or a receiving bank having notice that the funds-transfer system might be used in the funds transfer and of the choice of law by the system when the originator, other sender, or receiving bank issued or accepted a payment order. The beneficiary of a funds transfer is bound by the choice of law if, when the funds transfer is initiated, the beneficiary has notice that the funds-transfer system might be used in the funds transfer and of the choice of law by the system. The law of a jurisdiction selected pursuant to this subsection may govern, whether or not that law bears a reasonable relation to the matter in issue.

(d) In the event of inconsistency between an agreement under subsection (b) and a choice-of-law rule under subsection (c), the agreement under subsection (b) prevails.

(e) If a funds transfer is made by use of more than one funds-transfer system and there is inconsistency between choice-of-law rules of the systems, the matter in issue is governed by the law of the selected jurisdiction that has the most significant relationship to the matter in issue. (1993, c. 157, s. 1.)

Article 5.

Letters Of Credit.

§ 25-5-101. Short title.

This article may be cited as Uniform Commercial Code - Letters of Credit. (1999-73, s. 1.)

§ 25-5-102. Definitions.

(a) In this Article:

(1) "Adviser" means a person who, at the request of the issuer, a confirmer, or another adviser, notifies or requests another adviser to notify the beneficiary that a letter of credit has been issued, confirmed, or amended.

(2) "Applicant" means a person at whose request or for whose account a letter of credit is issued. The term includes a person who requests an issuer to issue a letter of credit on behalf of another if the person making the request undertakes an obligation to reimburse the issuer.

(3) "Beneficiary" means a person who under the terms of a letter of credit is entitled to have its complying presentation honored. The term includes a person to whom drawing rights have been transferred under a transferable letter of credit.

(4) "Confirmer" means a nominated person who undertakes, at the request or with the consent of the issuer, to honor a presentation under a letter of credit issued by another.

(5) "Dishonor" of a letter of credit means failure timely to honor or to take an interim action, such as acceptance of a draft, that may be required by the letter of credit.

(6) "Document" means a draft or other demand, document of title, investment security, certificate, invoice, or other record, statement, or representation of fact, law, right, or opinion (i) which is presented in a written or other medium permitted by the letter of credit or, unless prohibited by the letter of credit, by the standard practice referred to in G.S. 25-5-108(e) and (ii) which is capable of being examined for compliance with the terms and conditions of the letter of credit. A document may not be oral.

(7) "Good faith" means honesty in fact in the conduct or transaction concerned.

(8) "Honor" of a letter of credit means performance of the issuer's undertaking in the letter of credit to pay or deliver an item of value. Unless the letter of credit otherwise provides, "honor" occurs:

a. Upon payment;

b. If the letter of credit provides for acceptance, upon acceptance of a draft and, at maturity, its payment; or

c. If the letter of credit provides for incurring a deferred obligation, upon incurring the obligation and, at maturity, its performance.

(9) "Issuer" means a bank or other person that issues a letter of credit, but does not include an individual who makes an engagement for personal, family, or household purposes.

(10) "Letter of credit" means a definite undertaking that satisfies the requirements of G.S. 25-5-104 by an issuer to a beneficiary at the request or for the account of an applicant or, in the case of a financial institution, to itself or for its own account, to honor a documentary presentation by payment or delivery of an item of value.

(11) "Nominated person" means a person whom the issuer (i) designates or authorizes to pay, accept, negotiate, or otherwise give value under a letter of credit and (ii) undertakes by agreement or custom and practice to reimburse.

(12) "Presentation" means delivery of a document to an issuer or nominated person for honor or giving of value under a letter of credit.

(13) "Presenter" means a person making a presentation as or on behalf of a beneficiary or nominated person.

(14) "Record" means information that is inscribed on a tangible medium or that is stored in an electronic or other medium and is retrievable in perceivable form.

(15) "Successor of a beneficiary" means a person who succeeds to substantially all of the rights of a beneficiary by operation of law, including a corporation with or into which the beneficiary has been merged or consolidated, an administrator, executor, personal representative, trustee in bankruptcy, debtor in possession, liquidator, and receiver.

(b) Definitions in other Articles of this Chapter applying to this Article and the sections in which they appear are:

"Accept" or "Acceptance" G.S. 25-3-409.

"Value" G.S. 25-3-303, G.S. 25-4-209.

(c) Article 1 of this Chapter contains certain additional general definitions and principles of construction and interpretation applicable throughout this Article. (1999-73, s. 1.)

Article 5.

Letters of Credit.

(Revised)

§ 25-5-103. Scope.

(a) This Article applies to letters of credit and to certain rights and obligations arising out of transactions involving letters of credit.

(b) The statement of a rule in this Article does not by itself require, imply, or negate application of the same or a different rule to a situation not provided for, or to a person not specified, in this Article.

(c) With the exception of this subsection, subsections (a) and (d) of this section, G.S. 25-5-102(a)(9) and (10), 25-5-106(d), and 25-5-114(d), and except to the extent prohibited in G.S. 25-1-302 and G.S. 25-5-117(d), the effect of this Article may be varied by agreement or by a provision stated or incorporated by reference in an undertaking. A term in an agreement or undertaking generally excusing liability or generally limiting remedies for failure to perform obligations is not sufficient to vary obligations prescribed by this Article.

(d) Rights and obligations of an issuer to a beneficiary or a nominated person under a letter of credit are independent of the existence, performance, or nonperformance of a contract or arrangement out of which the letter of credit arises or which underlies it, including contracts or arrangements between the issuer and the applicant and between the applicant and the beneficiary. (1999-73, s. 1; 2006-112, s. 19.)

§ 25-5-104. Formal requirements.

A letter of credit, confirmation, advice, transfer, amendment, or cancellation may be issued in any form that is a record and is authenticated (i) by a signature or (ii) in accordance with the agreement of the parties or the standard practice referred to in G.S. 25-5-108(e). (1999-73, s. 1.)

§ 25-5-105. Consideration.

Consideration is not required to issue, amend, transfer, or cancel a letter of credit, advice, or confirmation. (1999-73, s. 1.)

§ 25-5-106. Issuance, amendment, cancellation, and duration.

(a) A letter of credit is issued and becomes enforceable according to its terms against the issuer when the issuer sends or otherwise transmits it to the person requested to advise or to the beneficiary. A letter of credit is revocable only if it so provides.

(b) After a letter of credit is issued, rights and obligations of a beneficiary, applicant, confirmer, and issuer are not affected by an amendment or cancellation to which that person has not consented except to the extent the letter of credit provides that it is revocable or that the issuer may amend or cancel the letter of credit without that consent.

(c) If there is no stated expiration date or other provision that determines its duration, a letter of credit expires one year after its stated date of issuance or, if none is stated, after the date on which it is issued.

(d) A letter of credit that states that it is perpetual expires five years after its stated date of issuance, or if none is stated, after the date on which it is issued. (1999-73, s. 1.)

§ 25-5-107. Confirmer, nominated person, and adviser.

(a) A confirmer is directly obligated on a letter of credit and has the rights and obligations of an issuer to the extent of its confirmation. The confirmer also has rights against and obligations to the issuer as if the issuer were an applicant, and the confirmer had issued the letter of credit at the request and for the account of the issuer.

(b) A nominated person who is not a confirmer is not obligated to honor or otherwise give value for a presentation.

(c) A person requested to advise may decline to act as an adviser. An adviser that is not a confirmer is not obligated to honor or give value for a presentation. An adviser undertakes to the issuer and to the beneficiary accurately to advise the terms of the letter of credit, confirmation, amendment, or advice received by that person and undertakes to the beneficiary to check the apparent authenticity of the request to advise. Even if the advice is inaccurate, the letter of credit, confirmation, or amendment is enforceable as issued.

(d)   A person who notifies a transferee beneficiary of the terms of a letter of credit, confirmation, amendment, or advice has the rights and obligations of an adviser under subsection (c) of this section. The terms in the notice to the transferee beneficiary may differ from the terms in any notice to the transferor beneficiary to the extent permitted by the letter of credit, confirmation, amendment, or advice received by the person who so notifies. (1999-73, s. 1.)

§ 25-5-108. Issuer's rights and obligations.

(a)   Except as otherwise provided in G.S. 25-5-109, an issuer shall honor a presentation that, as determined by the standard practice referred to in subsection (e) of this section, appears on its face strictly to comply with the terms and conditions of the letter of credit. Except as otherwise provided in G.S. 25-5-113 and unless otherwise agreed with the applicant, an issuer shall dishonor a presentation that does not appear so to comply.

(b)   An issuer has a reasonable time after presentation, but not beyond the end of the seventh business day of the issuer after the day of its receipt of documents:

(1)   To honor;

(2)   If the letter of credit provides for honor to be completed more than seven business days after presentation, to accept a draft or incur a deferred obligation; or

(3)   To give notice to the presenter of discrepancies in the presentation.

(c)   Except as otherwise provided in subsection (d) of this section, an issuer is precluded from asserting as a basis for dishonor any discrepancy if timely notice is not given or any discrepancy not stated in the notice if timely notice is given.

(d) Failure to give the notice specified in subsection (b) of this section or to mention fraud, forgery, or expiration in the notice does not preclude the issuer from asserting as a basis for dishonor (i) fraud or forgery as described in G.S. 25-5-109(a) or (ii) expiration of the letter of credit before presentation.

(e) An issuer shall observe standard practice of financial institutions that regularly issue letters of credit. Determination of the issuer's observance of the standard practice is a matter of interpretation for the court. The court shall offer the parties a reasonable opportunity to present evidence of the standard practice.

(f) An issuer is not responsible for:

(1) The performance or nonperformance of the underlying contract, arrangement, or transaction;

(2) An act or omission of others; or

(3) Observance or knowledge of the usage of a particular trade other than the standard practice referred to in subsection (e) of this section.

(g) If an undertaking constituting a letter of credit under G.S. 25-5-102(a)(10) contains nondocumentary conditions, an issuer shall disregard the nondocumentary conditions and treat them as if they were not stated.

(h) An issuer that has dishonored a presentation shall return the documents or hold them at the disposal of, and send advice to that effect to, the presenter.

(i) An issuer that has honored a presentation as permitted or required by this Article:

(1) Is entitled to be reimbursed by the applicant in immediately available funds not later than the date of its payment of funds;

(2) Takes the documents free of claims of the beneficiary or presenter;

(3) Is precluded from asserting a right of recourse on a draft under G.S. 25-3-414 and G.S. 25-3-415;

(4) Except as otherwise provided in G.S. 25-5-110 and G.S. 25-5-117, is precluded from restitution of money paid or other value given by mistake to the

extent the mistake concerns discrepancies in the documents or tender which are apparent on the face of the presentation; and

(5) Is discharged to the extent of its performance under the letter of credit unless the issuer honored a presentation in which a required signature of a beneficiary was forged. (1999-73, s. 1.)

§ 25-5-109. Fraud and forgery.

(a) If a presentation is made that appears on its face strictly to comply with the terms and conditions of the letter of credit, but a required document is forged or materially fraudulent, or honor of the presentation would facilitate a material fraud by the beneficiary on the issuer or applicant:

(1) The issuer shall honor the presentation, if honor is demanded by (i) a nominated person who has given value in good faith and without notice of forgery or material fraud, (ii) a confirmer who has honored its confirmation in good faith, (iii) a holder in due course of a draft drawn under the letter of credit which was taken after acceptance by the issuer or nominated person, or (iv) an assignee of the issuer's or nominated person's deferred obligation that was taken for value and without notice of forgery or material fraud after the obligation was incurred by the issuer or nominated person; and

(2) The issuer, acting in good faith, may honor or dishonor the presentation in any other case.

(b) If an applicant claims that a required document is forged or materially fraudulent or that honor of the presentation would facilitate a material fraud by the beneficiary on the issuer or applicant, a court of competent jurisdiction may temporarily or permanently enjoin the issuer from honoring a presentation or grant similar relief against the issuer or other persons only if the court finds that:

(1) The relief is not prohibited under the law applicable to an accepted draft or deferred obligation incurred by the issuer;

(2) A beneficiary, issuer, or nominated person who may be adversely affected is adequately protected against loss that it may suffer because the relief is granted;

(3)   All of the conditions to entitle a person to the relief under the law of this State have been met; and

(4)   On the basis of the information submitted to the court, the applicant is more likely than not to succeed under its claim of forgery or material fraud and the person demanding honor does not qualify for protection under subdivision (a)(1) of this section. (1999-73, s. 1.)

§ 25-5-110. Warranties.

(a)   If its presentation is honored, the beneficiary warrants:

(1)   To the issuer, any other person to whom presentation is made, and the applicant that there is no fraud or forgery of the kind described in G.S. 25-5-109(a); and

(2)   To the applicant that the drawing does not violate any agreement between the applicant and beneficiary or any other agreement intended by them to be augmented by the letter of credit.

(b)   The warranties in subsection (a) of this section are in addition to warranties arising under Articles 3, 4, 7, and 8 of this Chapter because of the presentation or transfer of documents covered by any of those Articles. (1999-73, s. 1.)

§ 25-5-111. Remedies.

(a)   If an issuer wrongfully dishonors or repudiates its obligation to pay money under a letter of credit before presentation, the beneficiary, successor, or nominated person presenting on its own behalf may recover from the issuer the amount that is the subject of the dishonor or repudiation. If the issuer's obligation under the letter of credit is not for the payment of money, the claimant may obtain specific performance or, at the claimant's election, recover an amount equal to the value of performance from the issuer. In either case, the claimant may also recover incidental but not consequential damages. The claimant is not obligated to take action to avoid damages that might be due from the issuer under this subsection. If, although not obligated to do so, the claimant avoids damages, the claimant's recovery from the issuer must be reduced by the amount of damages avoided. The issuer has the burden of proving the amount of damages avoided. In the case of repudiation the claimant need not present any document.

(b)   If an issuer wrongfully dishonors a draft or demand presented under a letter of credit or honors a draft or demand in breach of its obligation to the applicant, the applicant may recover damages resulting from the breach, including incidental but not consequential damages, less any amount saved as a result of the breach.

(c)   If an adviser or nominated person other than a confirmer breaches an obligation under this Article or an issuer breaches an obligation not covered in subsection (a) or (b) of this section, a person to whom the obligation is owed may recover damages resulting from the breach, including incidental but not consequential damages, less any amount saved as a result of the breach. To the extent of the confirmation, a confirmer has the liability of an issuer specified in this subsection and subsections (a) and (b) of this section.

(d)   An issuer, nominated person, or adviser who is found liable under subsection (a), (b), or (c) of this section shall pay interest on the amount owed thereunder from the date of wrongful dishonor or other appropriate date.

(e)   Reasonable attorneys' fees and other expenses of litigation must be awarded to the prevailing party in an action in which a remedy is sought under this Article, and G.S. 6-21.2 shall not apply.

(f)   Damages that would otherwise be payable by a party for breach of an obligation under this Article may be liquidated by agreement or undertaking, but only in an amount or by a formula that is reasonable in light of the harm anticipated. (1999-73, s. 1.)

§ 25-5-112. Transfer of letter of credit.

(a)   Except as otherwise provided in G.S. 25-5-113, unless a letter of credit provides that it is transferable, the right of a beneficiary to draw or otherwise demand performance under a letter of credit may not be transferred.

(b) Even if a letter of credit provides that it is transferable, the issuer may refuse to recognize or carry out a transfer if:

(1) The transfer would violate applicable law; or

(2) The transferor or transferee has failed to comply with any requirement stated in the letter of credit or any other requirement relating to transfer imposed by the issuer which is within the standard practice referred to in G.S. 25-5-108(e) or is otherwise reasonable under the circumstances. (1999-73, s. 1.)

§ 25-5-113. Transfer by operation of law.

(a) A successor of a beneficiary may consent to amendments, sign and present documents, and receive payment or other items of value in the name of the beneficiary without disclosing its status as a successor.

(b) A successor of a beneficiary may consent to amendments, sign and present documents, and receive payment or other items of value in its own name as the disclosed successor of the beneficiary. Except as otherwise provided in subsection (e) of this section, an issuer shall recognize a disclosed successor of a beneficiary as beneficiary in full substitution for its predecessor upon compliance with the requirements for recognition by the issuer of a transfer of drawing rights by operation of law under the standard practice referred to in G.S. 25-5-108(e) or, in the absence of such a practice, compliance with other reasonable procedures sufficient to protect the issuer.

(c) An issuer is not obliged to determine whether a purported successor is a successor of a beneficiary or whether the signature of a purported successor is genuine or authorized.

(d) Honor of a purported successor's apparently complying presentation under subsection (a) or (b) of this section has the consequences specified in G.S. 25-5-108(i) even if the purported successor is not the successor of a beneficiary. Documents signed in the name of the beneficiary or of a disclosed successor by a person who is neither the beneficiary nor the successor of the beneficiary are forged documents for the purposes of G.S. 25-5-109.

(e) An issuer whose rights of reimbursement are not covered by subsection (d) of this section or substantially similar law and any confirmer or nominated person may decline to recognize a presentation under subsection (b) of this section.

(f)   A beneficiary whose name is changed after the issuance of a letter of credit has the same rights and obligations as a successor of a beneficiary under this section. (1999-73, s. 1.)

§ 25-5-114. Assignment of proceeds.

(a)   In this section, "proceeds of a letter of credit" means the cash, check, accepted draft, or other item of value paid or delivered upon honor or giving of value by the issuer or any nominated person under the letter of credit. The term does not include a beneficiary's drawing rights or documents presented by the beneficiary.

(b)   A beneficiary may assign its right to part or all of the proceeds of a letter of credit. The beneficiary may do so before presentation as a present assignment of its right to receive proceeds contingent upon its compliance with the terms and conditions of the letter of credit.

(c)   An issuer or nominated person need not recognize an assignment of proceeds of a letter of credit until it consents to the assignment.

(d)   An issuer or nominated person has no obligation to give or withhold its consent to an assignment of proceeds of a letter of credit, but consent may not be unreasonably withheld if the assignee possesses and exhibits the letter of credit and presentation of the letter of credit is a condition to honor.

(e)   Rights of a transferee beneficiary or nominated person are independent of the beneficiary's assignment of the proceeds of a letter of credit and are superior to the assignee's right to the proceeds.

(f)   Neither the rights recognized by this section between an assignee and an issuer, transferee beneficiary, or nominated person nor the issuer's or nominated person's payment of proceeds to an assignee or a third person affect the rights between the assignee and any person other than the issuer, transferee beneficiary, or nominated person. The mode of creating and perfecting a security interest in or granting an assignment of a beneficiary's rights to proceeds is governed by Article 9 of this Chapter or other law. Against persons other than the issuer, transferee beneficiary, or nominated person, the rights and obligations arising upon the creation of a security interest or other assignment of a beneficiary's right to proceeds and its perfection are governed by Article 9 of this Chapter or other law. (1999-73, s. 1.)

§ 25-5-115. Statute of limitations.

An action to enforce a right or obligation arising under this Article must be commenced within one year after the expiration date of the relevant letter of credit or one year after the cause of action accrues, whichever occurs later. A cause of action accrues when the breach occurs, regardless of the aggrieved party's lack of knowledge of the breach. (1999-73, s. 1.)

§ 25-5-116. Choice of law and forum.

(a) The liability of an issuer, nominated person, or adviser for action or omission is governed by the law of the jurisdiction chosen by an agreement in the form of a record signed or otherwise authenticated by the affected parties in the manner provided in G.S. 25-5-104 or by a provision in the person's letter of credit, confirmation, or other undertaking. The jurisdiction whose law is chosen need not bear any relation to the transaction.

(b) Unless subsection (a) of this section applies, the liability of an issuer, nominated person, or adviser for action or omission is governed by the law of the jurisdiction in which the person is located. The person is considered to be located at the address indicated in the person's undertaking. If more than one address is indicated, the person is considered to be located at the address from which the person's undertaking was issued. For the purpose of jurisdiction, choice of law, and recognition of interbranch letters of credit, but not enforcement of a judgment, all branches of a bank are considered separate juridical entities and a bank is considered to be located at the place where its relevant branch is considered to be located under this subsection.

(c) Except as otherwise provided in this subsection, the liability of an issuer, nominated person, or adviser is governed by any rules of custom or practice, such as the Uniform Customs and Practice for Documentary Credits, to which the letter of credit, confirmation, or other undertaking is expressly made subject.

If (i) this Article would govern the liability of an issuer, nominated person, or adviser under subsection (a) or (b) of this section, (ii) the relevant undertaking incorporates rules of custom or practice, and (iii) there is conflict between this Article and those rules as applied to that undertaking, those rules govern except to the extent of any conflict with the nonvariable provisions specified in G.S. 25-5-103(c).

(d)   If there is conflict between this Article and Article 3, 4, 4A, or 9 of this Chapter, this Article governs.

(e)   Notwithstanding G.S. 22B-3, the forum for settling disputes arising out of an undertaking within this Article may be chosen in the manner and with the binding effect that governing law may be chosen in accordance with subsection (a) of this section. (1999-73, s. 1.)

§ 25-5-117. Subrogation of issuer, applicant, and nominated person.

(a)   An issuer that honors a beneficiary's presentation is subrogated to the rights of the beneficiary to the same extent as if the issuer were a secondary obligor of the underlying obligation owed to the beneficiary and of the applicant to the same extent as if the issuer were the secondary obligor of the underlying obligation owed to the applicant.

(b)   An applicant that reimburses an issuer is subrogated to the rights of the issuer against any beneficiary, presenter, or nominated person to the same extent as if the applicant were the secondary obligor of the obligations owed to the issuer and has the rights of subrogation of the issuer to the rights of the beneficiary stated in subsection (a) of this section.

(c)   A nominated person who pays or gives value against a draft or demand presented under a letter of credit is subrogated to the rights of:

(1)   The issuer against the applicant to the same extent as if the nominated person were a secondary obligor of the obligation owed to the issuer by the applicant;

(2)   The beneficiary to the same extent as if the nominated person were a secondary obligor of the underlying obligation owed to the beneficiary; and

(3) The applicant to the same extent as if the nominated person were a secondary obligor of the underlying obligation owed to the applicant.

(d) Notwithstanding any agreement or term to the contrary, the rights of subrogation stated in subsections (a) and (b) of this section do not arise until the issuer honors the letter of credit or otherwise pays and the rights in subsection (c) of this section do not arise until the nominated person pays or otherwise gives value. Until then, the issuer, nominated person, and the applicant do not derive under this section present or prospective rights forming the basis of a claim, defense, or excuse. (1999-73, s. 1.)

§ 25-5-118. Security interest of issuer or nominated person.

(a) An issuer or nominated person has a security interest in a document presented under a letter of credit to the extent that the issuer or nominated person honors or gives value for the presentation.

(b) So long as and to the extent that an issuer or nominated person has not been reimbursed or has not otherwise recovered the value given with respect to a security interest in a document under subsection (a) of this section, the security interest continues and is subject to Article 9 of this Chapter, but:

(1) A security agreement is not necessary to make the security interest enforceable under G.S. 25-9-203(b)(3);

(2) If the document is presented in a medium other than a written or other tangible medium, the security interest is perfected; and

(3) If the document is presented in a written or other tangible medium and is not a certificated security, chattel paper, a document of title, an instrument, or a letter of credit, the security interest is perfected and has priority over a conflicting security interest in the document so long as the debtor does not have possession of the document. (2000-169, s. 18.)

Article 6.

Bulk Transfers.

§§ 25-6-101 through 25-6-105: Repealed by Session Laws 2004-190, s. 1, effective January 1, 2005.

§ 25-6-106. Repealed by Session Laws 1967, c. 562, s. 1, effective at midnight June 30, 1967.

§§ 25-6-107 through 25-6-111: Repealed by Session Laws 2004-190, s. 1, effective January 1, 2005.

Article 7.

Documents of Title.

PART 1.

GENERAL.

§ 25-7-101. Short title.

This Article may be cited as Uniform Commercial Code - Documents of Title. (1965, c. 700, s. 1; 2006-112, s. 25.)

§ 25-7-102. Definitions and index of definitions.

(a) In this Article, unless the context otherwise requires:

(1) "Bailee" means a person that by a warehouse receipt, bill of lading, or other document of title acknowledges possession of goods and contracts to deliver them.

(2) "Carrier" means a person that issues a bill of lading.

(3) "Consignee" means a person named in a bill of lading to whom or to whose order the bill promises delivery.

(4) "Consignor" means a person named in a bill of lading as the person from whom the goods have been received for shipment.

(5) "Delivery order" means a record that contains an order to deliver goods directed to a warehouse, carrier, or other person that in the ordinary course of business issues warehouse receipts or bills of lading.

(6) Reserved for future codification purposes.

(7) "Goods" means all things that are treated as movable for the purposes of a contract for storage or transportation.

(8) "Issuer" means a bailee that issues a document of title or, in the case of an unaccepted delivery order, the person that orders the possessor of goods to deliver. The term includes a person for whom an agent or employee purports to act in issuing a document if the agent or employee has real or apparent authority to issue documents, even if the issuer did not receive any goods, the goods were misdescribed, or in any other respect the agent or employee violated the issuer's instructions.

(9) "Person entitled under the document" means the holder, in the case of a negotiable document of title, or the person to whom delivery of the goods is to be made by the terms of, or pursuant to instructions in a record under, a nonnegotiable document of title.

(10) Reserved for future codification purposes.

(11) "Sign" means, with present intent to authenticate or adopt a record:

a. To execute or adopt a tangible symbol; or

b. To attach to or logically associate with the record an electronic sound, symbol, or process.

(12) "Shipper" means a person that enters into a contract of transportation with a carrier.

(13) "Warehouse" means a person engaged in the business of storing goods for hire.

(b) Definitions in other Articles applying to this Article and the sections in which they appear are:

(1) "Contract for sale," G.S. 25-2-106.

(2) "Lessee in the ordinary course of business," G.S. 25-2A-103.

(3) "Receipt" of goods, G.S. 25-2-103.

(c) In addition, Article 1 of this Chapter contains general definitions and principles of construction and interpretation applicable throughout this Article. (1917, c. 37, s. 58; 1919, c. 65, s. 42; C.S., ss. 280, 4037; 1965, c. 700, s. 1; 2006-112, s. 25.)

§ 25-7-103. Relation of Article to treaty or statute.

(a) This Article is subject to any treaty or statute of the United States or regulatory statute of this State to the extent the treaty, statute, or regulatory statute is applicable.

(b) This Article does not modify or repeal any law prescribing the form or content of a document of title or the services or facilities to be afforded by a bailee or otherwise regulating a bailee's business in respects not specifically treated in this Article. However, violation of such a law does not affect the status of a document of title that otherwise is within the definition of a document of title.

(c) This Article modifies, limits, and supersedes the federal Electronic Signatures in Global and National Commerce Act (15 U.S.C. § 7001, et seq.) but does not modify, limit, or supersede section 101(c) of that Act (15 U.S.C. § 7001(c)) or authorize electronic delivery of any of the notices described in section 103(b) of that Act (15 U.S.C. § 7003(b)).

(d) To the extent there is a conflict between Article 40 of Chapter 66 of the General Statutes (the Uniform Electronic Transactions Act) and this Article, this Article governs. (1965, c. 700, s. 1; 1997-181, s. 21; 2006-112, s. 25.)

§ 25-7-104. Negotiable and nonnegotiable document of title.

(a) Except as otherwise provided in subsection (c) of this section, a document of title is negotiable if by its terms the goods are to be delivered to bearer or to the order of a named person.

(b) A document of title other than one described in subsection (a) of this section is nonnegotiable. A bill of lading that states that the goods are consigned to a named person is not made negotiable by a provision that the goods are to be delivered only against an order in a record signed by the same or another named person.

(c) A document of title is nonnegotiable if, at the time it is issued, the document has a conspicuous legend, however expressed, that it is nonnegotiable. (Rev., s. 3032; 1917, c. 37, ss. 4, 7; 1919, c. 65, ss. 3, 6, 7; C.S., ss. 285, 288, 289, 4044, 4045; 1965, c. 700, s. 1; 2006-112, s. 25.)

§ 25-7-105. Reissuance in alternative medium.

(a) Upon request of a person entitled under an electronic document of title, the issuer of the electronic document may issue a tangible document of title as a substitute for the electronic document if:

(1) The person entitled under the electronic document surrenders control of the document to the issuer; and

(2) The tangible document when issued contains a statement that it is issued in substitution for the electronic document.

(b) Upon issuance of a tangible document of title in substitution for an electronic document of title in accordance with subsection (a) of this section:

(1) The electronic document ceases to have any effect or validity; and

(2) The person that procured issuance of the tangible document warrants to all subsequent persons entitled under the tangible document that the warrantor was a person entitled under the electronic document when the warrantor surrendered control of the electronic document to the issuer.

(c) Upon request of a person entitled under a tangible document of title, the issuer of the tangible document may issue an electronic document of title as a substitute for the tangible document if:

(1) The person entitled under the tangible document surrenders possession of the document to the issuer; and

(2) The electronic document when issued contains a statement that it is issued in substitution for the tangible document.

(d) Upon issuance of an electronic document of title in substitution for a tangible document of title in accordance with subsection (c) of this section:

(1) The tangible document ceases to have any effect or validity; and

(2) The person that procured issuance of the electronic document warrants to all subsequent persons entitled under the electronic document that the warrantor was a person entitled under the tangible document when the warrantor surrendered possession of the tangible document to the issuer. (2006-112, s. 25.)

§ 25-7-106. Control of electronic document of title.

(a) A person has control of an electronic document of title if a system employed for evidencing the transfer of interests in the electronic document reliably establishes that person as the person to which the electronic document was issued or transferred.

(b) A system satisfies subsection (a) of this section, and a person is deemed to have control of an electronic document of title, if the document is created, stored, and assigned in such a manner that:

(1) A single authoritative copy of the document exists which is unique, identifiable, and, except as otherwise provided in subdivisions (4), (5), and (6) of this subsection, unalterable;

(2) The authoritative copy identifies the person asserting control as:

a. The person to whom the document was issued; or

b. If the authoritative copy indicates that the document has been transferred, the person to whom the document was most recently transferred;

(3) The authoritative copy is communicated to and maintained by the person asserting control or its designated custodian;

(4) Copies or amendments that add or change an identified assignee of the authoritative copy can be made only with the consent of the person asserting control;

(5) Each copy of the authoritative copy and any copy of a copy is readily identifiable as a copy that is not the authoritative copy; and

(6) Any amendment of the authoritative copy is readily identifiable as authorized or unauthorized. (2006-112, s. 25.)

PART 2.

WAREHOUSE RECEIPTS: SPECIAL PROVISIONS.

§ 25-7-201. Person that may issue a warehouse receipt; storage under bond.

(a) A warehouse receipt may be issued by any warehouse.

(b) If goods, including distilled spirits and agricultural commodities, are stored under a statute requiring a bond against withdrawal or a license for the issuance of receipts in the nature of warehouse receipts, a receipt issued for the goods is deemed to be a warehouse receipt even if issued by a person that is the owner of the goods and is not a warehouse. (1917, c. 37, s. 1; C.S., s. 4041; 1965, c. 700, s. 1; 2006-112, s. 25.)

§ 25-7-202. Form of warehouse receipt; effect of omission.

(a) A warehouse receipt need not be in any particular form.

(b) Unless a warehouse receipt provides for each of the following, the warehouse is liable for damages caused to a person injured by its omission:

(1) A statement of the location of the warehouse facility where the goods are stored;

(2) The date of issue of the receipt;

(3) The unique identification code of the receipt;

(4) A statement whether the goods received will be delivered to the bearer, to a named person, or to a named person or its order;

(5) The rate of storage and handling charges, unless goods are stored under a field warehousing arrangement, in which case a statement of that fact is sufficient on a nonnegotiable receipt;

(6) A description of the goods or the packages containing them;

(7) The signature of the warehouse or its agent;

(8) If the receipt is issued for goods that the warehouse owns, either solely, jointly, or in common with others, a statement of the fact of that ownership; and

(9) A statement of the amount of advances made and of liabilities incurred for which the warehouse claims a lien or security interest, unless the precise amount of advances made or liabilities incurred, at the time of the issue of the receipt, is unknown to the warehouse or to its agent that issued the receipt, in which case a statement of the fact that advances have been made or liabilities incurred and the purpose of the advances or liabilities is sufficient.

(c) A warehouse may insert in its receipt any terms that are not contrary to this Chapter and do not impair its obligation of delivery under G.S. 25-7-403 or its duty of care under G.S. 25-7-204. Any contrary provision is ineffective. (Rev., s. 3032; 1917, c. 37, ss. 2, 3; C.S., ss. 4042, 4043; 1965, c. 700, s. 1; 2006-112, s. 25.)

§ 25-7-203. Liability for nonreceipt or misdescription.

A party to or purchaser for value in good faith of a document of title, other than a bill of lading, that relies upon the description of the goods in the document may recover from the issuer damages caused by the nonreceipt or misdescription of the goods, except to the extent that:

(1) The document conspicuously indicates that the issuer does not know whether all or part of the goods in fact were received or conform to the description, such as a case in which the description is in terms of marks or labels or kind, quantity, or condition, or the receipt or description is qualified by "contents, condition, and quality unknown," "said to contain," or words of similar import, if the indication is true; or

(2) The party or purchaser otherwise has notice of the nonreceipt or misdescription. (1917, c. 37, s. 20; C.S., s. 4060; 1931, c. 358, s. 1; 1965, c. 700, s. 1; 2006-112, s. 25.)

§ 25-7-204. Duty of care; contractual limitation of warehouse's liability.

(a) A warehouse is liable for damages for loss of or injury to the goods caused by its failure to exercise care with regard to the goods that a reasonably careful person would exercise under similar circumstances. Unless otherwise agreed, the warehouse is not liable for damages that could not have been avoided by the exercise of that care.

(b) Damages may be limited by a term in the warehouse receipt or storage agreement limiting the amount of liability in case of loss or damage beyond which the warehouse is not liable. Such a limitation is not effective with respect to the warehouse's liability for conversion to its own use. On request of the bailor in a record at the time of signing the storage agreement or within a reasonable time after receipt of the warehouse receipt, the warehouse's liability may be increased on part or all of the goods covered by the storage agreement or the warehouse receipt. In this event, increased rates may be charged based on an increased valuation of the goods.

(c) Reasonable provisions as to the time and manner of presenting claims and commencing actions based on the bailment may be included in the warehouse receipt or storage agreement.

(d) This section does not modify or repeal any statute that imposes a higher responsibility upon the warehouse or invalidates a contractual limitation that would be permissible under this Article. (1917, c. 37, s. 21; C.S., s. 4061; 1965, c. 700, s. 1; 2006-112, s. 25.)

§ 25-7-205. Title under warehouse receipt defeated in certain cases.

A buyer in ordinary course of business of fungible goods sold and delivered by a warehouse that is also in the business of buying and selling such goods takes the goods free of any claim under a warehouse receipt even if the receipt is negotiable and has been duly negotiated. (1965, c. 700, s. 1; 2006-112, s. 25.)

§ 25-7-206. Termination of storage at warehouse's option.

(a) A warehouse, by giving notice to the person on whose account the goods are held and any other person known to claim an interest in the goods, may require payment of any charges and removal of the goods from the warehouse at the termination of the period of storage fixed by the document of title or, if a period is not fixed, within a stated period not less than 30 days after the warehouse gives notice. If the goods are not removed before the date specified in the notice, the warehouse may sell them pursuant to G.S. 25-7-210.

(b) If a warehouse in good faith believes that goods are about to deteriorate or decline in value to less than the amount of its lien within the time provided in subsection (a) of this section and G.S. 25-7-210, the warehouse may specify in the notice given under subsection (a) of this section any reasonable shorter time for removal of the goods and, if the goods are not removed, may sell them at public sale held not less than one week after a single advertisement or posting.

(c) If, as a result of a quality or condition of the goods of which the warehouse did not have notice at the time of deposit, the goods are a hazard to other property, the warehouse facilities, or other persons, the warehouse may sell the goods at public or private sale without advertisement or posting on reasonable notification to all persons known to claim an interest in the goods. If the warehouse, after a reasonable effort, is unable to sell the goods, it may dispose of them in any lawful manner and does not incur liability by reason of that disposition.

(d)   A warehouse shall deliver the goods to any person entitled to them under this Article upon due demand made at any time before sale or other disposition under this section.

(e)   A warehouse may satisfy its lien from the proceeds of any sale or disposition under this section but shall hold the balance for delivery on the demand of any person to whom the warehouse would have been bound to deliver the goods. (Rev., ss. 3036 to 3040; 1917, c. 37, ss. 33, 34; C.S., ss. 4073, 4074; 1965, c. 700, s. 1; 2006-112, s. 25.)

§ 25-7-207. Goods must be kept separate; fungible goods.

(a)   Unless the warehouse receipt provides otherwise, a warehouse shall keep separate the goods covered by each receipt so as to permit at all times identification and delivery of those goods. However, different lots of fungible goods may be commingled.

(b)   If different lots of fungible goods are commingled, the goods are owned in common by the persons entitled thereto and the warehouse is severally liable to each owner for that owner's share. If, because of overissue, a mass of fungible goods is insufficient to meet all the receipts the warehouse has issued against it, the persons entitled include all holders to whom overissued receipts have been duly negotiated. (Rev., s. 3034; 1917, c. 37, ss. 22 to 24; C.S., ss. 4062 to 4064; 1965, c. 700, s. 1; 2006-112, s. 25.)

§ 25-7-208. Altered warehouse receipts.

If a blank in a negotiable tangible warehouse receipt has been filled in without authority, a good-faith purchaser for value and without notice of the lack of authority may treat the insertion as authorized. Any other unauthorized alteration leaves any tangible or electronic warehouse receipt enforceable against the issuer according to its original tenor. (1917, c. 37, s. 13; C.S., s. 4053; 1965, c. 700, s. 1; 2006-112, s. 25.)

§ 25-7-209. Lien of warehouse.

(a) A warehouse has a lien against the bailor on the goods covered by a warehouse receipt or storage agreement or on the proceeds thereof in its possession for charges for storage or transportation, including demurrage and terminal charges, insurance, labor, or other charges, present or future, in relation to the goods, and for expenses necessary for preservation of the goods or reasonably incurred in their sale pursuant to law. If the person on whose account the goods are held is liable for similar charges or expenses in relation to other goods whenever deposited and it is stated in the warehouse receipt or storage agreement that a lien is claimed for charges and expenses in relation to other goods, the warehouse also has a lien against the goods covered by the warehouse receipt or storage agreement or on the proceeds thereof in its possession for those charges and expenses, whether or not the other goods have been delivered by the warehouse. However, as against a person to which a negotiable warehouse receipt is duly negotiated, a warehouse's lien is limited to charges in an amount or at a rate specified in the warehouse receipt or, if no charges are so specified, to a reasonable charge for storage of the specific goods covered by the receipt subsequent to the date of the receipt.

(b) A warehouse may also reserve a security interest against the bailor for the maximum amount specified on the receipt for charges other than those specified in subsection (a) of this section, such as for money advanced and interest. The security interest is governed by Article 9 of this Chapter.

(c) A warehouse's lien for charges and expenses under subsection (a) of this section or a security interest under subsection (b) of this section is also effective against any person that so entrusted the bailor with possession of the goods that a pledge of them by the bailor to a good-faith purchaser for value would have been valid. However, the lien or security interest is not effective against a person that before issuance of a document of title had a legal interest or a perfected security interest in the goods and that did not:

(1) Deliver or entrust the goods or any document of title covering the goods to the bailor or the bailor's nominee with:

a. Actual or apparent authority to ship, store, or sell;

b. Power to obtain delivery under G.S. 25-7-403; or

c. Power of disposition under G.S. 25-2-403, 25-2A-304(2), 25-2A-305(2), 25-9-320, or 25-9-321(c) or other statute or rule of law; or

(2) Acquiesce in the procurement by the bailor or its nominee of any document.

(d) A warehouse's lien on household goods for charges and expenses in relation to the goods under subsection (a) of this section is also effective against all persons if the depositor was the legal possessor of the goods at the time of deposit. In this subsection, "household goods" means furniture, furnishings, or personal effects used by the depositor in a dwelling.

(e) A warehouse loses its lien on any goods that it voluntarily delivers or unjustifiably refuses to deliver. (1917, c. 37, ss. 27 to 31, 41; 1919, c. 65, s. 31; C.S., ss. 313, 4067 to 4071, 4081; 1965, c. 700, s. 1; 1967, c. 562, s. 1; 2000-169, s. 20; 2006-112, s. 25.)

§ 25-7-210. Enforcement of warehouse's lien.

(a) Except as otherwise provided in subsection (b) of this section, a warehouse's lien may be enforced by public or private sale of the goods, in bulk or in packages, at any time or place and on any terms that are commercially reasonable, after notifying all persons known to claim an interest in the goods. The notification must include a statement of the amount due, the nature of the proposed sale, and the time and place of any public sale. The fact that a better price could have been obtained by a sale at a different time or in a method different from that selected by the warehouse is not of itself sufficient to establish that the sale was not made in a commercially reasonable manner. The warehouse sells in a commercially reasonable manner if the warehouse sells the goods in the usual manner in any recognized market therefore, sells at the price current in that market at the time of the sale, or otherwise sells in conformity with commercially reasonable practices among dealers in the type of goods sold. A sale of more goods than apparently necessary to be offered to ensure satisfaction of the obligation is not commercially reasonable, except in cases covered by the preceding sentence.

(b) A warehouse may enforce its lien on goods, other than goods stored by a merchant in the course of its business, only if the following requirements are satisfied:

(1) All persons known to claim an interest in the goods must be notified.

(2) The notification must include an itemized statement of the claim, a description of the goods subject to the lien, a demand for payment within a specified time not less than 10 days after receipt of the notification, and a conspicuous statement that unless the claim is paid within that time the goods will be advertised for sale and sold by auction at a specified time and place.

(3) The sale must conform to the terms of the notification.

(4) The sale must be held at the nearest suitable place to where the goods are held or stored.

(5) After the expiration of the time given in the notification, an advertisement of the sale must be published once a week for two weeks consecutively in a newspaper of general circulation where the sale is to be held. The advertisement must include a description of the goods, the name of the person on whose account the goods are being held, and the time and place of the sale. The sale must take place at least 15 days after the first publication. If there is no newspaper of general circulation where the sale is to be held, the advertisement must be posted at least 10 days before the sale in not fewer than six conspicuous places in the neighborhood of the proposed sale.

(c) Before any sale pursuant to this section, any person claiming a right in the goods may pay the amount necessary to satisfy the lien and the reasonable expenses incurred in complying with this section. In that event, the goods may not be sold but must be retained by the warehouse subject to the terms of the receipt and this Article.

(d) A warehouse may buy at any public sale held pursuant to this section.

(e) A purchaser in good faith of goods sold to enforce a warehouse's lien takes the goods free of any rights of persons against whom the lien was valid, despite the warehouse's noncompliance with this section.

(f) A warehouse may satisfy its lien from the proceeds of any sale pursuant to this section but shall hold the balance, if any, for delivery on demand to any person to whom the warehouse would have been bound to deliver the goods.

(g) The rights provided by this section are in addition to all other rights allowed by law to a creditor against a debtor.

(h) If a lien is on goods stored by a merchant in the course of its business, the lien may be enforced in accordance with subsection (a) or (b) of this section.

(i) A warehouse is liable for damages caused by failure to comply with the requirements for sale under this section and, in case of willful violation, is liable for conversion. (Rev., ss. 3036 to 3038, 3041; 1917, c. 37, ss. 32, 33, 35; C.S., ss. 4072, 4073, 4075; 1965, c. 700, s. 1; 2006-112, s. 25.)

PART 3.

BILLS OF LADING: SPECIAL PROVISIONS.

§ 25-7-301. Liability for nonreceipt or misdescription; "said to contain"; "shipper's weight, load, and count"; improper handling.

(a) A consignee of a nonnegotiable bill of lading which has given value in good faith, or a holder to which a negotiable bill has been duly negotiated, relying upon the description of the goods in the bill or upon the date shown in the bill, may recover from the issuer damages caused by the misdating of the bill or the nonreceipt or misdescription of the goods, except to the extent that the bill indicates that the issuer does not know whether any part or all of the goods in fact were received or conform to the description, such as in a case in which the description is in terms of marks or labels or kind, quantity, or condition or the receipt or description is qualified by "contents or condition of contents of packages unknown," "said to contain," "shipper's weight, load, and count," or words of similar import, if that indication is true.

(b) If goods are loaded by the issuer of a bill of lading:

(1) The issuer shall count the packages of goods if shipped in packages and ascertain the kind and quantity if shipped in bulk; and

(2) Words such as "shipper's weight, load, and count," or words of similar import indicating that the description was made by the shipper are ineffective except as to goods concealed in packages.

(c) If bulk goods are loaded by a shipper that makes available to the issuer of a bill of lading adequate facilities for weighing those goods, the issuer shall ascertain the kind and quantity within a reasonable time after receiving the shipper's request in a record to do so. In that case, "shipper's weight" or words of similar import are ineffective.

(d) The issuer of a bill of lading, by including in the bill the words "shipper's weight, load, and count," or words of similar import, may indicate that the goods were loaded by the shipper, and, if that statement is true, the issuer is not liable for damages caused by the improper loading. However, omission of such words does not imply liability for damages caused by improper loading.

(e) A shipper guarantees to an issuer the accuracy at the time of shipment of the description, marks, labels, number, kind, quantity, condition, and weight, as furnished by the shipper, and the shipper shall indemnify the issuer against damage caused by inaccuracies in those particulars. This right of indemnity does not limit the issuer's responsibility or liability under the contract of carriage to any person other than the shipper. (1919, c. 65, ss. 20 to 22; C.S., ss. 302 to 304; 1965, c. 700, s. 1; 1967, c. 24, s. 12; 2006-112, s. 25.)

§ 25-7-302. Through bills of lading and similar documents of title.

(a) The issuer of a through bill of lading, or other document of title embodying an undertaking to be performed in part by a person acting as its agent or by a performing carrier, is liable to any person entitled to recover on the bill or other document for any breach by the other person or the performing carrier of its obligation under the bill or other document. However, to the extent that the bill or other document covers an undertaking to be performed overseas or in territory not contiguous to the continental United States or an undertaking including matters other than transportation, this liability for breach by the other person or the performing carrier may be varied by agreement of the parties.

(b) If goods covered by a through bill of lading or other document of title embodying an undertaking to be performed in part by a person other than the issuer are received by that person, the person is subject, with respect to its own performance while the goods are in its possession, to the obligation of the issuer. The person's obligation is discharged by delivery of the goods to another person pursuant to the bill or other document and does not include liability for breach by any other person or by the issuer.

(c) The issuer of a through bill of lading or other document of title described in subsection (a) of this section is entitled to recover from the performing carrier, or other person in possession of the goods when the breach of the obligation under the bill or other document occurred:

(1)   The amount it may be required to pay to any person entitled to recover on the bill or other document for the breach, as may be evidenced by any receipt, judgment, or transcript of judgment; and

(2)   The amount of any expense reasonably incurred by the issuer in defending any action commenced by any person entitled to recover on the bill or other document for the breach. (1965, c. 700, s. 1; 2006-112, s. 25.)

§ 25-7-303. Diversion; reconsignment; change of instructions.

(a)   Unless the bill of lading otherwise provides, a carrier may deliver the goods to a person or destination other than that stated in the bill or may otherwise dispose of the goods, without liability for misdelivery, on instructions from:

(1)   The holder of a negotiable bill;

(2)   The consignor on a nonnegotiable bill, even if the consignee has given contrary instructions;

(3)   The consignee on a nonnegotiable bill in the absence of contrary instructions from the consignor, if the goods have arrived at the billed destination or if the consignee is in possession of the tangible bill or in control of the electronic bill; or

(4)   The consignee on a nonnegotiable bill, if the consignee is entitled as against the consignor to dispose of the goods.

(b)   Unless instructions described in subsection (a) of this section are included in a negotiable bill of lading, a person to whom the bill is duly negotiated may hold the bailee according to the original terms. (1919, c. 65, ss. 9, 10; C.S., ss. 291, 292; 1965, c. 700, s. 1; 2006-112, s. 25.)

§ 25-7-304. Tangible bills of lading in a set.

(a) Except as customary in international transportation, a tangible bill of lading may not be issued in a set of parts. The issuer is liable for damages caused by violation of this subsection.

(b) If a tangible bill of lading is lawfully issued in a set of parts, each of which contains an identification code and is expressed to be valid only if the goods have not been delivered against any other part, the whole of the parts constitutes one bill.

(c) If a tangible negotiable bill of lading is lawfully issued in a set of parts and different parts are negotiated to different persons, the title of the holder to which the first due negotiation is made prevails as to both the document of title and the goods even if any later holder may have received the goods from the carrier in good faith and discharged the carrier's obligation by surrendering its part.

(d) A person that negotiates or transfers a single part of a tangible bill of lading issued in a set is liable to holders of that part as if it were the whole set.

(e) The bailee shall deliver in accordance with Part 4 of this Article against the first presented part of a tangible bill of lading lawfully issued in a set. Delivery in this manner discharges the bailee's obligation on the whole bill. (1919, c. 65, s. 4; C.S., s. 286; 1965, c. 700, s. 1; 2006-112, s. 25.)

§ 25-7-305. Destination bills.

(a) Instead of issuing a bill of lading to the consignor at the place of shipment, a carrier, at the request of the consignor, may procure the bill to be issued at destination or at any other place designated in the request.

(b) Upon request of any person entitled as against a carrier to control the goods while in transit and on surrender of possession or control of any outstanding bill of lading or other receipt covering the goods, the issuer, subject to G.S. 25-7-105, may procure a substitute bill to be issued at any place designated in the request. (1965, c. 700, s. 1; 2006-112, s. 25.)

§ 25-7-306. Altered bills of lading.

An unauthorized alteration or filling in of a blank in a bill of lading leaves the bill enforceable according to its original tenor. (1919, c. 65, s. 13; C.S., s. 295; 1965, c. 700, s. 1; 2006-112, s. 25.)

§ 25-7-307. Lien of carrier.

(a)   A carrier has a lien on the goods covered by a bill of lading or on the proceeds thereof in its possession for charges after the date of the carrier's receipt of the goods for storage or transportation, including demurrage and terminal charges, and for expenses necessary for preservation of the goods incident to their transportation or reasonably incurred in their sale pursuant to law. However, against a purchaser for value of a negotiable bill of lading, a carrier's lien is limited to charges stated in the bill or the applicable tariffs or, if no charges are stated, a reasonable charge.

(b)   A lien for charges and expenses under subsection (a) of this section on goods that the carrier was required by law to receive for transportation is effective against the consignor or any person entitled to the goods unless the carrier had notice that the consignor lacked authority to subject the goods to those charges and expenses. Any other lien under subsection (a) of this section is effective against the consignor and any person that permitted the bailor to have control or possession of the goods unless the carrier had notice that the bailor lacked authority.

(c)   A carrier loses its lien on any goods that it voluntarily delivers or unjustifiably refuses to deliver. (1919, c. 65, s. 25; C.S., s. 307; 1965, c. 700, s. 1; 2006-112, s. 25.)

§ 25-7-308. Enforcement of carrier's lien.

(a)   A carrier's lien on goods may be enforced by public or private sale of the goods, in bulk or in packages, at any time or place and on any terms that are commercially reasonable, after notifying all persons known to claim an interest in the goods. The notification must include a statement of the amount due, the nature of the proposed sale, and the time and place of any public sale. The fact that a better price could have been obtained by a sale at a different time or in a method different from that selected by the carrier is not of itself sufficient to establish that the sale was not made in a commercially reasonable manner. The carrier sells goods in a commercially reasonable manner if the carrier sells the goods in the usual manner in any recognized market therefor, sells at the price current in that market at the time of the sale, or otherwise sells in conformity with commercially reasonable practices among dealers in the type of goods sold. A sale of more goods than apparently necessary to be offered to ensure satisfaction of the obligation is not commercially reasonable, except in cases covered by the preceding sentence.

(b)   Before any sale pursuant to this section, any person claiming a right in the goods may pay the amount necessary to satisfy the lien and the reasonable expenses incurred in complying with this section. In that event, the goods may not be sold but shall be retained by the carrier, subject to the terms of the bill of lading and this Article.

(c)   A carrier may buy at any public sale pursuant to this section.

(d)   A purchaser in good faith of goods sold to enforce a carrier's lien takes the goods free of any rights of persons against which the lien was valid, despite the carrier's noncompliance with this section.

(e)   A carrier may satisfy its lien from the proceeds of any sale pursuant to this section but shall hold the balance, if any, for delivery on demand to any person to whom the carrier would have been bound to deliver the goods.

(f)   The rights provided by this section are in addition to all other rights allowed by law to a creditor against a debtor.

(g)   A carrier's lien may be enforced pursuant to either subsection (a) of this section or the procedure set forth in G.S. 25-7-210(b).

(h)   A carrier is liable for damages caused by failure to comply with the requirements for sale under this section and, in case of willful violation, is liable for conversion. (1965, c. 700, s. 1; 2006-112, s. 25.)

§ 25-7-309. Duty of care; contractual limitation of carrier's liability.

(a) A carrier that issues a bill of lading, whether negotiable or nonnegotiable, shall exercise the degree of care in relation to the goods which a reasonably careful person would exercise under similar circumstances. This subsection does not affect any statute, regulation, or rule of law that imposes liability upon a common carrier for damages not caused by its negligence.

(b) Damages may be limited by a term in the bill of lading or in a transportation agreement that the carrier's liability may not exceed a value stated in the bill or transportation agreement if the carrier's rates are dependent upon value and the consignor is afforded an opportunity to declare a higher value and the consignor is advised of the opportunity. However, such a limitation is not effective with respect to the carrier's liability for conversion to its own use.

(c) Reasonable provisions as to the time and manner of presenting claims and commencing actions based on the shipment may be included in a bill of lading or a transportation agreement. (1965, c. 700, s. 1; 2006-112, s. 25.)

PART 4.

WAREHOUSE RECEIPTS AND BILLS OF LADING: GENERAL OBLIGATIONS.

§ 25-7-401. Irregularities in issue of receipt or bill or conduct of issuer.

The obligations imposed by this Article on an issuer apply to a document of title even if:

(1) The document does not comply with the requirements of this Article or of any other statute, rule, or regulation regarding its issuance, form, or content;

(2) The issuer violated laws regulating the conduct of its business;

(3) The goods covered by the document were owned by the bailee when the document was issued; or

(4) The person issuing the document is not a warehouse but the document purports to be a warehouse receipt. (1917, c. 37, s. 20; 1919, c. 65, ss. 21, 22; C.S., ss. 303, 304, 4060; 1931, c. 358, s. 1; 1965, c. 700, s. 1; 2006-112, s. 25.)

§ 25-7-402. Duplicate document of title; overissue.

A duplicate or any other document of title purporting to cover goods already represented by an outstanding document of the same issuer does not confer any right in the goods, except as provided in the case of tangible bills of lading in a set of parts, overissue of documents for fungible goods, substitutes for lost, stolen, or destroyed documents, or substitute documents issued pursuant to G.S. 25-7-105. The issuer is liable for damages caused by its overissue or failure to identify a duplicate document by a conspicuous notation. (1917, c. 37, s. 6; 1919, c. 65, s. 5; C.S., ss. 287, 4047; 1965, c. 700, s. 1; 2006-112, s. 25.)

§ 25-7-403. Obligation of bailee to deliver; excuse.

(a) A bailee shall deliver the goods to a person entitled under a document of title if the person complies with subsections (b) and (c) of this section, unless and to the extent that the bailee establishes any of the following:

(1) Delivery of the goods to a person whose receipt was rightful as against the claimant;

(2) Damage to or delay, loss, or destruction of the goods for which the bailee is not liable;

(3) Previous sale or other disposition of the goods in lawful enforcement of a lien or on a warehouse's lawful termination of storage;

(4) The exercise by a seller of its right to stop delivery pursuant to G.S. 25-2-705 or by a lessor of its right to stop delivery pursuant to G.S. 25-2A-526;

(5) A diversion, reconsignment, or other disposition pursuant to G.S. 25-7-303;

(6) Release, satisfaction, or any other personal defense against the claimant; or

(7) Any other lawful excuse.

(b) A person claiming goods covered by a document of title shall satisfy the bailee's lien if the bailee so requests or if the bailee is prohibited by law from delivering the goods until the charges are paid.

(c) Unless a person claiming the goods is a person against whom the document of title does not confer a right under G.S. 25-7-503(a):

(1) The person claiming under a document shall surrender possession or control of any outstanding negotiable document covering the goods for cancellation or indication of partial deliveries; and

(2) The bailee shall cancel the document or conspicuously indicate in the document the partial delivery or the bailee is liable to any person to whom the document is duly negotiated. (1917, c. 37, ss. 8, 9, 11, 12, 36; 1919, c. 65, ss. 8, 9, 11, 12, 26; C.S., ss. 290, 291, 293, 294, 308, 4048, 4049, 4051, 4052, 4076; 1965, c. 700, s. 1; 2006-112, s. 25.)

§ 25-7-404. No liability for good-faith delivery pursuant to document of title.

A bailee that in good faith has received goods and delivered or otherwise disposed of the goods according to the terms of a document of title or pursuant to this Article is not liable for the goods even if:

(1) The person from whom the bailee received the goods did not have authority to procure the document or to dispose of the goods; or

(2) The person to whom the bailee delivered the goods did not have authority to receive the goods. (1917, c. 37, s. 10; 1919, c. 65, s. 10; C.S., ss. 292, 4050; 1965, c. 700, s. 1; 2006-112, s. 25.)

PART 5.

WAREHOUSE RECEIPTS AND BILLS OF LADING: NEGOTIATION AND TRANSFER.

§ 25-7-501. Form of negotiation and requirements of due negotiation.

(a) The following rules apply to a negotiable tangible document of title:

(1) If the document's original terms run to the order of a named person, the document is negotiated by the named person's indorsement and delivery. After the named person's indorsement in blank or to bearer, any person may negotiate the document by delivery alone.

(2) If the document's original terms run to bearer, it is negotiated by delivery alone.

(3) If the document's original terms run to the order of a named person and it is delivered to the named person, the effect is the same as if the document had been negotiated.

(4) Negotiation of the document after it has been indorsed to a named person requires indorsement by the named person and delivery.

(5) A document is duly negotiated if it is negotiated in the manner stated in this subsection to a holder that purchases it in good faith, without notice of any defense against or claim to it on the part of any person, and for value, unless it is established that the negotiation is not in the regular course of business or financing or involves receiving the document in settlement or payment of a monetary obligation.

(b) The following rules apply to a negotiable electronic document of title:

(1) If the document's original terms run to the order of a named person or to bearer, the document is negotiated by delivery of the document to another person. Indorsement by the named person is not required to negotiate the document.

(2) If the document's original terms run to the order of a named person and the named person has control of the document, the effect is the same as if the document had been negotiated.

(3) A document is duly negotiated if it is negotiated in the manner stated in this subsection to a holder that purchases it in good faith, without notice of any defense against or claim to it on the part of any person, and for value, unless it is established that the negotiation is not in the regular course of business or

financing or involves taking delivery of the document in settlement or payment of a monetary obligation.

(c) Indorsement of a nonnegotiable document of title neither makes it negotiable nor adds to the transferee's rights.

(d) The naming in a negotiable bill of lading of a person to be notified of the arrival of the goods does not limit the negotiability of the bill or constitute notice to a purchaser of the bill of any interest of that person in the goods. (1917, c. 37, ss. 37 to 40, 47; 1919, c. 65, ss. 3, 7, 27 to 30, 37; C.S., ss. 285, 289, 309 to 312, 319, 4077 to 4080, 4087; 1931, c. 358, ss. 2, 3; 1965, c. 700, s. 1; 2006-112, s. 25.)

§ 25-7-502. Rights acquired by due negotiation.

(a) Subject to G.S. 25-7-205 and G.S. 25-7-503, a holder to which a negotiable document of title has been duly negotiated acquires thereby:

(1) Title to the document;

(2) Title to the goods;

(3) All rights accruing under the law of agency or estoppel, including rights to goods delivered to the bailee after the document was issued; and

(4) The direct obligation of the issuer to hold or deliver the goods according to the terms of the document free of any defense or claim by the issuer except those arising under the terms of the document or under this Article, but in the case of a delivery order, the bailee's obligation accrues only upon the bailee's acceptance of the delivery order, and the obligation acquired by the holder is that the issuer and any indorser will procure the acceptance of the bailee.

(b) Subject to G.S. 25-7-503, title and rights acquired by due negotiation are not defeated by any stoppage of the goods represented by the document of title or by surrender of the goods by the bailee and are not impaired even if:

(1) The due negotiation or any prior due negotiation constituted a breach of duty;

(2) Any person has been deprived of possession of a negotiable tangible document or control of a negotiable electronic document by misrepresentation, fraud, accident, mistake, duress, loss, theft, or conversion; or

(3) A previous sale or other transfer of the goods or document has been made to a third person. (1917, c. 37, ss. 41, 47 to 49; 1919, c. 65, ss. 31, 37 to 39; C.S., ss. 313, 319 to 321, 4081, 4087 to 4089; 1931, c. 358, s. 3; 1965, c. 700, s. 1; 1998-217, s. 4(b); 2006-112, s. 25.)

§ 25-7-503. Document of title to goods defeated in certain cases.

(a) A document of title confers no right in goods against a person that before issuance of the document had a legal interest or a perfected security interest in the goods and that did not:

(1) Deliver or entrust the goods or any document of title covering the goods to the bailor or the bailor's nominee with:

a. Actual or apparent authority to ship, store, or sell;

b. Power to obtain delivery under G.S. 25-7-403; or

c. Power of disposition under G.S. 25-2-403, 25-2A-304(2), 25-2A-305(2), 25-9-320, or 25-9-321(c) or other statute or rule of law; or

(2) Acquiesce in the procurement by the bailor or its nominee of any document.

(b) Title to goods based upon an unaccepted delivery order is subject to the rights of any person to whom a negotiable warehouse receipt or bill of lading covering the goods has been duly negotiated. That title may be defeated under G.S. 25-7-504 to the same extent as the rights of the issuer or a transferee from the issuer.

(c) Title to goods based upon a bill of lading issued to a freight forwarder is subject to the rights of any person to which a bill issued by the freight forwarder is duly negotiated. However, delivery by the carrier in accordance with Part 4 of this Article pursuant to its own bill of lading discharges the carrier's obligation to deliver. (1917, c. 37, s. 41; 1919, c. 65, s. 31; C.S., ss. 313, 4081; 1965, c. 700, s. 1; 2000-169, s. 20; 2006-112, s. 25.)

§ 25-7-504. Rights acquired in absence of due negotiation; effect of diversion; stoppage of delivery.

(a)   A transferee of a document of title, whether negotiable or nonnegotiable, to which the document has been delivered but not duly negotiated, acquires the title and rights that its transferor had or had actual authority to convey.

(b)   In the case of a transfer of a nonnegotiable document of title, until but not after the bailee receives notice of the transfer, the rights of the transferee may be defeated:

(1)   By those creditors of the transferor which could treat the transfer as void under G.S. 25-2-402 or G.S. 25-2A-308;

(2)   By a buyer from the transferor in ordinary course of business if the bailee has delivered the goods to the buyer or received notification of the buyer's rights;

(3)   By a lessee from the transferor in ordinary course of business if the bailee has delivered the goods to the lessee or received notification of the lessee's rights; or

(4)   As against the bailee, by good-faith dealings of the bailee with the transferor.

(c)   A diversion or other change of shipping instructions by the consignor in a nonnegotiable bill of lading which causes the bailee not to deliver the goods to the consignee defeats the consignee's title to the goods if the goods have been delivered to a buyer in ordinary course of business or a lessee in ordinary course of business and, in any event, defeats the consignee's rights against the bailee.

(d)   Delivery of the goods pursuant to a nonnegotiable document of title may be stopped by a seller under G.S. 25-2-705 or a lessor under G.S. 25-2A-526, subject to the requirements of due notification in those sections. A bailee that honors the seller's or lessor's instructions is entitled to be indemnified by the seller or lessor against any resulting loss or expense. (1917, c. 37, s. 42; 1919, c. 65, s. 32; c. 290; C.S., ss. 314, 4082; 1965, c. 700, s. 1; 2006-112, s. 25.)

§ 25-7-505. Indorser not guarantor for other parties.

The indorsement of a tangible document of title issued by a bailee does not make the indorser liable for any default by the bailee or previous indorsers. (1917, c. 37, s. 45; 1919, c. 65, s. 35; C.S., ss. 317, 4085; 1965, c. 700, s. 1; 2006-112, s. 25.)

§ 25-7-506. Delivery without indorsement; right to compel indorsement.

The transferee of a negotiable tangible document of title has a specifically enforceable right to have its transferor supply any necessary indorsement, but the transfer becomes a negotiation only as of the time the indorsement is supplied. (1917, c. 37, s. 43; 1919, c. 65, s. 33; C.S., ss. 315, 4083; 1965, c. 700, s. 1; 2006-112, s. 25.)

§ 25-7-507. Warranties on negotiation or delivery of document of title.

If a person negotiates or delivers a document of title for value, otherwise than as a mere intermediary under G.S. 25-7-508, unless otherwise agreed, the transferor, in addition to any warranty made in selling or leasing the goods, warrants to its immediate purchaser only that:

(1)   The document is genuine;

(2)   The transferor does not have knowledge of any fact that would impair the document's validity or worth; and

(3)   The negotiation or delivery is rightful and fully effective with respect to the title to the document and the goods it represents. (1917, c. 37, s. 44; 1919, c. 65, s. 34; C.S., ss. 316, 4084; 1965, c. 700, s. 1; 1998-217, s. 4(c); 2006-112, s. 25.)

§ 25-7-508. Warranties of collecting bank as to documents of title.

A collecting bank or other intermediary known to be entrusted with documents of title on behalf of another or with collection of a draft or other claim against delivery of documents warrants by the delivery of the documents only its own good faith and authority even if the collecting bank or other intermediary has purchased or made advances against the claim or draft to be collected. (1917, c. 37, s. 46; 1919, c. 65, s. 36; C.S., ss. 318, 4086; 1965, c. 700, s. 1; 2006-112, s. 25.)

§ 25-7-509. Adequate compliance with commercial contract.

Whether a document of title is adequate to fulfill the obligations of a contract for sale, a contract for lease, or the conditions of a letter of credit is determined by Article 2, 2A, or 5 of this Chapter. (1965, c. 700, s. 1; 2006-112, s. 25.)

PART 6.

WAREHOUSE RECEIPTS AND BILLS OF LADING: MISCELLANEOUS PROVISIONS.

§ 25-7-601. Lost, stolen, or destroyed documents of title.

(a)   If a document of title is lost, stolen, or destroyed, a court may order delivery of the goods or issuance of a substitute document, and the bailee may without liability to any person comply with the order. If the document was negotiable, a court may not order delivery of the goods or issuance of a substitute document without the claimant's posting security unless it finds that any person that may suffer loss as a result of nonsurrender of possession or control of the document is adequately protected against the loss. If the document was nonnegotiable, the court may require security. The court may also order payment of the bailee's reasonable costs and attorneys' fees in any action under this subsection.

(b)   A bailee that, without a court order, delivers goods to a person claiming under a missing negotiable document of title is liable to any person injured thereby. If the delivery is not in good faith, the bailee is liable for conversion. Delivery in good faith is not conversion if the claimant posts security with the bailee in an amount at least double the value of the goods at the time of posting to indemnify any person injured by the delivery that files a notice of claim within one year after the delivery. (1917, c. 37, ss. 11, 14; 1919, c. 65, ss. 11, 14; C.S., ss. 293, 296, 4051, 4054; 1965, c. 700, s. 1; 2006-112, s. 25.)

§ 25-7-602. Judicial process against goods covered by negotiable document of title.

Unless a document of title was originally issued upon delivery of the goods by a person that did not have power to dispose of them, a lien does not attach by virtue of any judicial process to goods in the possession of a bailee for which a negotiable document of title is outstanding unless possession or control of the document is first surrendered to the bailee or the document's negotiation is enjoined. The bailee may not be compelled to deliver the goods pursuant to process until possession or control of the document is surrendered to the bailee or to the court. A purchaser of the document for value without notice of the process or injunction takes free of the lien imposed by judicial process. (1917, c. 37, s. 25; 1919, c. 65, s. 23; C.S., ss. 305, 4065; 1965, c. 700, s. 1; 2006-112, s. 25.)

§ 25-7-603. Conflicting claims; interpleader.

If more than one person claims title to or possession of the goods, the bailee is excused from delivery until the bailee has a reasonable time to ascertain the validity of the adverse claims or to commence an action for interpleader. The bailee may assert an interpleader either in defending an action for nondelivery of the goods or by original action. (1917, c. 37, ss. 17, 18; 1919, c. 65, ss. 17, 18; C.S., ss. 299, 300, 4057, 4058; 1965, c. 700, s. 1; 2006-112, s. 25.)

Vision Books Order Form

Fax Orders:	1-980-299-5965
Phone Orders:	1-704-898-0770
E-mail Orders:	www.visionbooks.org
Mail Orders:	Vision Books, LLC P.O. Box 42406 Charlotte, NC 28215

Shipp To:
Name_____
Address_____
City_____State_____Zip_____
Phone_____Fax_____
Email_____@_____

Bill To: We can bill a third party on your behalf.
Name_____
Address_____
City_____State_____Zip_____
Phone____(_____)_____Fax_____
Email_____@_____

Pamphlet Number ($15.00 Each)	Qty	Total Cost
_____	_____	_____
_____	_____	_____
_____	_____	_____
_____	_____	_____
_____	_____	_____
_____	_____	_____
_____	_____	_____
_____	_____	_____
<u>Full Volume Set 1-92</u>	<u>92 Pamphlets</u>	<u>1,380.00</u>

Free Shipping Shipping & Handling on Full Volume Orders
Add $1.00 Shipping & Handling per pamphlet $_____

Total Cost $_____

<u>Thank You for Your Support. Management!</u>

DID YOU ENJOY THIS BOOK?

Vision Books would like to hear from you! If you or someone you know has been falsely imprisoned, we would like to hear your story. If the 'North Carolina Criminal Law and Procedure' has had an effect in your life or if you have suggestions, we would like to hear from you. Send your letters to:

Vision Books, LLC
Attn: Staff Writers
P.O. Box 42406
Charlotte, NC 28215
Email: staff@visionbooks.org

Order Additional Copies:

Fax Orders: 1-980-299-5965

Phone Orders: 1-704-898-0770

E-mail Orders: www.visionbooks.org

Mail Orders: Vision Books, LLC
                    P.O. Box 42406
                    Charlotte, NC 28215

www.ingramcontent.com/pod-product-compliance
Lightning Source LLC
Chambersburg PA
CBHW071359170526
45165CB00001B/109